BUBBLENOMICS

A CRASH COURSE IN COMMON CENTS

LAWRENCE LEE ROWE JR.

Denver

BY LAWRENCE ROWE

FICTION
Tempus Fugit (Time Flies)
Stumbling Towards Oblivion [2012]
The Founding Fathers Return II: Pax Americana [2012]

NONFICTION
Bubblenomics: A Crash Course in Common Cents
Bubblenomics II: A PhD in Common Cents
UFOs for the Sane [2011]

VISIT LAWRENCE ON THE WORLD WIDE WEB
www.lawrencerowe.com

Printed in the United States of America by MDR Press.

ISBN 978-0-9767668-1-0

LCCN 2011937772

Bubblenomics may be purchased at special bulk quantity discounts for educational or promotional use. For information, e-mail: specialmarkets@mdrpress.com.

First paperback printing: September 2011.

10   9   8   7   6   5   4   3   2   1

"We are not afraid to entrust the American people with unpleasant facts, foreign ideas, alien philosophies, and competitive values. For a nation that is afraid to let its people judge the truth and falsehood in an open market is a nation that is afraid of its people."

—John F. Kennedy

"There are a thousand hacking at the branches of evil to one who is striking at the root."

—Henry David Thoreau

"So you think that money is the root of all evil. Have you ever asked what is the root of all money?"

—Ayn Rand

Contents

BACHELOR'S IN BUBBLENOMICS

Introduction

"If you want to make someone angry, tell him a lie; if you want to make him furious, tell him the truth."

—Arthur Schopenhauer

I will never forget the moment I first glimpsed the truth about our money system. I was studying engineering, a friend was taking a Master's-Degree course in finance, and I read a section of his textbook that he had left open on his desk. It detailed a banking practice called fractional reserve lending, which allows banks to create loan money out of thin air on a computer.

I was blown away. Such a practice was actually legal?

My friend explained that creating money for loans was accepted banking procedure. The textbook was used at universities nationwide. It was all perfectly legitimate.

I wasn't so sure. I had never pondered how money is created, who benefits from its creation, or the effects of fluctuating the supply of money. I had assumed that banks made loans using pre-existing money which they already possessed. I hadn't known banks created money for loans, so how could I ponder effects of their money creation? I couldn't. I hadn't. But now, in a life-changing instant, I did.

If banks created money for loans, was money uncreated when loans were repaid? Why was creating money a crime called counterfeiting for me, but "perfectly legitimate" for bankers? What kept banks from issuing gluts of loans with fortunes conjured out of thin air? If banks did so, wouldn't the economy crash when everyone was drowning in debt and refused to take out additional loans?

Previously, only my personal supply of money seemed important, but now the total supply of money seemed critical. I had rarely considered business cycles, except to hope that I had a job. I had believed the conventional explanation, that economic crashes were unavoidable tragedies like hurricanes, the inevitable result of a natural human tendency for greed and irrational exuberance. Yet now a curdling realization struck: maybe recessions were an artificially engineered—and therefore preventable—phenomenon.

I felt stupid. Duped. And later, as I learned more, angry.

My friend wanted to graduate, get a job, and buy an engagement ring for his girlfriend. To him, discussions about monetary philosophy or the morality of banking were frivolous. I was consumed by curiosity. I engaged this monetary puzzle, and solved it, but realized that most people were like my old friend: they work hard, and spend their limited free time with people they love, not studying economics.

Ah, the suffering that could be avoided if people understood more about money! Most people entrust their life savings with, and spend their lives making loan payments to, banks whose operating principles they don't understand. This ignorance is not accidental.

The information presented in this book may seem unconventional, perhaps even radical, but it is factual. To prepare this manuscript, I read hundreds of books, and interviewed dozens of investment bankers, Federal Reserve economists, politicians, and soldiers. Exhaustive documentation would have resulted in a several thousand page manuscript. I have provided some documentation, and additional resources for those who wish to research further.

Economic bubbles have been engineered throughout history. The housing bubble of the Roaring 2000s which preceded the current Depression has the same cause as the stock-market bubble of the Roaring 20s which preceded the Great Depression. Each bubble is not new and unique, but rather a repetition of the same old pattern. Thus the term bubblenomics:

bub•ble•nom•ics, noun, the study of the general principles of inflating and deflating economic bubbles.

Please don't let the term bubblenomics scare you. This is a crash course in common cents, in monetary principles which are depressingly simple when expressed in plain language. The ultra-rich mystify economic bubbles to increase their profit and power, and perpetuate debt serfdom.

I have labored to demystify the truth, and distill it down to a simple form so that you obtain maximum wisdom with minimum effort. Picture pages with supplementary content are outlined to separate them from chapters. Some picture page sections are long. Readers who want a quick summary can skip these pages.

Millions of honest, hardworking Americans played by the rules, toiled, saved, paid taxes, nonetheless lost everything, and don't understand why. One reader who lived in a tent with his family for a year told me *Bubblenomics* helped him finally find peace; he said he finally understood how the economy actually collapsed, and felt empowered. I can't promise that this book will bring you such joy. Sometimes the truth must dishearten you before it sets you free.

LR
September, 2011

ELEMENTARY

BUBBLENOMICS

INFLATION

"All the perplexities, confusion and distress in America arise, not from defects in their Constitution or Confederation, not from want of honor or virtue, so much as from the downright ignorance of the nature of coin, credit and circulation."

—John Adams

Our journey to understanding begins with money. Not money the way the average person views it, but from the point of view of billionaire bankers. To billionaire bankers, money is debt. Billionaire bankers created a money system where every dollar that exists is created to fund a loan. A confusing idea, just keep it in mind without bending your brain into a pretzel.

Assume the federal government needs more money. Or wants it. Governments always do. Politicians love spending other people's money. The government can raise taxes, but this is unpopular, and doesn't lead to what politicians want most: reelection.

What to do?

Say the government needs $3 billion. It has the United States Treasury print up ornate pieces of paper with images of heroes like George Washington and Thomas Jefferson, and calls these pieces of paper BONDS. Face value of the Treasury bonds: $3 billion. Bonds are fancy IOUs. Give us $3 billion now, says government, and we'll pay it back later. We'll also pay you interest on the $3 billion in the meantime.

There are 3 types of banks: commercial, investment, and Central Banks. Nations can have many commercial or investment banks, but they only have one Central Bank. America's Central Bank is the Federal Reserve or FED. The Federal Reserve is like the Supreme Court. It is the Supreme Bank. The Federal Reserve is to commercial banks what the Supreme Court is to lower courts. Lower courts operate somewhat independent of the Supreme Court, but it also controls their behaviors. Just as a Supreme Court can overturn the verdict of a lower court and make rulings that bind all lower courts, the Central Bank can set MONETARY POLICY that binds all banks. Monetary policy usually involves increasing or decreasing the supply of money.

The Federal Reserve creates $3 billion. This is in addition to all money that currently exists. It is new money printed specifically because the government created $3 billion in bonds. If you or I printed money, we would be convicted of counterfeiting. But it is legal for the Fed to create money be cause the government has given them this power and denied it to everyone else.

2

This power to print money can be confusing. Someone has to print money for it to exist and circulate, and a society with circulating money is more prosperous than one without it. But abuse of the money printing power is an evil like the counterfeiting you or I would go to prison for. Deciding how money will be created, and what form it will take, is one of the most important choices a nation makes, and much of history is a struggle for control of this all-important power.

So the Federal Reserve creates $3 billion and trades this new money to government for the bonds. Bling bling baby! The government now has $3 billion to spend on wars, Medicare, Medicaid, Social Security, Homeland Security, and job security.

Fun stuff.

Somethin' for nothin'.

At first.

The Federal Reserve now owns the Treasury bonds which entitle it to interest payments. And in theory, at some future point, the government will pay the original loan amount back to the Fed.

This will never happen. It is never intended to happen.

A loan designed to never be repaid? Huh?

Suppose there is $100 billion in circulation on Monday. That is, the total number of dollars in existence. But government decided to gladly pay on some future Tuesday for expenditures today, and had Fed create $3 billion, increasing the total supply of money to $103 billion.

$$\$100 \text{ billion} \quad + \quad \$3 \text{ billion} \quad = \quad \$103 \text{ billion}$$
$$\text{(existing)} \qquad\qquad \text{(created)} \qquad \text{(3\% increase)}$$

The money supply has increased by 3%. No big deal, right?

Wrong.

The term for what just happened is INFLATION. The supply of money has been increased, or inflated. Like a balloon.

You may have thought that rising prices are some unstoppable event like sunrise or the tides. Some of the smartest men on Earth, humble public servants like Alan Greenspan and Ben Bernanke, tell you so. Such caring geniuses laboring to keep prices low, yet every year they rise.

How strange.

The scam begins with inflation, the printing of more money out of thin air.

Misery always follows.

TO SKIP THE PICTURE PAGES AFTER THIS CHAPTER, PLEASE TURN TO PAGE 7

T-DEBTS: SWINDLING FUTURITY ON A LARGE SCALE

"I sincerely believe that banking establishments are more dangerous than standing armies; and that the principle of spending money to be paid by posterity, under the name of funding, is but swindling futurity on a large scale."—Thomas Jefferson

ABOVE A $100 U.S. Savings Bond with an image of Thomas Jefferson. Jefferson is doubtless ecstatic to be pictured on the debt instruments which are "swindling futurity on a large scale."

NEXT PAGE A 30-year $1,000,000 U.S. Treasury Bond with an image of Teddy Roosevelt. In 1977, a lender handed the U.S. government $1,000,000 and it gave them this piece of paper. The coupons below the bond were ripped off and presented to the federal government twice a year for interest payments. The bond paid 7.625% a year, which the government broke into 2 annual payments of 3.8125% or $38,125, paid on Feb. and Aug. 15th each year. 30 years later in 2007, the government paid the holder of the bond their $1,000,000 back. Taxpayers paid $2,287,500 in interest on this $1,000,000 loan. Government's inability to balance the budget and live within its means required futurity to pay $3.28 for a $1 spent today.

3 types of IOUs are sold by the United States government:
U.S. Treasury Bills (T-bills) mature in 1 year or less.
U.S. Treasury Notes (T-notes) mature in 2 to 10 years.
U.S. Treasury Bonds (T-bonds) mature in 30 years.

T-bills, T-notes and T-bonds are all government debts, so they will be referred to as T-DEBTS. Many T-debts are computerized and not issued in physical form. In 2008, the U.S. government issued $1.08 trillion worth of T-debt IOUs. That is, the U.S. government spent $1.08 trillion more than it collected in revenues. In 2009, $1.89 trillion T-debts were issued. In 2010, $1.65 trillion. By the end of 2011, U.S. federal debt will exceed $15 trillion, $50,000 per American. Definitely a "large scale." Current generations of Americans have no intention of paying this debt off. They are content to let unborn members of "futurity" foot the bill.

3 Species of Banks and the Mass Extinction of 2008

There are 3 types of banks: commercial banks, investment banks and Central Banks. A COMMERCIAL BANK accepts deposits from individuals and small businesses. It holds these deposits in checking and savings accounts, and makes home, car and small business loans with these deposits. The largest U.S. commercial banks were:

In 2008, several large commercial banks either went bankrupt, or entered shotgun weddings with other banks to avoid bankruptcy. This included Wachovia and Washington Mutual, formerly the 4th and 6th largest banks in America, with $600 billion in deposits between them—8% of the $8 trillion U.S. money supply.

A corporation that needs $3 billion can't walk into Wells Fargo and obtain a loan. It has an INVESTMENT BANK raise investment money by selling stocks or bonds. Investment banks also manage the mergers of companies, and finance purchases of companies by selling stocks and bonds. The "Big Five" U.S. investment banks included:

Investment banks like Merrill Lynch, Bear Stearns and Lehman Brothers were as much a symbol of American greatness as the Statue of Liberty or stealth bomber. In less than a year, they either went bankrupt or were forced into shotgun weddings with other banks to keep from going bankrupt.

These were huge banks with trillions of dollars of assets. To destroy so much wealth so quickly requires gargantuan greed. One is tempted to add stupidity. Except none of these banks paid the price for their greed. Sheeple did.

A CENTRAL BANK controls the supply of money in a nation. Citizens create commercial and investment banks. Government creates a Central Bank and gives it power to control all other banks. Central Banks are supposedly created to stabilize prices and the economy. They accomplish neither. Central Banks are actually created to bail out commercial and investment banks, and to inflate the money supply for government.

The Business Cycle

"I know of no severe Depression, in any country or any time, that was not accompanied by a sharp decline in the stock of money and equally of no sharp decline in the stock of money that was not accompanied by a severe Depression."
—Milton Friedman, Nobel Prize Winner in Economics

Inflation has counterintuitive consequences which cause a good portion of all human suffering. Let's examine these consequences using Robinson Crusoe economics. Robinson Crusoe economics places a few individuals in simplified situations which illustrate basic principles.

You're an orange farmer, I'm an apple farmer. We are the only two businesses in the economy. Everyone works producing apples and oranges, everyone buys only apples and oranges. There is one million dollars in circulation. Each year you grow a half million oranges, I grow a half million apples, each sold for a dollar apiece.

Enter a third character, Speculato, and cue the evil theme music. Speculato prints $100,000. To keep it simple, no bonds are involved. The money supply has been increased, or inflated, by 10%:

$$\begin{array}{ccc} \$1,000,000 & + \quad \$100,000 & = \quad \$1,100,000 \\ \text{(existing)} & \text{(printed)} & \text{(10\% increase)} \end{array}$$

Unfortunately, the apples and oranges don't reproduce like rabbits and magically increase their supply by 10%. So there is a problem. The supply of money has increased, but not the supply of goods & services. Each dollar is therefore worth less. And eventually, if enough new money is printed, worthless.

Prices are a balance between the supply of money and the goods it can be traded for. In creating more money but not more goods, Speculato disturbed this balance, and prices must adjust to restore it.

If you and I knew the supply of money had been increased 10% we would have immediately raised prices 10%. Each apple and orange would immediately cost $1.10 rather than $1.00. But we don't know the money supply was inflated. Speculato didn't tell us new money was printed. He lends this new money out to citizens who also do not know more money has been created.

I work 50 weeks per year. I sell 500,000 apples per year, or 10,000 apples per week. At $1 per apple, that is $10,000 income per week. Same for you but with oranges.

Speculato's newly created money increases these sales amounts. He spends

$10,000 of his newly created money per week, half on apples, half on oranges. I sell $15,000 worth of apples the next week and you sell $15,000 worth of oranges. It continues a 2nd week. Then a 3rd week. Then a 4th week...

In this example I could simply talk to you and we might deduce that the supply of money had increased. In the real world with millions of businesses such communication is not possible. So assume we don't talk to each other.

How, I ask myself, is such an increase in business possible? Only one way. People have decided they like my apples better than your oranges. I think demand has shifted. In my mind, I sold 15,000 apples this week because you only sold 5,000.

Week after week I am selling 50% more apples than before. But my inventory dwindles because it is based on the previous 10,000 apples per week sales projections. To meet this long term shift in demand, I must buy more land and seed, hire more employees, plant more trees, expand at all levels. I am selling 5,000 more apples a week, there are 50 weeks in my work year, 50 x 5,000 = 250,000. 250,000 more apples sold next year. In my mind, my 500,000 annual apple sales will increase to 750,000. I leverage myself accordingly, and grow more apples. You do the same with oranges.

We think we made good investments in the future of our businesses. But we made bad investments: MALINVESTMENT. Increasing the supply of money resulted in inaccurate price signals that tricked us.

Soon everyone feels richer. Those who sold us land, financed it, seed producers, the laborers tilling our new land. The economy is booming.

Until week 11, when Speculato's magic money runs out and our business plummets back to 10,000 apples and oranges per week. Just a hiccup, we try to tell ourselves.

Until week 13, when nothing has changed. We look at our new apple and orange trees, realize no one ever really wanted more apples or oranges, and cry. We are ruined. We begin firing employees, apples and oranges sit rotting, and Crusoeville is far worse off than before Speculato's infusion of new money.

The formal economic name for this travesty is THE BUSINESS CYCLE. Any normal economy will have some businesses that fail. But inflating the money supply increases the severity of these waves, turning mild ripples into tsunamis.

Substitute houses for apples and a $4.76 trillion money supply for Crusoeville's $1 million, inflate that money supply by $2.03 trillion rather than $100,000, and you have the U.S. housing bubble.

Our optimistic Crusoeville scenario assumes that Speculato chooses not to speculate. A presumption which borders on delusion, as we will see.

TO SKIP THE PICTURE PAGES AFTER THIS CHAPTER, PLEASE TURN TO PAGE 18

THE GREAT DEPRESSION: THE MOST INFAMOUS "BUSINESS CYCLE"

The most infamous example of the "business cycle" is the Great Depression of the 1930s. America's money supply was $45 billion in 1921, $73 billion by 1929, a 62% increase which created the "Roaring 20s" boom. When money creation was halted, the Great Depression resulted. There were several causes, but inflation was the primary. America has endured 8 Depressions. Monetary inflation preceded each one. The "recession" that began in 2006 is America's 9th Depression. As long as the money supply can be yo-yo-ed, booms and busts will result. The question is not if there will be an 10th American Depression, but when?

UPPER LEFT Speculators flood Wall Street after the 1929 Stock Market Crash. The Dow peaked at 381 in 1929, and bottomed out at 38 in 1932, losing 90% of its value. It hit a high of 14,164 in 2007, bottomed out at 6,547 in early 2009, and had lost 54% of its value.

MIDDLE A 1930s soup line. Hardworking citizens reduced to beggars. 25%-37% of America was unemployed in the 1930s, in late 2011 the actual rate was 22%.

BOTTOM Then as now, the Depression was a puzzling contradiction to most people. Few deduced the actual causes. Those who cannot remember history are condemned to repeat it. Of course, to remember history, you have to understand it a first time.

INFLATING THE MONEY SUPPLY CAUSED EVERY U.S. DEPRESSION

The money supply is inflated, creating a boom. Inflation is stopped, creating a bust. All U.S. Depressions were created this way. Are there other factors? Of course. But inflation is the primary cause. Depressions will be identified by:

$$\text{Depression } vNumber.YearBegan\text{-}YearEnded$$

For example, Depression v8.1929-1942 was America's 8th Depression, which began in 1929 and ended in 1942.

DEPRESSION v0.1777-1781

America wasn't a nation yet, thus the v0. Colonies created money called Continentals to fund the Revolution. From 1775-1779, the Continental supply was increased from 12 million to 237 million, 1875%. This led to the saying, "Not worth a Continental." George Washington wrote, "A wagonload of money will scarcely purchase a wagonload of provisions." Continentals were rejected as money.

DEPRESSION v1.1819-1823

From 1816-1818, America's money supply was increased from $67.3 million to $103.5 million, 54%. From 1818-1819, the money supply decreased from $103.5 million to $74.2 million. A steamboat and farm bubble popped. Paper money could be redeemed for gold. America's Central Bank printed paper money in excess of gold reserves, feared bankruptcy if gold was demanded, so stopped issuing new loans and called in existing loans, contracting the money supply. Historian W. Gouge summed it up best: "The bank was saved, and the people were ruined."

DEPRESSION v2.1837-1843

From 1830-1837, America's money supply was increased from $134 million to $311 million, 132%. From 1837-1843, the money supply decreased from $311 million to $171 million. Andrew Jackson abolished America's Central Bank and created an honest money system. America's transition to an honest money system required liquidation of malinvestment. This was healthy. Faulty price signals were corrected and the market re-allocated resources to reflect actual supply and demand. The economy stabilized and prosperity returned. Had America adhered to this honest money system, there would have been no future Depressions.

DEPRESSION v3.1857-1861

From 1847-1860, America's money supply was increased from $283 million to $630 million, 123%. The California Gold Rush was underway. Banks inflated the supply of paper money expecting influxes of gold to back it. The mines dried and the SS Central America, a ship carrying 15 tons of gold, was sunk in a hurricane.

People doubted banks ability to redeem paper notes for gold and mobbed banks. Bank runs. Major American banks were bankrupted, except Peabody & Company, which obtained loans from the Rothschild Bank of England. Peabody & Co. was run by Speculato JP Morgan, the inspiration for the mustached magnate in the game Monopoly. Morgan became a Rothschild underling and bought up slices of America for pennies on the dollar. The Banking Panic of 1857 was ended by the Civil War..

Depression v4.1873-1879

From 1869-1873, America's money supply was increased from $1,280 million to $1,620 million, 27%. Speculato Jay Cooke made a fortune peddling bonds that funded the Civil War. "As rich as Jay Cooke," became a saying. America's first transcontinental railroad was completed in 1869. Cooke created money to fund a second transcontinental railroad. A railroad bubble similar to the housing bubble was created. Cooke went bankrupt, popping the bubble. This Depression was exacerbated by abandoning silver as money. Gold *and* silver had been used for money, The Coinage Act of 1873 decreed that only gold could be used. This decreased the money supply. More than 10,000 businesses failed.

Depression v5.1893-1896

From 1886-1893, America's money supply was increased from $3,100 million to $4,430 million, 43%. Banks created money to fund the ongoing railroad craze. Railroads were overbuilt. The Reading Railroad went bankrupt. Confidence vanished. Depositors mobbed banks demanding gold. Banks didn't have it. 500 banks were rupted. The Northern Pacific, Union Pacific, and Santa Fe Railroads went bankrupt. Unemployment approached 20%.

Depression v6.1907-1908

From 1904-1907, America's money supply was increased from $9,240 million to $11,600 million, 26%. Bad derivative bets by Speculato Otto Heinze bankrupted him, triggering a chain reaction of bank collapses. John D. Rockefeller, JP Morgan and Rothschilds lent banks money to weather runs, bailing out the economy. This irritated them. Taxpayers should bail out banks, not bank owners. America needed a Central Bank. The Federal Reserve was created in 1913, supposedly to prevent Depressions. The second Depression on Fed's watch was America's worst.

Depression v7.1919-1921

From 1915 to 1920, America's money supply was doubled from $20.6 billion to $39.8 billion. This was done to fund World War I. When World War I ended in 1918, inflation of the money supply was halted and the economy collapsed. World War I was the first modern industrial war which America entered; it required the entire U.S. economy to be channeled to the production of weapons. When World

War I ended in 1919, millions of Americans soldiers who returned home had no jobs, and there was a brief period of stagnation while factories which had been producing weapons were retooled for peacetime.

DEPRESSION V8.1929-1942

From 1921-1929, America's money supply was increased from $45 billion to $73 billion, 62%. This was done to create lower interest rates in America than in Britain and create a movement of gold from American banks to British banks. The British monetary unit was the pound. The waning British Empire had a massive military and welfare state, was unwilling to reduce spending, and so had to fund itself by printing pounds relentlessly. Gold was money. People deposited gold money in banks, were paid interest on gold deposits in the form of paper money, and moved gold to banks which paid higher interest rates. British paper pounds were backed by gold, meaning any paper pound could be presented to the British government and redeemed for a fixed weight of gold. Britain had issued far more paper pounds than it had gold to honor them, and would face demands for gold which would reveal its fraud and collapse its empire—if it didn't receive a gold transfusion. Americans never would have supported a bailout of Britain, and Congress never would have passed such a bill, so a covert bailout was arranged by Speculatos who inflated America's currency faster than Britain's. Interest rates are the price of money, and that price is subject to supply and demand like any other price; more money means a lower price, lower interest rates. In creating more dollars than pounds, Central Bankers engineered lower interest rates in America than in Britain, the opposite of the interest rates the free market had set. Gold flowed from America to Britain as depositors seeking higher interest rates withdrew gold from banks in America and deposited it at banks in Britain. The stock market bubble of the Roaring '20s was an inevitable secondary effect of America's bailout of Britain. The mountains of dollars which America created to artificially lower its interest rates were used to buy stocks on margin. Speculators put up $1 they'd saved, borrowed $9 conjured out of thin air, and bought $10 worth of stocks. An amount of money equal to 78% of America's World War I expenditures—a fortune sufficient to fund the dominant combatant in the second most expensive war in history—was created out of thin air and spent almost entirely on stocks. Stock prices of course skyrocketed and a gargantuan bubble resulted. In 1929, Fed suddenly cut off the supply of money for stock margin loans, collapsing the economy. Every Depression in American history prior to Depression v8.1929-1942 lasted 6 years or less because the free market was allowed to liquidate malinvested resources and no "bailouts" or other "countercyclical" policies of monetary inflation were attempted. FDR made Depression v8.1929-1942 "Great" by implementing America's first "stimulus" program, The New Deal. The New Deal provided some jobs, but failed to end the Great Depression. The Great Depression was ended by World War II.

DEPRESSION V9.2006-201X

From 1987-2006, Inflator General (Federal Reserve Chairman) Alan Greenspan increased America's money supply by $6.6 trillion, creating or bailing out the '87 Stock Market Crash, '90s S&L Scandal, '97Asian Crisis, '98 LTCM rescue, '00 Dot-com Crash, and Roaring 2000s Housing Bubble. People who thought they were millionaires on the verge of retirement because of 1990s dot.com stock "profits" spent money on luxuries they couldn't afford. When the dot.com stock bubble popped in early 2000, gaggles of these "millionaires" saw their fortunes vanish and began withdrawing money from bank accounts to survive. Banks had promised this money to depositors while simultaneously embezzling it and lending it out, and therefore didn't have it, so Federal Reserve Chairman Alan Greenspan created it out of thin air for them. Numerous ex-"millionaires" also stopped spending, which should have created a recession. Greenspan created money to artificially lower interest rates and induce people who had stopped spending to start spending again. They could do so only by borrowing, mortgaging their futures, and America's. Greenspan's inflation prevented a recession in 2000, but insured a Depression at some later date—2006 to be precise. From April 2000 to April 2006 Greenspan increased the U.S. money supply from $4.76 trillion to $6.79 trillion, by 43%. Greenspan created $2.03 trillion out of thin air, $926 million per day on average, every day for 6 years. $1.8 trillion of this $2.03 trillion was loanable by commercial banks, enough money to issue 7.2 million mortgages at $250,000 apiece, or 3,287 $250,000 mortgages per day on average, every day for 6 years. This conjured $1.8 trillion did not merely cause the housing bubble, in the most literal and absolute sense, it was the housing bubble. Without money creation, mortgage loan money would had to have come from the pool of pre-existing money which was saved. If Greenspan had not created money, the money supply would have remained at $4.76 trillion. To obtain $2.03 trillion in loan money from a $4.76 trillion money supply without conjuring money would have required a 43% savings rate. America's savings rate is well under 10%. The housing bubble never could have occurred under an honest money system, and absolutely positively would have been impossible without Greenspan's Great Inflation. Fed reduced the supply of new mortgage money starting in April 2006, popping the housing bubble. A future historian may note, "Citigroup, Goldman Sachs, AIG and GM were saved, and the people were ruined."

DEPRESSION V10.20XX-20XX
DEPRESSION V11.21XX-21XX
DEPRESSION V12.22XX-22XX
DEPRESSION V13.23XX-23XX. . .

Sheeple have learned nothing. Inflating the money supply causes Depressions. Reforms have not eliminated inflation. The next fleecing may be a carbon credit crash, moon crater mania, or asteroid belt bubble. But there will be future Depressions.

BANKING PANICS BECOME DEPRESSIONS BECOME RECESSIONS

The Panic on Wall Street in 1907. Bank failures led to a lack of confidence in the economy as a whole, including the stock market.

Prior to the Great Depression, Depressions were called Panics, and usually Banking Panics—an honest term which indicates the true cause, bank money creation. Even the watered down term Panic was too accurate. Admitting there was a Panic caused more panic. Herbert Hoover invented a less threatening term for the 1929 Banking Panic, calling it "merely a Depression." The connotation was of a small pothole in the road. Propagandists quickly adopted the term.

Today the term Depression results in petrifying comparisons to the Great Depression, so propagandists use the less threatening term recession. No matter how severe Depression v9.2006-201x becomes, the establishment will continue to call it a recession.

This scene looks a lot like the Great Crash of 1929, doesn't it? That's because it is a lot like it. Depressions are the same basic formula repeated again and again and again and again and again. . .

Banking Panics in Pop Culture

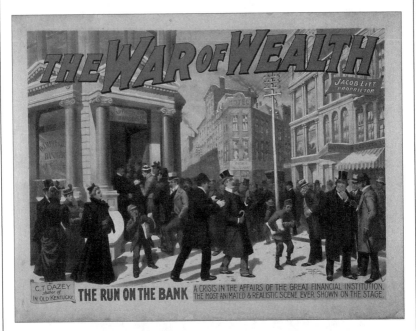

A poster advertising an 1896 Broadway melodrama based on the Banking Panic of 1893. 500 banks failed during the Banking Panic of 1893. Sheeple didn't understand why. Plays and books purporting to offer an inside glimpse of the crisis had popular appeal. The poster says: "THE RUN ON THE BANK a crisis in the affairs of the great financial institution. the most animated and realistic scene ever shown on the stage."

During the Banking Panics of 1893 and 1907, Speculatos like J.P. Morgan personally bailed out the U.S. economy and government. This 1911 political cartoon appeared in *Puck* magazine. It is entitled, "The Helping Hand." Morgan and Uncle Sam are rowing a boat. Morgan is larger than Uncle Sam, indicating his power dwarfs even that of the United States.

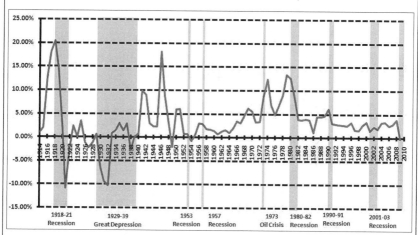

Every Depression and Recession Since 1913 Coincides With a Decrease in the Money Supply/Price Level

The percentage change in the inflation rate is shown on the left. Shaded sections are Depressions and recessions. A negative percentage is a decrease in the money supply, as during 1920-1921 and 1929-1931. Suddenly decreasing the rate of new money creation also implodes the economy if it is accustomed to a higher rate of money creation; for example, Fed inflated the money supply by 20% in 1918 but reduced this rate to 10% in 1919. The money supply increased in 1919, but because the increase was smaller than in previous years, the economy tanked.

The only modern recession or Depression not caused by a sudden decrease in the rate of money creation was the 1970s Oil Crisis in which OPEC constricted America's oil supply.

The only sharp decrease in the inflation rate which did not cause a recession or Depression was the one which occurred after World War II. America inflated its money supply egregiously to fund World War II, and stopped suddenly when the war ended, but its economy did not collapse because of several unique factors. America was the only major industrial economy on Earth not physically destroyed in World War II. Foreign nations with decimated economies purchased American products, keeping demand for them robust. America also used its economic output to help rebuild the world via the Marshall plan. The sharp drop off in demand usually created by a sudden contraction of the money supply was therefore averted. There was also not a period of stagnation while factories producing armaments were retooled to produce peacetime goods, as was the case after World War I; America did not retool as many factories after World War II because it maintained a permanent military industrial complex and became an empire.

Banking Panic Mad Lib

Banks created _____ dollars out of thin air,
LARGE NUMBER

and lent this money to people who bought _____,
PLURAL NOUN

causing prices of these to skyrocket. Banks created so much

money that any dumb _____ could get a loan.
BODY PART

Banks _____ stopped creating new money, prices
ADVERB

plummeted _____, and loans were defaulted upon.
ADVERB

Broke banks blamed the crash on irrational _____
AN EMOTION

and _____, not money creation. The banks
SOMETHING MYTHICAL

bribed _____ politicians to _____ the
ADJECTIVE   SEXUAL ACT

people by passing a bailout that made the people pay bank losses.

This was the _____th Banking Panic in American
NUMBER

history. It is also called the _____ Depression.
SUPERLATIVE

Rising Prices

"The wisdom of man, in my humble opinion, cannot at this time devise a plan by which the credit of paper money would be long supported; consequently, depreciation keeps pace with the quantity of the emission, and [prices of] articles for which it is exchanged rise in a greater ratio than the sinking value of the money. Wherein, then, is the farmer, the planter, the artisan benefited? An evil equally great is the door it immediately opens for speculation, by which the least designing and perhaps most valuable part of the community are preyed upon by the more knowing and crafty speculators."

—George Washington

You and I didn't raise prices when Speculato printed more money, but they will increase anyway. I bought wooden barrels to store apples, wooden carts to transport apples, and wooden ladders to pick apples. Producers of these goods received similar orders from you. They might deduce the oddity we didn't notice. Or maybe the provider of wood who sees everyone demanding more lumber.

Eventually producers of core commodities like lumber, steel and coal raise prices, either out of greed or due to scarcity of resources. When the lumber mill charges more for wood, cart makers charge more for a wooden cart, and you and I pay more for it. With everyone hiring more workers, labor also rises in price. Eventually an apple which once cost 50¢ to produce costs 60¢ to produce, and I raise prices 10¢ per apple to compensate. Same with you and your oranges.

Speculato sent a money wave out into the economy, and like radar being pinged back, it will return in the form of higher prices. An increase in the supply of money is MONETARY INFLATION. Monetary inflation leads to rising prices, or PRICE INFLATION. Monetary inflation is the cause, price inflation the effect.

Speculato knows the money supply has been inflated before anyone else does. He knows prices must rise. Why not buy apples at the low price of $1.00, and sell them later for $1.10. Or more...

Why more than $1.10? Wasn't $1.10 the price that should have been set when Speculato's new money was created? If every apple sold for $1.10, yes. But once some apples are sold for less than $1.10, other apples must be sold for more than $1.10 to balance out total revenue.

I begin with 500,000 apples. Once Speculato prints more money, I need to sell apples for $1.10 on average, or a total of $550,000, to maintain existing profit levels.

Suppose Speculato doesn't loan his newly created money out, but buys 100,000 apples from me for $1.00 apiece, being careful to use middlemen to disguise his intent. Money spent before prices have adjusted buys goods at old, lower prices. Involuntary sale prices. By not raising prices, I offer a blue light special and don't know it. Speculato knows it, and spends new money fast, making purchases before prices rise.

I need to sell 500,000 apples for a total of $550,000. I have sold 100,000 apples for $100,000. I have 400,000 apples remaining which must be sold for $450,000 total. $450,000 ÷ 400,000 apples = $1.125 per apple. $1.125 per apple! 12.5% percent more than people paid before Speculato inflated the money supply. 2.5% more than people would pay if you and I had immediately raised prices to $1.10 when Speculato printed more money.

This math does not factor in human emotion. You and I are not smart enough to deduce that Speculato printed more money, but we know something is amiss. We raise prices more than the mathematically exact 10% to provide a buffer against rapidly rising costs. This is what George Washington meant by "[prices of] articles for which it is exchanged rise in a greater ratio than the sinking value of the money."

In Crusoeville only the prices of apples and oranges rise, but this is a metaphor for what happens to the price of everything in a real economy. Money is the common denominator of all transactions, the one thing in the economy that can simultaneously alter the perceived value of everything else.

If prices of everything rise next year, you can't print more money like Speculato, and your income stays the same, you have effectively taken a pay cut. How big a pay cut? Pop a Prozac, and let's look at some real world price inflation data.

CPI: A Crime Scene

"[Vladimir] Lenin is said to have declared that the best way to destroy the Capitalist System was to debauch the currency. Lenin was certainly right. There is no subtler, no surer means of overturning the existing basis of society than to debauch the currency. By a continuing process of inflation, governments can confiscate, secretly and unobserved, an important part of the wealth of their citizens. The process engages all the hidden forces of economic law on the side of destruction, and does it in a manner which not one man in a million can diagnose."

—John Maynard Keynes, Father of Macroeconomics

"The way to crush the bourgeoisie [middle class] is to grind them between the millstones of taxation and inflation."

—Vladimir Lenin

In 1931 a one-pound loaf of white bread cost 7.7¢. Today that loaf costs at least 100¢. A dollar. We are talking plain-Jane white bread, not the $4.00-a-loaf organic 49-grain variety. Technology allows a farmer today to produce more wheat than a farmer in 1931. Computers, robotics, pesticides, tractors, irrigation. All sorts of productivity improvements have become commonplace, and should have made bread cheaper, yet here it sits at a buck a loaf.

As the opposing chart indicates, bread rose in price steadily since 1931. Similar price increases occurred for most every good & service in America.

Prices of a few goods or services can rise abnormally. Like Cabbage Patch Kids, X-Boxes, and Superbowl tickets. Or oil during the 1970s. But when the prices of everything rise decade after decade, century after century, inflation of the money supply is the cause.

On average, the price of bread—and all other goods and services—rose 3.3% per year.. Anyone who did not receive a 3.3% raise took a pay cut in terms of the goods & services their wages bought. 2% raise in 1933? Subtract the 3.3% inflation, it is a 1.3% paycut, effectively. 6% raise in 1957? It was actually only 2.7%.

Bread did not rise in price because it became more valuable. Nor did the 10¢ cup of coffee, $1,000 new car, or $7,500 house from the Leave-It-To-Beaver era. Prices rose because dollars were devalued at a rate of 3.3% per year.

Note the Purchasing Power Lost column in the chart. Suppose you buried a dollar in 1931, time travelled to the present, and dug the dollar up. Bread is still 7.7¢ a loaf, right? A dollar still buys 13 loaves of bread, doesn't it?

13 loaves then, 1 now. Your dollar has 1/13th its original purchasing power, or

PRICES RISE AS MORE MONEY IS PRINTED

A loaf of bread cost 8¢ in 1931, but rose in price as additional money was printed and each dollar lost value. This perpetual devaluing of the dollar causes *everything* to rise in price at an average rate of 3.3% per year. 92% of the dollar's purchasing power has been confiscated by this inflation tax since 1931, and the perpetual process of devaluation is ongoing, eroding purchasing power further.

Year	Price of a Loaf of Bread	Purchasing Power Lost Since 1931
1931	$0.08	0%
1940	$0.10	20%
1950	$0.14	43%
1960	$0.20	63%
1970	$0.27	70%
1980	$0.38	79%
1990	$0.52	85%
2000	$0.72	89%
2011	$1.00	92%

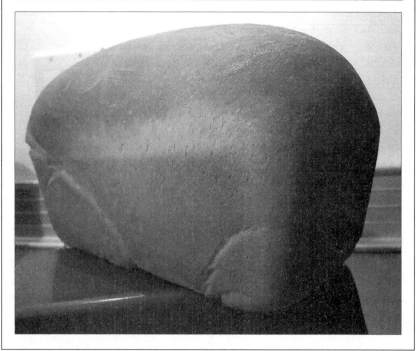

7.7%. 92.3% of its value was taken from you when more money was printed year after year. It's a good thing you didn't bury 8¢ and plan on coming forward in time to buy a single loaf of bread. That won't buy a slice of bread today. The lost 92% can be confusing. How can 3.3% inflation confiscate more wealth than an income tax that is 10 times larger? The income tax takes a percentage of what you earned this year. Inflation takes a percentage of everything you've ever earned. Circulating money has a claim to your home, car, savings, the whole enchilada, and inflation devalues all of it.

Haven't wages risen, negating some of the inflationary losses? Yep. An entry-level accountant made $2,250 in 1931, $24,500 today. 10.9 times as much. Bread increased in price 13-fold, an accountant's wages increased 11-fold. A 15% pay cut, effectively. If you're an accountant earning an average income buying only bread. What if you bought something else, are an unaverage accountant, or have a different job? How bad have you been screwed then?

You could consult government's Consumer Price Index, or CPI. It monitors price changes for a sample of goods, and gives a general sense of overall price increases. Problem is, the CPI is the basis for Social Security cost-of-living increases. The U.S. Congress embezzled trillions of dollars from Social Security and used this money to fund the federal government. Retirees actually expect this money, so there is a problem. Bill Clinton's solution: fudge the CPI so it understates rising prices and cost-of-living increases are smaller. This helps Social Security screw retirees via inflation, but doesn't help us, because the CPI is now a Fantasia.

You could also examine the money supply over time. Prices would rise in proportion to money supply increases. The total amount of dollars in existence is called the M3 money supply. In 1959, when M3 was first reported, it was $288 billion. When last reported by Fed in February, 2006, M3 was $10,300 billion. In 47 years, the money supply was increased by $10 trillion. Inflation tax, indeed.

The Federal Reserve stopped publishing M3 money supply data in March, 2006. Said it was too costly to produce the information and they wanted to "de-emphasize" it. Counting the money you create out of thin air and loan. Phew. Sounds arduous. Wouldn't want them to go broke. Now that M3 isn't published do banks lend new money without counting it?

A cynic might think the Fed saw the housing crash coming. If you're planning to create trillions of dollars out of thin air, it isn't smart to give markets confirmation. Such a great-flood inflation might make people panic. Well, panic more. Private economists think M3 was $15 trillion as of September 2011.

The money supply is inflated to transfer wealth to the holder of newly created money, which is government. When government confiscates wealth from you, what is this process called? Taxation. So inflation is a tax. A sneaky tax, levied in a clever way which most people can't deduce. Inflation isn't a natural occurrence like the tides or sunrise, but an engineered phenomenon!

This may be a shocking revelation to you. It is neither shocking nor a revelation to the Federal Reserve Chairman, Secretary of the Treasury, or any other Wall Street Speculato. Nor the President, nor your Senator or Congressman. Every politician in Washington understands the true nature of inflation.

If inflation is a tax, why doesn't the government acknowledge it like other taxes it levies? Put it on your pay stub every week?

You know how much income tax you pay. You can't pay your income tax unless government tells you the rate. Not so with the INFLATION TAX. No IRS, tax code, auditors, or police are necessary to levy inflation. All you need is a printing press.

You probably didn't know inflation was a tax until now. Most people will never know. How are they going to demand inflation reform then? Even if they realize inflation is a tax, it is much harder to understand than other taxes. A doubling of the inflation tax won't make them as mad as a doubling of an income or sales tax, even though the inflation tax will confiscate far more wealth. This is why governments love the inflation tax.

TO SKIP THE PICTURE PAGES AFTER THIS CHAPTER, PLEASE TURN TO PAGE **33**

LYING ABOUT INFLATION SCREWS SOCIAL SECURITY RETIREES

To understand how lying about the inflation rate screws sheeple, take a Social Security retiree receiving $100 per year who buys only apples. Apples cost $1. The Social Security cost of living increase is 3%, meaning the retiree's check increases 3% per year. Prices actually rise 6% per year.

Year 2, the retiree's $100 check increases 3% to $103, but apple prices increase 6%, from $1.00 to $1.06. The retiree's check buys 3% less apples, or 3 apples less, 97 apples total.

Year 3, the retiree's $103 check increases 3% to $106.09, but apple prices increase 6%, from $1.06 to $1.12. The retiree's check buys 3% less apples, or 3 apples less, 94 apples total.

Year 4, the retiree's $106.09 check increases 3% to $109.27, but apple prices increase 6%, from $1.12 to $1.19. The retiree's check buys 3% less apples, or 2 apples less, 92 apples total.

25 years later, the poor retiree can only buy 50 apples—half as many as originally.

Year	Amount of Social Security Check	Apple Price	Number of Apples Social Security Check Buys
1	$100.00	$1.00	100
2	$103.00	$1.06	97
3	$106.09	$1.12	94
4	$109.27	$1.19	92
5	$112.55	$1.26	89
6	$115.93	$1.34	87
7	$119.41	$1.42	84
8	$122.99	$1.50	82
9	$126.68	$1.59	79
10	$130.48	$1.69	77
11	$134.39	$1.79	75
12	$138.42	$1.90	73
13	$142.58	$2.01	71
14	$146.85	$2.13	69
15	$151.26	$2.26	67
16	$155.80	$2.40	65
17	$160.47	$2.54	63
18	$165.28	$2.69	61
19	$170.24	$2.85	60
20	$175.35	$3.03	58
21	$180.61	$3.21	56
22	$186.03	$3.40	55
23	$191.61	$3.60	53
24	$197.36	$3.82	52
25	$203.28	$4.05	50

When this mechanism is grasped, the legions of poverty stricken senior citizens struggling to make ends meet makes much more sense. Unfortunately, these suffering senior citizens are hardly victims. Only morons would entrust their retirement to politicians. The only surprise is that this government thievery is surprising to people.

Guv'ment Doctors Statistics to Conceal Price Inflation

Different Ways of Measuring Inflation

During the Reagan and Clinton administrations, the method of calculating rising prices was altered in ways that lowered the official inflation rate. The graph below shows how the inflation rate would look if it were measured by the former methods.

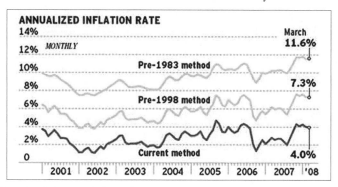

Note that the fudging of the inflation rate was instituted by both a Republican President (Reagan) and a Democratic President (Clinton). The inflation tax is a tool of both political parties, a fraud more fundamental than mere Democrat or Republican. Anyone buying gas, groceries and Big Macs—or living anywhere in the real world—knows that prices are rising much faster than the fictional rate being reported by the government's current inflation calculation method.

Even the pre-1983 method underestimates the true wealth confiscation engineered by rising prices. All data in the chart above assumes a 0% price increase as a baseline. Technology is astounding, and over the last few centuries, it has allowed people to produce much, much more goods & services in the same amount of time. If people produce more goods & services each year—which they usually do—and the money supply stays fixed, prices would decline. If the supply of goods & services increases but prices stay the same, government has printed money, buying up the additional goods & services created.

Very roughly, 3% is the annual growth rate for a healthy industrialized economy. 3% growth means 3% more goods & services produced each year. Had no additional money been printed from 2001-2008, prices would have decreased 3% per year. The actual inflation rate would not be the difference between the price increase and a baseline of zero (no change in prices). The actual inflation rate would be the difference between the price increase and the price decrease that should have occurred. Thus the true inflation rate in 2008 would not have been 11.6%, but rather 11.6%-(-3%), or 14.9%. And the discrepancy is cumulative, as shown on the chart on the opposing page.

Year	# of Apples	Fixed Money Supply	Apple Price	3% increase in Money Supply	Apple Price	6% Increase in Money Supply	Apple Price
1	100	$100	$1.00	$100.00	$1.00	$100.00	$1.00
2	103	$100	$0.97	$103.00	$1.00	$106.00	$1.03
3	106	$100	$0.94	$106.09	$1.00	$112.36	$1.06
4	109	$100	$0.92	$109.27	$1.00	$119.10	$1.09
5	113	$100	$0.89	$112.55	$1.00	$126.25	$1.12
6	116	$100	$0.86	$115.93	$1.00	$133.82	$1.15
7	119	$100	$0.84	$119.41	$1.00	$141.85	$1.19
8	123	$100	$0.81	$122.99	$1.00	$150.36	$1.22
9	127	$100	$0.79	$126.68	$1.00	$159.38	$1.26
10	130	$100	$0.77	$130.48	$1.00	$168.95	$1.29
11	134	$100	$0.74	$134.39	$1.00	$179.08	$1.33
12	138	$100	$0.72	$138.42	$1.00	$189.83	$1.37
13	143	$100	$0.70	$142.58	$1.00	$201.22	$1.41
14	147	$100	$0.68	$146.85	$1.00	$213.29	$1.45
15	151	$100	$0.66	$151.26	$1.00	$226.09	$1.49
16	156	$100	$0.64	$155.80	$1.00	$239.66	$1.54
17	160	$100	$0.62	$160.47	$1.00	$254.04	$1.58
18	165	$100	$0.61	$165.28	$1.00	$269.28	$1.63
19	170	$100	$0.59	$170.24	$1.00	$285.43	$1.68
20	175	$100	$0.57	$175.35	$1.00	$302.56	$1.73
21	181	$100	$0.55	$180.61	$1.00	$320.71	$1.78
22	186	$100	$0.54	$186.03	$1.00	$339.96	$1.83
23	192	$100	$0.52	$191.61	$1.00	$360.35	$1.88
24	197	$100	$0.51	$197.36	$1.00	$381.97	$1.94
25	203	$100	**$0.49**	$203.28	**$1.00**	$404.89	**$1.99**

Begin with 100 apples and $100, apples cost $1. No need to read every number on this chart, just observe trends. People are productive and inventive and increase apple output 3% per year. If the money supply remains fixed at $100, apple prices decline; a dollar buried for 25 years buys twice as many apples when dug up, as they are $1 when it is buried, 49¢ when it is unearthed. Since money buys more in the future, people save, creating an economy that invests in its future. If government increases the money supply 3% each year, apple prices stay constant and government confiscates all additional apples created by sheeple. If government increases the money supply 6% per year, it confiscates all the additional apples created by sheeple, plus some of the original 100 apples they used to consume each year. Focus on year 2. With no money creation, apples would have dropped in price to 97¢. Government inflation statistics assume the price would have stayed constant at $1.00 Prices have risen to $1.03. Government inflation statistics would call this a 3% inflation rate—a rise in prices from $1.00 to $1.03. A more realistic inflation rate is 6%—a rise in prices from 97¢ to $1.03. That is, the difference between what prices would have dropped to with no inflation, and what they rose to because of inflation. Summed over years, the cumulative effect of this discrepancy is monstrous. Focus on year 25. Apple prices should be 49¢, but they are $1.99—a 306% difference. Government inflation statistics say that prices doubled and wages buy 1/2 as many apples. Prices actually quadrupled and wages buy 1/4 as many apples.

THE INFLATION TAX ALSO SCREWS SHEEPLE VIA BRACKET CREEP

Year 1: 30% rate above $125

	Income	Bracket	Paid
Person 1	$100	20%	$20
Person 2	$110	20%	$22
Person 3	$120	20%	$24
Person 4	$130	30%	$39
Person 5	$140	30%	$42
Person 6	$150	30%	$45
Total	**$750**		**$192**
% of Money Supply Confiscated			25.60%

Year 2: 30% rate above $125

	Income	Bracket	Paid
Person 1	$110	20%	$22
Person 2	$121	20%	$24
Person 3	$132	30%	$40
Person 4	$143	30%	$43
Person 5	$154	30%	$46
Person 6	$165	30%	$50
Total	**$825**		**$224**
% of Money Supply Confiscated			27.20%

Year 3: 30% rate above $125

	Income	Bracket	Paid
Person 1	$121	20%	$24
Person 2	$133	30%	$40
Person 3	$145	30%	$44
Person 4	$157	30%	$47
Person 5	$169	30%	$51
Person 6	$182	30%	$54
Total	**$908**		**$260**
% of Money Supply Confiscated			28.67%

Year 4: 30% rate above $125

	Income	Bracket	Paid
Person 1	$133	30%	$40
Person 2	$146	30%	$44
Person 3	$160	30%	$48
Person 4	$173	30%	$52
Person 5	$186	30%	$56
Person 6	$200	30%	$60
Total	**$998**		**$299**
% of Money Supply Confiscated			30.00%

30% rate above $125

	Income	Bracket	Paid
Person 1	$100	20%	$20
Person 2	$110	20%	$22
Person 3	$120	20%	$24
Person 4	$130	30%	$39
Person 5	$140	30%	$42
Person 6	$150	30%	$45
Total	**$750**		**$192**
% of Money Supply Confiscated			25.60%

30% rate above $137.50

	Income	Bracket	Paid
Person 1	$110	20%	$22
Person 2	$121	20%	$24
Person 3	$132	20%	$26
Person 4	$143	30%	$43
Person 5	$154	30%	$46
Person 6	$165	30%	$50
Total	**$825**		**$211**
% of Money Supply Confiscated			25.60%

30% rate above $151.25

	Income	Bracket	Paid
Person 1	$121	20%	$24
Person 2	$133	20%	$27
Person 3	$145	20%	$29
Person 4	$157	30%	$47
Person 5	$169	30%	$51
Person 6	$182	30%	$54
Total	**$908**		**$232**
% of Money Supply Confiscated			25.60%

30% rate above $166.38

	Income	Bracket	Paid
Person 1	$133	20%	$27
Person 2	$146	20%	$29
Person 3	$160	20%	$32
Person 4	$173	30%	$52
Person 5	$186	30%	$56
Person 6	$200	30%	$60
Total	**$998**		**$256**
% of Money Supply Confiscated			25.60%

Increasing the money supply pushes taxpayers into higher income tax brackets. In the upper 4 charts, money supply is increased 10% a year and increases income 10% per year. Tax brackets remain the same. Each year, a taxpayer creeps into a higher income tax bracket, paying 30% instead of their old rate of 20%. This allows government to confiscate more tax revenue—30% of the money supply after bracket creep, as opposed to 25.6% before it. To prevent bracket creep, tax brackets should be increased at the same rate as the money supply, as in the lower 4 charts in which government confiscates the same 25.6% of the money supply annually. Tax brackets are never increased as fast as the money supply is inflated. Government thus confiscates a greater percent of the money supply each year. Yet another way inflation screws sheeple.

MULTITUDINOUS MS: MEASURES OF THE U.S. MONEY SUPPLY

Economists use four main measures of the U.S. money supply, which are called M0, M1, M2 and M3:

> M0: All physical currency, including paper notes and coins, plus bank accounts at the Fed which can be exchanged for physical currency.

> M1: All physical currency, including paper notes and coins, plus checking accounts at commercial banks.

> M2: M1 + savings accounts at commercial banks, money market accounts, retail money market mutual funds, and small denomination time deposits (certificates of deposit under $100,000).

> M3: M2 + all other CDs (large denomination time deposits, institutional money market mutual fund balances), deposits of eurodollars, and repurchase agreements.

M0 is the monetary base, or base money. It is money Fed creates initially, which commercial banks fraction into loans. M0 is the base of the money "pyramid," and determines the amount of money which commercial banks can create.

M1 is meant to approximate the supply of money which Americans spend for day to day commerce.

M2 is meant to approximate the supply of money which is held by individuals in the United States. As previously stated, there is no exact measure of the internal U.S. money supply, but M2 is the best estimate.

M3 is the most inclusive money supply measure. Pension funds, corporations, and governments have *massive* deposits at U.S. banks totalling trillions of dollars; these are the "large denomination time deposits" and "institutional money market mutual fund balances" in M3. Eurodollars are dollars circulating outside America. Much of the money Fed creates circulates overseas or becomes large "institutional" deposits. By refusing to report M3, Fed hides this money.

The Fed reports money stock measures weekly in release H.6. On August 15, 2011, H.6 listed an M1 money supply of $2.08 trillion and an M2 money supply of $9.52 trillion. Fed no longer reports M3, but an economist who compiles M3 at www.shadowstats.com estimated M3 at $15 trillion. By refusing to report M3, Fed essentially hid $5.48 trillion.

CREATING MORE DOLLARS ERODES THE VALUE OF EACH DOLLAR

PURCHASING POWER OF THE U.S. DOLLAR

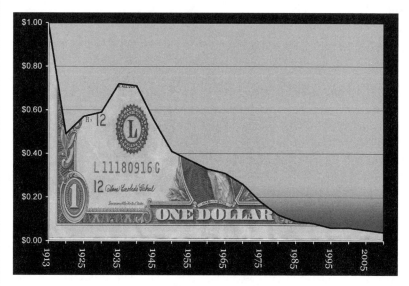

The dollar has lost 95.4% of its value since 1913 when Fed was created. Its decline has accelerated since gold backing was removed in 1971. The dollar lost 76% of its value 1913-1971, in 68 years. The dollar lost 81% of its value 1971-2009, in 28 years. The dollar is being devalued 2.6 times as fast since 1971. The amount of goods a dollar buys is called its purchasing power. As the same dollar purchases less goods each year, its purchasing power is eroding.

CUMULATIVE INFLATION RATE SINCE 1913 BY DECADE

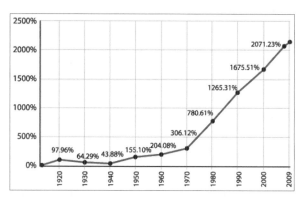

And this uses guv'ment's bogus Consumer Price Index data, which understates actual inflation. More than 2,000%!

INFLATION: THE HIDDEN TAX

| John Q. Debtor | | SS# | | | 123-45-6789 |
| | | Date | | | 12/28/2050 |

Earnings	rate	hours	this period	year to date
regular	17.76	40.00	710.40	35,520.00
overtime	26.64	10.00	266.40	13,320.00
holiday	35.52	0.00	0.00	1,704.96
	Gross Pay		$ 976.80	50,544.96

Deductions	this period	
Federal Income Tax	179.73	18.4%
Social Security Tax	81.07	8.3%
State Income Tax	70.33	7.2%
State Unemployment/Disability	14.65	1.5%
City Income Tax	6.84	0.7%
Inflation Tax	32.23	3.3%
401K	0.00	
Net Pay	$ 591.94	

If guv'ment were honest, inflation would appear on sheeple's paystubs with other taxes. This inflation payroll deduction is inaccurate because the inflation tax confiscates 3.3% of all wealth sheeple have accumulated, not just 3.3% of their wages.

When Will a Big Mac Cost $10?

To make price inflation more digestible, it can be trimmed down to a simple question about the price of something everyone can relate to: when will a Big Mac cost $10?

The Big Mac was 49¢ when introduced in 1968. A Big Mac combo meal with fries and a drink was less than $3.00 in the 1990s, now a Big Mac by itself is $3.57 and a combo meal exceeds $6.00. McDonald's has been serving the same tasty Big Mac for decades, and earning the same profit margin on that tasty Big Mac for decades. The price of Big Macs has risen not because buns or meat have become scarce or inherently more valuable, but because the supply of money has increased.

If inflation continues at its historical pace, here are future Big Mac prices:

1968	49¢
1997	$1.90
2009	$3.57
2038	$13.84
2050	$26.01

These prices may seem absurd viewed from the perspective of today, but a $3.57 Big Mac would seem just as absurd to someone in 1968. Most people read about drastically cheaper goods & services in the old days, but do not comprehend the perpetual wealth confiscation engineered via ever-rising prices.

PRICES IN THE GOOD OLD DAYS

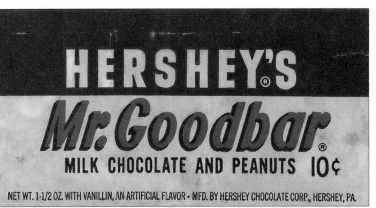

HERSHEY'S

Mr. Goodbar®

MILK CHOCOLATE AND PEANUTS 10¢

NET WT. 1-1/2 OZ. WITH VANILLIN, AN ARTIFICIAL FLAVOR • MFD. BY HERSHEY CHOCOLATE CORP., HERSHEY, PA.

McDonald's

the drive-in with the arches

McDonald's

McDonald's Amazing Menu

Pure Beef Hamburger	15¢
Tempting Cheeseburger	19¢
Triple-Thick Shakes	20¢
Golden French Fries	10¢
Thirst-Quenching Coke	10¢
Delightful Root Beer	10¢
Steaming Hot Coffee	10¢
Full-Flavor Orange Drink	10¢
Refreshing Cold Milk	12¢

JUNGLE

Hot Dog Buns	Pkg. 19c	Meat Pies	3 Cn. 3/49c
Boston Cream Pies	Ea. 59c	Grits (Quick or Reg.)	24 Oz. 10c
Pound Cakes	Ea. 39c	Hi-Ho Crackers	16 Oz. 21c
Biscuits (Sm. or Lge.)	5/39c	Marshmallows	2 Cn. 2/33c
Purex	½ Gal. 2/59c	Syrup (Reg. in Glass)	No. 5 39c

JITNEY JUNGLE

Margarine 1 Lb. — 2 FOR 29c

LARGE
Tide — 2 FOR 49c

U.S. NO. 1 ARIZONA RIPE—LARGE SIZE
Cantaloupes — 3 FOR 49c

FRESH—HOME GROWN—BUTTER
Beans — 2 Lbs. 19c

DRINK

Coca-Cola

TRADE MARK

IN BOTTLES 5¢

EMPEROR SPECULATO

"The decrease in purchasing power incurred by holders of money due to inflation imparts gains to the issuers of money."
—*1975 Annual Review*, Federal Reserve Bank of St. Louis

Back to Crusoeville. Let's look at things from Speculato's perspective. We pay higher prices, but he pays lower. Those who buy soon after a monetary inflation rather than later always will.

Immediately after printing new money, Speculato bought 100,000 apples for $100,000 at the original dollar price. Once the price rose he sold them for a tidy profit.

Speculato never planted an apple or broke a sweat, merely exploited insider knowledge that prices must rise. And the next time he prints money out of thin air, he can buy apples with all of it, plus the profit from the previous sale. He may then own 0.1% of the society. The next year 0.3%. The next year 0.6%. The year after 1%...

Oversimplified? Yes.

Inaccurate? No.

And the poor cart maker and apple picker, the ignorant but honest hard working sucker, now pays more for everything. For Speculato to have more, workers must have less, and rising prices are the mechanism by which this wealth transferal is achieved.

You might call Speculato a skumbag. The modern world calls him a genius, issues him accolades, and puts him on the covers of magazines. For by the time he controls a significant proportion of the wealth of society, Speculato is a dangerous man to criticize. And he owns most magazines and newspapers anyway.

Buying apples low and selling them high is but one way Speculato can help himself. Or you.

Your son Hans is a ladies' man. Nordic, athletic, good hearted. Speculato is at the market, an orange rolls out of a barrel, and his daughter accidentally steps on it and catapults herself into the air. Hans catches her and it is love at first swoop. They marry, and you and Speculato are soon chums. He encourages you to grow apples. Call yourself the One Stop Fruit Shop. Crush my apple business and become a monopoly. You tell Speculato you could never afford that. As if by magic, $200,000 appears. The two of you could be partners, Speculato the silent one...

The more complex the economy, the more pronounced Speculato's advantage grows. The power to lend newly created money is the power to help those he likes or who do his bidding, and to destroy those who oppose him by denying them cheap credit.

Speculato can issue loans only for apples. Or deny credit to anyone looking to buy oranges. This allows him to send a flurry of customers to your business one week, cause a drop off the next. Or fund your competitors.

Speculato can refuse to issue loans for more apple farms. Or issue loans for many orange farms. He then knows that orange supply will rise and orange prices will drop, and places bets on the change.

These manipulative principles can be applied to wood, carts, ladders, barrels. . .

Maybe Speculato prints money and buys local politicians instead of your apples, or stocks, or land, or apple future contracts. Speculato's speculative possibilities are limitless, and as hard as it is to believe, often more profitable than the printing of the money itself.

Speculato need do only two things to end up owning and running Crusoeville. First, not get too greedy, and print so much money that the ruse becomes obvious or the economy self destructs. Second, keep a very, very low profile. Speculato doesn't want to be a celebrity. He never flaunts his wealth and power. Speculato is like a mobster, content to issue economic hits from the shadows.

OCEANLOADS OF MONEY

"Paper money eventually returns to its intrinsic value—zero."

—Voltaire

Why didn't Speculato print another $100,000 for week 11? This would have prevented the crash of Crusoeville and he would have another free pile of money. But can Speculato honestly print $100,000 every ten weeks? Or dishonestly, even?

Yes. For awhile. But if he prints too much money, people will realize the currency is being devalued, and reject it.

Suppose Speculato increases the money supply 10% every ten weeks. We started out with $1 million and Speculato added 10%, or $100,000, resulting in $1,100,000. 10% of this resulting $1,100,000 is $110,000, for a new total of $1,210,000. 10% of this resulting $1,210,000 is $121,000, for a new total of $1,331,000. . .

Eventually Speculato has added 10% to the money supply 100 times. 20 years of continuous inflation. $12.5 billion dollars are in circulation. An apple that once cost $1 is now $12,500.

By the time an apple increases in price to even $10, what is a dollar really worth anymore? The sarcastic might say 1/10th an apple, but the point is that with evermore dollars buying ever-less goods, they cease to be a reliable store or measure of value. Businesses have difficulty planning, calculating, writing contracts, because a dollar in a few weeks is worth less than a dollar now.

You want to buy 100 apples, and pay me over 50 months. Monthly payments, interest free since we're buds. But the money supply is increasing. You and I don't know the size of the inflations the way Speculato does, merely that prices are always rising.

Since you know dollars are always worth less, you are happy to pay $10 per apple for 100 apples, $1,000 total, or $20 a month for 50 months. I'm less enthusiastic. If apple prices weren't going up, your offer would be fair. Apples cost $20 or $40 or $60 each when you make later payments, yet you're still paying $10 each for them. If I carefully record the number of apples each of your payments buys at the time you pay, I find that you've effectively gotten 100 apples for the price of 10 or 20. I got shafted.

Inflation helps debtors because they can repay loans in devalued dollars, cheating the lender. This happened to George Washington and Thomas Jefferson during the American Revolution. They accepted devalued money in settlement of debts, but their creditors refused this devalued money in payment of debts. Screwed on both ends. They lost a lot of wealth, but obviously had more pressing concerns. We're friends. You don't want to screw me, just finance apples. Even if we understood inflation and knew how much money Speculato printed, we might not be able to determine what was fair. Life was simpler when an apple was always worth a dollar!

We decide dollars are the problem, and attempt the transaction without them. You have an extra cart I want, but it is worth more than 100 apples. We arrange a 4-party barter in which the cart is traded for barrels which are traded for ladders which are traded for apples. What a hassle. Many other people want to trade, but don't because they can't arrange barters that work out equitably. And soon, with everyone wasting time bartering, productivity drops, trade slows even more, and the economy declines.

If Speculato was dumb enough to print $100,000 daily instead of every 10 weeks, you'd soon need a wheelbarrow full of dollars to buy an apple. Even the densest rube would wise up to the scam. Such excessive monetary creation is called HYPERINFLATION, and the classic example is Germany in the 1920s.

Germany lost World War I, owed the Allies obscene reparations payments as part of the peace settlement, was broke, and printed enough to pay their bills. We owe Britain 2,000 gajillion marks? Fire up the presses. Heil Gutenberg! Here you go limeys, 222 metric tons of marks, 2,000 gajillion, give or take a gajillion. That might buy a loaf of bread. They were printed an hour ago, make that a quarter loaf. Marks always make good wallpaper or kindling.

Pretty shady, huh? What sort of fraudulent nation would try something crooked like that? You might be surprised.

Imagine Crusoeville before Speculato. Apple prices stayed constant for centuries, fluctuating a penny or two occasionally, but always returning to a dollar. You knew what a dollar was worth in terms of a real good. It meant an apple. To your grandfather and his grandfather and his grandfather's grandfather. A dollar would still buy an apple 100 years from now. If you wanted an apple a day during retirement, you needed to save a dollar per day.

With Speculato inflating the money supply, retirement—and every other economic calculation—is trickier. What will the price of an apple be when you retire? Will a dollar buy a darkened rind? A spoonful of applesauce? The worm? You don't know!

This uncertainty forces you to trust your dollars to people you don't know, in a doomed attempt to get them to reproduce like rabbits. Stock markets, mutual funds, individual retirement accounts. These are your only hope of reclaiming the wealth Speculato relentlessly confiscates via inflation. You don't understand the first thing about these havens, but there are now plenty of Speculatos that do. They have multiplied like rabbits, and are your shepherds on this pilgrimage to prosperity.

As you hand your life savings to the Harvard MBA with the used-car-sales-man smile, you yearn for that simpler world where an IRA was a buried coffee can and a savings account was gold coins hidden in a mattress. Long for thieves that stole your retirement the good-old-fashioned way: by breaking into your house at 4 am and drubbing your brains in. There was more dignity in it that way. At least you understood the way you were robbed, and had a chance to defend yourself.

That world is gone. It wasn't stolen, but given away. We must deal with the world as it is, not as it was or should be. And with an army of Speculatos in this real world instead of just one, things will get much, much worse for you and me.

To SKIP THE PICTURE PAGES AFTER THIS CHAPTER, PLEASE TURN TO PAGE 42

POST WORLD WAR I GERMANY
THE MOST INFAMOUS HYPERINFLATION

The 1920s Weimar Republic hyperinflation. Germany printed so much money that it was used as wallpaper, kindling for stoves, or toys for children. A wheelbarrow full of marks scarcely bought a loaf of bread. 1,783 money printing presses ran around the clock. In 1921, a single dollar bought 75 marks, by 1923 the same dollar bought 4.2 trillion marks. That's trillion, with a T. This is the most infamous hyperinflation in history, but far from the worst. In recent times, nations such as Yugoslavia and Zimbabwe have abused their money printing power even more severely.

BANKNOTES ISSUED DURING HYPERINFLATIONS

TOP 5 million Zaire banknote issued by Zaire in 1992. It bought 3-4 pineapples at a market in Bukavu.

MIDDLE 10 quadrillion Pengo banknote issued by Hungary in 1946. At the height of this hyperinflation, prices tripled daily. If you pocketed this note for 1 day, it bought $1/3^{rd}$ as much. 2 days, $1/9^{th}$ as much. 3 days, $1/27^{th}$ as much. 4 days, $1/81^{st}$ as much. 1 week, $1/2,187^{th}$ as much. 1 month, $1/617,673,396,283,947^{th}$ as much…

BOTTOM 1 million Peso banknote issued by Argentina in 1981. Grocery stores didn't bother writing prices on items, as prices rose 30% every few hours.

TOP 100 million mark banknote issued by Germany's Weimar Republic in 1923. 1 pound of bread cost 3 billion marks (30 of these notes), 1 beer cost 4 billion marks (40 of these notes), and 1 pound of meat cost 36 billion marks (360 of these notes)."
MIDDLE 500 billion dinar banknote issued by Yugoslavia in 1993. Yugoslavians lucky enough to find food on shelves could use this note to buy 10 loaves of bread, 4 ounces of pork, or 1 gallon of milk.
BOTTOM 100 billion Zimbabwe-dollar banknote issued by Zimbabwe in 2008. It bought three eggs at a market in Harare.

SUPERMARKET PHOTOS OF 2008 ZIMBABWE HYPERINFLATION

TOP LEFT A can of mixed fruit jam cost 560,500 Zimbabwe-dollars (Z$) in 2008. The average government worker had their wages frozen at a "mere" Z$120,000 per month. A can of jam cost more than four months wages!

TOP RIGHT Prices skyrocketing this fast are enough to drive one to drink. Unfortunately, a fifth of Johnnie Walker Red Label Whiskey cost Z$8,129,350. 8 million Zimbawe dollars! The cheaper Vat 69 Whiskey was only Z$4,150,000.

BOTTOM LEFT Guv'ments which hyperinflate freeze prices to keep them from skyrocketing. This completes the destruction of their economy. $10, 10 apples, $1 apples. After $90 of hyperinflation, $100 and 10 apples, apple prices should increase to $10. Guv'ment freezes apple prices at $6. 10 apples x $6 = $60. $60 buys all apples in the economy. The other $40 can't be spent. People realize that price freezes have turned the entire economy into a game of musical chairs. They rush to stores, buy everything they can, and empty shelves. Americans take it for granted that they can buy a Coca Cola on a 100 degree day. So did Zimbabweans—prior to hyperinflation. That couldn't happen here, right? Wrong. After Richard Nixon removed gold backing from the dollar in 1971, people spent dollars to escape the inflation tax. Nixon tried freezing prices, creating the "stagflation" of the 1970s.

BOTTOM RIGHT Once shelves of every store in Zimbabwe emptied, people realized they would never be able to buy anything with their money and threw it away.

ELEMENTARY BUBBLENOMICS

That concludes Elementary Bubblenomics. Maybe you're smart and grasped everything easily, but for some people it's hard. So let's summarize:

Printing more money out of thin air is inflation. Inflation is NOT higher prices. Inflation causes higher prices. Inflation is expanding the money supply as if inflating a balloon.

Inflation skews the price signal that is the backbone of the free market. People mistake rapid increases in the supply of money for increases in demand or shifts in demand. This creates a euphoria or economic boom in which people incur debt to satisfy this illusory demand, or think themselves richer and spend wealth they never really had. Once the spigot of new money is shut off, the illusion is shattered, the boom ends and a bust occurs. These booms and busts are called the business cycle, and the primary cause of the business cycle is inflation. No inflation, no big business cycle. Period.

Inflation causes price increases because printing more money devalues each unit of it. The owner of newly printed money siphons wealth from everyone holding existing money. New money has value because all the old money has less value. The value the old money lost is equal to the value the new money gained.

Inflation creates opportunities for speculators with inside knowledge of its real cause. Those who buy immediately get bargains, those who buy later pay higher prices and are defrauded.

Those who wield a society's money printing power own and control the society. Such Speculatos are smart enough to keep a very, very low profile.

Now onward, to goldsmiths and fractional reserve lending.

Junior High

Bubblenomics

GOLDSMITHS

"We are in danger of being overwhelmed with irredeemable paper, mere paper, representing not gold nor silver; no sir, representing nothing but broken promises, bad faith, bankrupt corporations, cheated creditors, and a ruined people. Of all contrivances for cheating the laboring classes of mankind, none has been more effective than that which deludes them with paper money."

—Daniel Webster

We started in the middle but must revisit the beginning. Man the hunter-gatherer developed agriculture. Some people were better at hunting, some farming. So hunters hunted, farmers farmed. The hunter had to trade with the farmer. There was no money. All trade was barter, goods exchanged for other goods.

This created problems of portability, divisibility, and durability. Hauling a wooly mammoth to trade for grain was tiring. Mammoth meat was not worth as much as a mammoth tusk, and mammoth carcasses rotted.

Money was created to solve these problems. Shells, seeds, jewels, tobacco. It was different commodities in different places and times, but always a scarce commodity of irrefutable value. Yet in all times one commodity came to be preferred as money.

Gold.

Gold has high unit value; a small amount buys much. It is scarce; seawater would not make good money. Unlike mammoths, gold is portable and durable. Gold is uniformly divisible; melting gold doesn't result in tusks and t-bones. Gold is also a commodity; if not used as money, it is still desired for jewelry and other uses.

Yet there was still the problem of the third oldest profession: thievery. The first bankers were goldsmiths who required safes to run their businesses. Citizens began storing gold in these safes, and the goldsmiths would give them receipts used to redeem the gold.

Such a receipt is a PROMISSORY NOTE. The goldsmith promised to keep gold in his safe, do nothing else with it, and redeem it upon demand. Rather than go to the goldsmith, get their gold, and use it to buy something, people began using the receipts to make purchases. Gold promissory notes circulated as money and were accepted in place of gold because they could always be exchanged for gold. A goldsmith who issued 100 one-ounce gold notes had 100 ounces of gold in his vault.

As everyone had confidence in the goldsmith's ability to cough up the gold, only 10% of his notes were redeemed. Goldsmiths were approached for loans because of their hoards of wealth. The 10% redemption rate allowed them to create more receipts than they had gold, and lend these extra receipts out at interest.

Fraud, in other words. A goldsmith with 100 ounces of gold in his vault could create 1,000 one-ounce gold receipts, 100 issued to the gold owners, 900 lent at interest. Only 10% of the 1,000 receipts would be redeemed for gold—100 ounces worth.

The goldsmith is careful and only circulates 500 receipts, 100 to the gold owners, 400 lent at interest. He keeps 20% reserves (100 oz. per 500 receipts) instead of 10% reserves (100 oz. per 1000 receipts). If more people than normal demand gold, he still has plenty. The goldsmith doesn't own the gold in his vault, isn't legally allowed to lend it, but is collecting interest on it five separate times! He produces nothing of value, but uses gold receipts he receives as interest payments to purchase goods & services which others labor to create.

No one knew how much gold the goldsmiths actually had. If they didn't get greedy and print oodles of receipts they were safe. But the money creation power proved too tempting. Goldsmiths flooded the market with bogus notes. Say a goldsmith with 100 ounces of gold circulates 2,000 one-ounce gold notes. People suspect a scam and mob his vault. 100 people get their ounce of gold, the other 1900 get screwed. This is the origin of the term "run on a bank." And the game of musical chairs. Goldsmiths were sometimes hung or dismembered. Quite a contrast to the golden parachutes and bailouts today.

History is a nauseating repetition of this fraud. The sleight of hand grows ever more sophisticated, but the basic mechanism remains depressingly simple: money is created out of thin air.

Paper money is a promissory note. Or should be. Holders expect to exchange it for something of value. This doesn't always happen. Inflation, of course, but at a deeper level, why?

Paper money is not wealth, it is exchanged for wealth. A gold note is not a commodity, only the gold it is redeemed for is. If gold is money, there is little risk of inflation because the effort it takes to mine gold can't be counterfeited. In every civilization in every time, gold bought real goods, and that won't change anytime soon.

The value of paper promissory notes is based not upon intrinsic wealth, but a promise. This is a risk. How good is the word of the person making the promise? In the case of dollars, government is making the promise. So to assess the integrity of the dollar, we might ask how much you trust government?

Rut roh raggy!

This is why nations made gold and silver money, as the U.S. Constitution specifies, for example. Not specified, specifies. Speculatos hate such systems because every new dollar must be dug up. Can't make much money that way.

Nations move to a goldsmith-like system in which banks accept gold deposits and issue promissory notes for that gold. Speculatos hate this system too, because if government does its job and enforces contracts, they'll go to prison if they issue more gold notes than gold. It is fraud, after all.

If Speculato is stuck in an honest nation that enforces contracts, he makes government a partner in the scam, and gets them to suspend the enforcement of gold contracts. Once he and GUV'MENT are in cahoots, he prints more notes than he has gold, and in time abandons gold backing altogether. Eventually gold is forgotten, and worthless paper is "money."

The term "guv'ment" may have jumped out at you. Vocabulary must keep pace with human ingenuity, and to avoid confusion while teaching bubblenomics, we'll be creating new words and defining them:

> guv'•ment, noun, a corrupt government which teams with Speculatos to pervert money. Governments create only enough money to facilitate trade. Guv'ments create an excess of money to levy a hidden inflation tax.

As we'll see later, the American government became a guv'ment in 1913. The American government levied an inflation tax sporadically before 1913, but the practice was institutionalized in 1913 and became permanent.

Speculatos who team up with guv'ments can't help chuckling at the stupidity of sheeple. To Speculatos, only a commodity with intrinsic value is money. To Speculatos, a promissory note with no value as a commodity is just paper, not money.

Sheeple is obviously a demeaning term, but this is how Speculatos view you and me:

> sheep•le, noun, people who do not understand bubblenomics, and can therefore be exploited by Speculatos and guv'ments. Combination of the words sheeple and people. Derogatory term used by Speculatos and guv'ments to describe the working class, which they consider a mindless herd that is meek and docile.

Once commodity money is a fable and sheeple have accepted worthless paper as "money," Speculato gets even more creative. He only had enough reserves— enough gold—to honor a fraction of his circulating paper notes. Once paper notes are used as reserves instead of gold, Speculato can circulate accounting entries as money instead of paper notes. He doesn't have to physically print most circulating money anymore! Virtual dollars become most of the money supply, and these virtual dollars are redeemed for paper note reserves. The charade Speculato has been engaging in is FRACTIONAL RESERVE LENDING, but he can't use it to shaft sheeple as much as he'd like until he's freed from the shackles of gold.

TO SKIP THE PICTURE PAGES AFTER THIS CHAPTER, PLEASE TURN TO PAGE 49

WHAT IS THE DIFFERENCE BETWEEN A $1 BILL AND A $100 BILL?

The difference between a $1 bill and a $100 bill is 2 zeros. The labor required to create either bill is equal, yet a $100 bill claims 100 times more goods than a $1 bill.

The difference between 1 ounce of gold and 100 ounces of gold is 99 ounces of gold. The effort required to create either amount of gold is not equal:

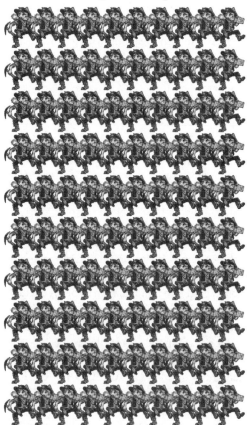

Creating 100 times more commodity money requires 100 times more labor. The labor required to create commodity money cannot be counterfeited. The supply of commodity money can therefore not be inflated monstrously the way the supply of paper money can.

THE **GHOST** OF A **DOLLAR** OR THE **BANKERS SURPRIZE**

Surely my eyes do not deceive me — It certainly must be a DOLLAR! — I declare I have not seen such a thing since I sold the last I had in my Vaults at 18 per Cent premium — If thou art a real DOLLAR do drop in my till and let me hear thee Chink — As I have been sued for payment of part of my notes in Specie I must collect some to pay them for quietnefs sake or the game would be up at once —

STEPHEN GEASPALL.
Banker & Shaver.
Paper Wholesale & Retail

NB — No foreign Bank notes taken on Deposit except such as are about 5 per cent above par —

W. Charles Del et Sculp

THE GHOST of a DOLLAR or the BANKERS SURPRIZE.

This sarcastic 1813 cartoon mocks bankers who circulated more "gold backed" notes than they had gold to honor them. The upper left portion reads: "Surely my eyes do not deceive me. It certainly must be a DOLLAR! I declare I have not seen such a thing since I sold the last I had in my vaults at 18 per cent premium. If thou art a real DOLLAR do drop in my till and let me hear thee clink. As I have been sued for payment for part of my notes in Specie I must collect some to pay them for quietnefs sake or the game would be up at once". At this time a dollar was a precious metal coin, not worthless paper. Specie is precious metal coin money. The upper right portion reads, "STEPHEN GEASPALL, Banker and Shaver, Paper Wholesale & Retail, No foreign Bank notes taken on Deposit except such as are about 5 percent above par." Shaver was a colonial term for a swindler or extortioner, and the term was applied to crooked bankers. Bankers in this era were sued for fraud if they could not honor all deposits—an impossibility today because bank fraud has been legalized and institutionalized.

FRACTIONAL RESERVE LENDING

"The people must be helped to think naturally about money. They must be told what it is, and what makes it money, and what are the possible tricks of the present system which put nations and peoples under control of the few."

—Henry Ford

Paper dollars were once backed by gold. For every paper dollar that existed, there was supposed to be a fixed weight of gold in a vault, and a dollar bill could be redeemed for this fixed weight of gold. This is no longer the case. Now banks create money out of thin air.

In the first chapter, the Federal Reserve Bank printed $3 billion and guv'ment traded bonds for this physical currency. The author lied like a goldsmith. No physical money is printed. It is done virtually, on computers. We need another new word. Computer exists as a noun (a thing), we'll be using it as a verb (an action):

com•put•er, verb, to create money out of thin air on a computer ledger. Also: computered, computering.

Physical money is roughly 10% of America's money supply, 90% is computered. 9 virtual dollars per paper dollar. Paper money in this system serves the purpose that gold did in the goldsmith scam. Speculatos have indeed made progress.

Imagine the Federal Reserve Chairman sitting down, opening a ledger, and penciling $1,000,000,000 in the credit column. Or picture "Fedwire," a kind of Western Union for thieves. The Fed Chairman types $1,000,000,000 into a computer ledger, hits the enter key, and $1,000,000,000 springs into existence in a distant guv'ment bank account.

Guv'ment would issue payments with this money and payees would deposit funds, but make the simplistic assumption that Uncle Sam races to the taxmobile. Fire shoots out the back and he zips across Gotham to deposit his $1 billion at First Fraud Bank. The author pictures Eminem's "Get Down to Business" blaring, and The Riddler as bank manager, but whatever works for you.

First Fraud Bank opens a $1 billion account for Uncle Sam. Sam's deposit is a RESERVE, something the bank is supposed to set aside and store for him. It is also called a DEMAND DEPOSIT, as it can be demanded anytime. Demand deposits should be like a coat in a coat check, sitting waiting to be picked up. As opposed to a TIME DEPOSIT, which the bank lends out and returns to the depositor after a period of time.

Misrepresenting a time deposit as a demand deposit is fraud. If a coat check rents out a stored coat, he can be sued or jailed. Giving the fraud a respectable name like "fractional reserve coat checking" shouldn't change this fact. And doesn't change this fact—in any business besides banking. Unfortunately, bankers have had fractional reserve lending legalized and elevated to an economic principle. Banking is the only profession where counterfeiting and embezzling are legal.

Uncle Sam thinks his money will be kept 100% in reserve, but fractional reserve lending means that only a fraction must be kept in reserve, and the rest can be lent out. The reserve rate averages 10%, but the Federal Reserve can alter it by decree.

Uncle Sam deposited $1 billion, so only 10% or $100 million of this must be kept as a reserve. First Fraud Bank can lend 90% or $900 million out. This should leave $100 million in Uncle Sam's account. When he wins that aircraft carrier on e-bay and tries to pay for it, he finds $900 million missing from his account and freaks out, right?

Wrong. First Fraud Bank keeps $1 billion in Sam's account and creates $900 million in a new account. $900 million is computered. One moment $1,000 million exists, the next $1,900 million.

First Fraud Bank cannot spend the new money like normal cash. It is classified as an "excess" reserve and can only be used for loans. To turn the new money into profit, First Fraud Bank must lend it out and "earn" interest.

Bill Gates needs some chump change, so borrows $900 million from First Fraud Bank and deposits the loan check at Steal Second Bank.

Steal Second Bank repeats the fractional reserve process. $900 million deposited, 10% or $90 million kept as reserves, leaving 90% or $810 million to lend. Donald Trump needs a loan, so Steal Second Bank computers $810 million. One moment $1,900 million exists, the next $2,710 million. Trump deposits his loan check at Third Thievery Bank.

Third Thievery Bank repeats the fractional reserve process. $810 million deposited, 10% or $81 million kept as reserves, leaving 90% or $729 million to lend. Warren Buffet wants credit, so Third Thievery Bank computers $729 million. One moment $2,710 million exists, the next $3,439 million. Buffet deposits his loan check at Fourth Filch Bank. . .

On it goes. Each new deposit fractioned, money computered, loans issued. It is obscene, and almost unbelievable, but this is actually how it works.

At a 10% reserve rate, the theoretical limit for new money creation is 9 times the original deposit. In practice this limit is not reached, but a lower multiple can still pummel your purchasing power. Every time a new loan is spent by a borrower, money enters the economy and begins competing with yours. Your dollars are worth 1/11th of an apple instead of 1/10th. Or whatever the math works out to. New money buys existing goods & services, meaning less are available for remaining money to claim.

$1 billion was deposited. Banks fraction this into $9 billion, lent at say 5% interest. Sheeple think banks lend the original deposit once, earning 5% interest. Banks actually lend it 9 times, earning 45% interest. In just 2 years, banks earn $1.102 billion in interest, more than doubling the initial deposit. Legalized loan sharking.

In the boom phase of this fractional reserve lending system, so much money is created out of thin air that you can dress a chimp up in a suit, give him a business plan written in crayon, and he'll get a loan. To understand why, we must view the scam from a banker's perspective. So put on your Chachi Versace, and let's take a stroll to Bankerville.

TO SKIP THE PICTURE PAGES AFTER THIS CHAPTER, PLEASE TURN TO PAGE 54

FRACTIONAL RESERVE LENDING

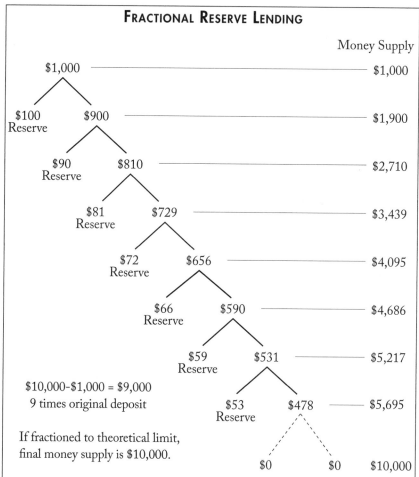

Money Supply

$1,000 ——————————————— $1,000

$100 Reserve $900 ——————————————— $1,900

$90 Reserve $810 ——————————————— $2,710

$81 Reserve $729 ——————————————— $3,439

$72 Reserve $656 ——————————————— $4,095

$66 Reserve $590 ——————————————— $4,686

$59 Reserve $531 ——————————————— $5,217

$10,000-$1,000 = $9,000
9 times original deposit

$53 Reserve $478 ——— $5,695

If fractioned to theoretical limit,
final money supply is $10,000.

$0 $0 $10,000

Only fractions of deposits must be kept by banks as reserves, the remainder can be lent out. The Federal Reserve decrees the reserve ratio, which averages 10%. 10% is chosen because experience has shown that this is the percentage of deposits which will be withdrawn. For a $1,000 deposit, 10% or $100 must be kept as reserves, 90% or $900 can be lent. The $900 is not subtracted from the depositor's account, an additional $900 is created out of thin air, increasing the money supply to $1,900. When the $900 loan is spent and deposited, it can also be fractioned and relent. The process repeats recursively, and at a 10% reserve ratio can reach a theoretical maximum of 9 times the original deposit. Deposits are rarely fractioned this much, but 1/3rd of the potential is reached after the 4th fractioning, 1/2 after the 7th. Fractional reserve lending is portrayed as a legitimate economic principle, but it is just a confusing term that makes embezzlement and counterfeiting seem respectable to the ignorant. Honest banking requires 100% reserves—no fractional reserve lending is allowed.

DAILY FRACTIONAL RESERVE LENDING DURING HOUSING BUBBLE

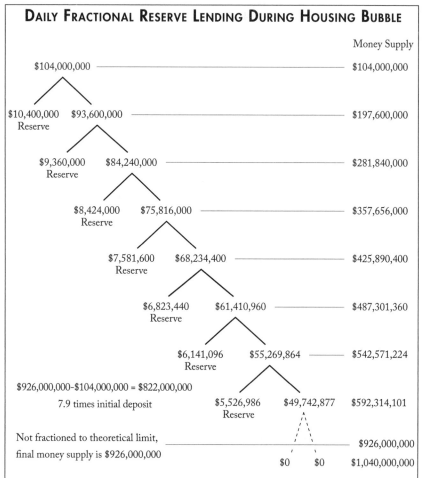

Money Supply

$104,000,000 ——————————————————— $104,000,000

$10,400,000 $93,600,000 ——————————————— $197,600,000
Reserve

$9,360,000 $84,240,000 ——————————— $281,840,000
Reserve

$8,424,000 $75,816,000 ——————— $357,656,000
Reserve

$7,581,600 $68,234,400 ——————— $425,890,400
Reserve

$6,823,440 $61,410,960 ——————— $487,301,360
Reserve

$6,141,096 $55,269,864 ——————— $542,571,224
Reserve

$926,000,000-$104,000,000 = $822,000,000

7.9 times initial deposit $5,526,986 $49,742,877 $592,314,101
Reserve

Not fractioned to theoretical limit, ——————————— $926,000,000
final money supply is $926,000,000 $0 $0 $1,040,000,000

The origin of the initial deposit was not mentioned. Fed can computer money and make purchases, usually T-debts. Fed buys newly-created T-debts from guv'ment or pre-existing T-debts owned by 3rd parties, and pays by computering money into commercial banks to pay sellers, literally creating money out of thin air. Banks fraction these computered deposits into additional deposits. The money Fed creates initially is called base money. From April 2000 to April 2006, Fed increased the base money supply from $572 billion to $801 billion, by $229 billion or 40%. Fed created $104 million per day on average, every day for 6 years. Commercial banks created an additional $1.8 trillion via fractional reserve lending, $822 million per day on average, every day for 6 years. Commercial banks could have created $936 million per day, or 9 times the initial Fed deposit of $104 million. They "only" created $822 million per day, 7.9 times the initial Fed deposit. Commercial banks created $822 million out of thin air each and every day for 6 years, lent it, and charged interest to suckers who actually have to work for money!

A World of Pure Imagination

"Come with me, and you'll be, in a world of pure imagination."
—Willy Wonka introducing his chocolate factory
In *Willy Wonka and the Chocolate Factory*

Welcome to Bankerville. How was the double mocha choka choca frappa crappa sextuple espresso? Good to get the old heart twitchin'. So you need $100,000 to be a Barbie psychologist? Provide therapy to dolls? No problem. No credit history? No worries. Never run a business? Gotta start somewhere. Looking to buy a few houses while you're at it? Already have three, huh. How about renovations for those houses? Maybe a pool or three...

Take an honest bank, Infinite Integrity. Infinite Integrity doesn't create money out of thin air or misrepresent time deposits as demand deposits. Running this honest bank takes skill. The marketplace is a tough place. Even smart individuals are bested by it. Infinite Integrity won't lend to any chimp that puts on a tie and presents a Ponzi scheme. Its deposits can't easily be replaced.

Computered money wasn't earned or saved. When First Fraud Bank creates new dollars, it picks the pocket of every American and siphons wealth from each dollar in their wallet. This wealth is used to make the loan. First Fraud Bank's mentality is that there is always another pocket to pick. More money can always be computered.

Imagine a swimming pool full of Kool Aid. Hard working suckers produce mix and have only cups to drink with. They toil harder and longer every year. More and more mix is poured into the pool, yet the Kool Aid is always weaker and more diluted.

Bankers have water and pitchers. Creating more money is like adding water to the pool. Fractional reserve lending is like scooping a pitcher of Kool Aid out and selling it. The Kool Aid is diluted, but bankers don't care because they stole a pitcher of it.

Suppose bankers add water and remove pitchers secretly and offer bogus explanations for the dilution. The pool is in Florida and alligators love Kool Aid. The heat evaporates water, diluting the Kool Aid. It has rained more. A Kool-Aid laborer would have to be pretty dumb not to figure things out, right? That's what Speculatos think of you and me. Such an obvious scam, seemingly. Yet sheeple don't deduce it.

Great gig, for the bankers. Confiscate wealth from sheeple via the inflation tax, and then loan them the wealth just confiscated. And charge them interest to boot.

Sheeple think they are borrowing pre-existing funds. If this were the case, someone would have surrendered money, and its claim to real goods & services. If the lender retains use of their money, and the borrower can also use it, then the process isn't a loan as honest people define the term.

If borrowers were told that money for loans is created out of thin air, they might ask why the bank wields this power? Shouldn't people giving up the wealth for the loan be paid interest? Why should a bank that didn't create the wealth which the loan utilizes receive interest payments on that wealth?

Sheeple don't ask these questions, so the fractional reserve charade continues. A fractional reserve bank will give a loan to any chimp because the wealth being lent isn't theirs. Loan officers ignore risk and approve loans which generate the highest issuing fees and interest payments. These profits are quickly paid to bank executives and owners as bonuses, dividends and stock options. These riches never have to be paid back, even if borrowers default and the bank goes bankrupt.

And who can resist the temptation of easy credit? Stuff for practically free, right? Only when it is too late do sheeple realize their error. And often times, as troubles during Depression v9.2006-201x indicate, not even then.

If you were a millionaire would you lend huge sums of money to someone with bad credit who is drowning in debt? If you wouldn't lend such people money, why are banks willing to? If sheeple thought it through on this level, they would realize something is fundamentally wrong.

The chilling thing about the fractional reserve system is that it takes on a life of its own. The Federal Reserve is a banker's bank. You can't sit down in front of your friendly neighborhood Alan Greenspan or Ben Bernanke, and open a Federal Reserve Checking Account. Print me $10,000, wouldya Ben? Normal banks for mere mortals are commercial banks, and this is where fractional reserve lending occurs. The Fed and guv'ment begin bubbles by creating money and depositing it in commercial banks, but once commercial banks start fractioning reserves, the bubble is beyond the Fed's control to a significant degree.

So commercial banks make risky loans because they care mainly about interest and fees. Borrowers borrow, never asking where all the magic credit came from, oblivious to the long term consequences of massive debt. Reserve upon reserve, loaned, deposited, fractioned, re-loaned. Billions of dollars spring into existence. The monetary bubble expands rapidly. Everyone feels richer, just like in Crusoeville.

Sheeple think bubbles can expand forever, but Speculatos know better and plan ahead. They computer money and loan it to you for a mortgage, but you put up the house as collateral for the loan. If you default on the loan, they get the house. This is always in the back of bankers' minds as they make loans they know can never be repaid.

TO SKIP THE PICTURE PAGES AFTER THIS CHAPTER, PLEASE TURN TO PAGE 61

FRACTIONAL RESERVE LENDING GENERATES MASSIVE PROFITS

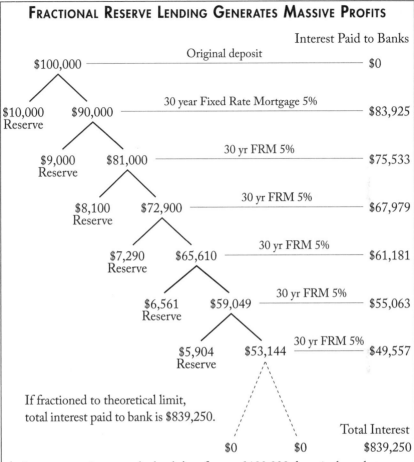

Interest Paid to Banks

$100,000	Original deposit		$0
$10,000 Reserve	$90,000	30 year Fixed Rate Mortgage 5%	$83,925
	$9,000 Reserve	$81,000	30 yr FRM 5%	$75,533
		$8,100 Reserve	$72,900	30 yr FRM 5%	$67,979
			$7,290 Reserve	$65,610	30 yr FRM 5%	$61,181
				$6,561 Reserve	$59,049	30 yr FRM 5%	$55,063
					$5,904 Reserve	$53,144	30 yr FRM 5%	$49,557

If fractioned to theoretical limit,
total interest paid to bank is $839,250.

Total Interest
$0 $0 $839,250

As interest rates increase, the banks' profit on a $100,000 deposit skyrockets:

30 yr FRMs 5%	$839,250	8 times original deposit
30 yr FRMs 6%	$1,042,542	10 times original deposit
30 yr FRMs 7%	$1,255,572	12 times original deposit
30 yr FRMs 8%	$1,477,350	14 times original deposit
30 yr FRMs 9%	$1,706,940	17 times original deposit

You sell your house for $100,000 and deposit the check in a bank. Banks pyramid your deposit via fractional reserve lending and issue 30 year mortgages at a fixed interest rate of 5%. Banks have lent none of their own assets, can earn more than 8 times your deposit in interest, and own each mortgaged house until paid off. If these mortgages are defaulted upon, taxpayers bailout banks. People toil much of their lives paying mortgages which are bookkeeping entries conjured by bankers.

DAILY PROFIT ON CONJURED LOANS DURING THE HOUSING BUBBLE

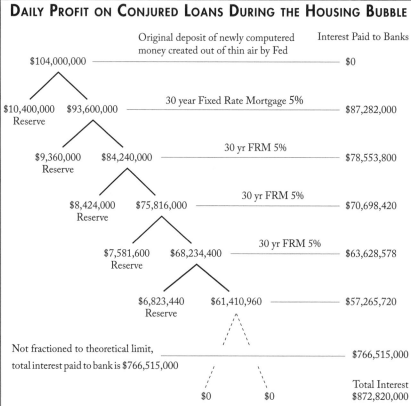

Original deposit of newly computered
money created out of thin air by Fed

Interest Paid to Banks

$104,000,000 — $0

$10,400,000 $93,600,000
Reserve

30 year Fixed Rate Mortgage 5% — $87,282,000

$9,360,000 $84,240,000
Reserve

30 yr FRM 5% — $78,553,800

$8,424,000 $75,816,000
Reserve

30 yr FRM 5% — $70,698,420

$7,581,600 $68,234,400
Reserve

30 yr FRM 5% — $63,628,578

$6,823,440 $61,410,960
Reserve

$57,265,720

Not fractioned to theoretical limit,
total interest paid to bank is $766,515,000

$766,515,000

$0 $0

Total Interest
$872,820,000

Banks don't fraction $104 million into one $87 million loan, they issue many loans. Loans besides mortgages were issued, including car loans, credit card loans, etc. Many loans were issued at rates far above 5%, assuming a 5% average rate is conservative. On average, everyday for 6 years, commercial banks created $822 million out of thin air and issued loans which would pay them $766 million in interest. During the 6 years of the housing bubble, commercial banks created $1.8 trillion worth of loans which paid $1.68 trillion dollars in interest payments, $11,200 in interest for every working American. The average American income is $45,000. In very rough terms, on average, Greenspan's Great Inflation and the fractional reserve lending it allowed, enabled bankers to confiscate $11,200 from every working American, or about 1/4 of a year of their labor. As mortgages are for 30 years, this is about 2 days of labor per year for every American, or 1% of their annual pay. Two days of labor or 1% of annual pay for 30 years may not seem like much, until you sum up the labor or pay of 150 million people: it is a year's labor from 37.5 million Americans! Via this esoteric fractional reserve mechanism, a cabal of bankers confiscated two days of labor from 150 million people every year for 30 years. Fractional reserve lending allows bankers to secretly tithe a percentage of the labor and wealth of an entire nation or civilization. Fractional reserve bankers are modern pharaohs.

An Interest-Only Housing Bubble Mortgage

AMORTIZATION SCHEDULE

NAME: ███████████████ PROD: 1358
LN AMT: $216,000 DESC: (32737) FS-FNMA 30 YEAR INTEREST
TERM: 360

PMT #	PAYMENT AMOUNT	INT RATE	DISTRIBUTION PRIN	INT	ENDING BALANCE
1	$1,147.50	6.375%		$1,147.50	$216,000.00
2	$1,147.50	6.375%		$1,147.50	$216,000.00
3	$1,147.50	6.375%		$1,147.50	$216,000.00
4	$1,147.50	6.375%		$1,147.50	$216,000.00
5	$1,147.50	6.375%		$1,147.50	$216,000.00
6	$1,147.50	6.375%		$1,147.50	$216,000.00
7	$1,147.50	6.375%		$1,147.50	$216,000.00
8	$1,147.50	6.375%		$1,147.50	$216,000.00
9	$1,147.50	6.375%		$1,147.50	$216,000.00
10	$1,147.50	6.375%		$1,147.50	$216,000.00
11	$1,147.50	6.375%		$1,147.50	$216,000.00
12	$1,147.50	6.375%		$1,147.50	$216,000.00
13	$1,147.50	6.375%		$1,147.50	$216,000.00
14	$1,147.50	6.375%		$1,147.50	$216,000.00
15	$1,147.50	6.375%		$1,147.50	$216,000.00
16	$1,147.50	6.375%		$1,147.50	$216,000.00
17	$1,147.50	6.375%		$1,147.50	$216,000.00
18	$1,147.50	6.375%		$1,147.50	$216,000.00
19	$1,147.50	6.375%		$1,147.50	$216,000.00
20	$1,147.50	6.375%		$1,147.50	$216,000.00
21	$1,147.50	6.375%		$1,147.50	$216,000.00
22	$1,147.50	6.375%		$1,147.50	$216,000.00
23	$1,147.50	6.375%		$1,147.50	$216,000.00
24	$1,147.50	6.375%		$1,147.50	$216,000.00
25	$1,147.50	6.375%		$1,147.50	$216,000.00
26	$1,147.50	6.375%		$1,147.50	$216,000.00
27	$1,147.50	6.375%		$1,147.50	$216,000.00
28	$1,147.50	6.375%		$1,147.50	$216,000.00
29	$1,147.50	6.375%		$1,147.50	$216,000.00
30	$1,147.50	6.375%		$1,147.50	$216,000.00
31	$1,147.50	6.375%		$1,147.50	$216,000.00
32	$1,147.50	6.375%		$1,147.50	$216,000.00
33	$1,147.50	6.375%		$1,147.50	$216,000.00
34	$1,147.50	6.375%		$1,147.50	$216,000.00
35	$1,147.50	6.375%		$1,147.50	$216,000.00

IF THIS AMORTIZATION SCHEDULE IS FOR AN ADJUSTABLE RATE MORTGAGE LOAN, IT ASSUMES HYPOTHETICAL INTEREST RATE AND PAYMENT CHANGES THAT MAY DIFFER FROM ACTUAL CHANGES.

PAGE 1

This is an actual mortgage issued during the Roaring 2000s housing bubble. It was interest-only for the first 15 years. No honest bank would ever issue such a loan. Imagine conjuring $216,000 for a mortgage out of thin air, and having some sucker toil to pay you $1,147.50 in interest per month on the loan. Or conjuring trillions for loans, and having millions of suckers toil to pay tens of billions of dollars in interest payments per month. Money for nothing. Literally.

AMORTIZATION SCHEDULE

NAME: ▉▉▉▉▉▉▉▉▉▉▉   PROD: 1358
LN AMT: $216,000   DESC: (32737) FS-FNMA 30 YEAR INTEREST
TERM: 360

PMT #	PAYMENT AMOUNT	INT RATE	DISTRIBUTION PRIN	INT	ENDING BALANCE
176	$1,147.50	6.375%		$1,147.50	$216,000.00
177	$1,147.50	6.375%		$1,147.50	$216,000.00
178	$1,147.50	6.375%		$1,147.50	$216,000.00
179	$1,147.50	6.375%		$1,147.50	$216,000.00
180	$1,147.50	6.375%		$1,147.50	$216,000.00
181	$1,866.78	6.375%	$719.28	$1,147.50	$215,280.72
182	$1,866.78	6.375%	$723.10	$1,143.68	$214,557.62
183	$1,866.78	6.375%	$726.94	$1,139.84	$213,830.68
184	$1,866.78	6.375%	$730.80	$1,135.98	$213,099.88
185	$1,866.78	6.375%	$734.69	$1,132.09	$212,365.19
186	$1,866.78	6.375%	$738.59	$1,128.19	$211,626.60
187	$1,866.78	6.375%	$742.51	$1,124.27	$210,884.09
188	$1,866.78	6.375%	$746.46	$1,120.32	$210,137.63
189	$1,866.78	6.375%	$750.42	$1,116.36	$209,387.21
190	$1,866.78	6.375%	$754.41	$1,112.37	$208,632.80
191	$1,866.78	6.375%	$758.42	$1,108.36	$207,874.38
192	$1,866.78	6.375%	$762.45	$1,104.33	$207,111.93
193	$1,866.78	6.375%	$766.50	$1,100.28	$206,345.43
194	$1,866.78	6.375%	$770.57	$1,096.21	$205,574.86
195	$1,866.78	6.375%	$774.66	$1,092.12	$204,800.20
196	$1,866.78	6.375%	$778.78	$1,088.00	$204,021.42
197	$1,866.78	6.375%	$782.92	$1,083.86	$203,238.50
198	$1,866.78	6.375%	$787.08	$1,079.70	$202,451.42
199	$1,866.78	6.375%	$791.26	$1,075.52	$201,660.16
200	$1,866.78	6.375%	$795.46	$1,071.32	$200,864.70
201	$1,866.78	6.375%	$799.69	$1,067.09	$200,065.02
202	$1,866.78	6.375%	$803.93	$1,062.85	$199,261.08
203	$1,866.78	6.375%	$808.21	$1,058.57	$198,452.88
204	$1,866.78	6.375%	$812.50	$1,054.28	$197,640.38
205	$1,866.78	6.375%	$816.82	$1,049.96	$196,823.56
206	$1,866.78	6.375%	$821.15	$1,045.63	$196,002.41
207	$1,866.78	6.375%	$825.52	$1,041.26	$195,176.89
208	$1,866.78	6.375%	$829.90	$1,036.88	$194,346.99
209	$1,866.78	6.375%	$834.31	$1,032.47	$193,512.68
210	$1,866.78	6.375%	$838.74	$1,028.04	$192,673.93

PAGE 6

15 years into the 30-year mortgage, this borrower had made 180 monthly payments totalling $206,550—an amount almost equal to the face value of the mortgage. Not one nickel of principal had been paid off. To begin paying principal halfway through the loan, the payment increased by 63% or $719.28, from $1,147.50 to $1,866.78. The borrower paid another $120,020 in interest during its next 15 years or 180 months of payments, bringing the total interest paid to $326,570. This borrower could actually afford a 63% higher payment, but many borrowers couldn't and planned on selling or refinancing once housing prices rose from the stratosphere into the mesosphere.

PMT #	PAYMENT AMOUNT	INT RATE	DISTRIBUTION PRIN	DISTRIBUTION INT	ENDING BALANCE
		AMORTIZATION SCHEDULE			
1	$1,344.32	6.375%	$196.82	$1,147.50	$215,280.72
2	$1,344.32	6.375%	$200.64	$1,143.68	$215,080.08
3	$1,344.32	6.375%	$201.71	$1,142.61	$214,878.37
4	$1,344.32	6.375%	$202.78	$1,141.54	$214,675.59
5	$1,344.32	6.375%	$203.86	$1,140.46	$214,471.74
...	...	...	...	...	...
356	$1,344.33	6.375%	$1,309.26	$35.07	$5,292.70
357	$1,344.33	6.375%	$1,316.21	$28.12	$3,976.49
358	$1,344.33	6.375%	$1,323.20	$21.13	$2,653.28
359	$1,344.33	6.375%	$1,330.23	$14.10	$1,323.05
360	$1,330.08	6.375%	$1,323.05	$7.03	$0

Had a conventional 30-year mortgage which paid principal throughout its duration been issued, monthly payments would have been $1,344.32, as shown in the amortization schedule above. This schedule shows only the first and last five years of payments, but you get the point. As the outstanding loan amount decreases, so does the interest paid each month, and a larger percentage of each successive payment is allocated to paying off the loan principal.

Had this mortgage been chosen, total interest paid would have been $268,474. The bank "earned" $58,096 in additional interest by creating a loan which paid only interest for 15 years. The sheeple with the mortgage shown on the previous two pages earned $50,000 per year and paid $10,000 for various taxes. Their after-tax income was $40,000 per year. The $326,570 in interest paid on their mortgage was 8.16 years of their after-tax labor. The $268,474 interest on the conventional mortgage shown above would have been 6.71 years of their after-tax labor. $58,096 in additional interest was an additional 1.45 years of their after-tax labor. By getting sheeple to agree to an interest-only mortgage, banks confiscated an additional 1.45 years of their labor! Even the conventional mortgage represents a staggering wealth confiscation of 6.71 years. Most people begin work at age 18, retire at age 65, and work 47 years. 6.71 years is 14% of 47 years. 14% of this borrower's lifetime income, tithed by a bank which produced nothing, simply conjured loan money out of thin air, and charged interest on that conjured loan money. Most Americans toil paying mortgages and other loans, and most all are conjured out of thin air by bankers who practice fractional reserve lending. The totality of banker's wealth confiscation is sickening, and is essentially form of serfdom. Of course, sheeple rarely think in these terms.

The sheeple who agreed to this mortgage also took out a $40,000 home equity credit line which they used to purchase a boat and other luxuries. They weren't even paying the principal on the house they "owned," yet leveraged it to buy a fishing boat! Such insanity was typical during the housing bubble.

Pimp My Economy

"When you're high you never, ever want to come down."

—Guns n' Roses

A spiraling economic bubble is a mental ward. All fiscal sanity is jettisoned. You go into a fractional reserve bank with change from lunch, and use it as a down payment on a house. An honest banker wanted 20% of the house value as a down payment, but no such absurd restrictions here. Would you like a 30 year mortgage, 40 year mortgage, or prefer to pay only the interest and never own your house?

Why, never own my house, of course.

A house in your neighborhood was valued at $100,000 ten years ago, $285,000 last year, and sold for $305,000 this year. Never mind interest, mortgages, debt. Buy as many houses as you can. Wait 10 years and sell them for 10 times what you paid. Or wait 10 weeks and turn a quick 10% profit. It's as sure as the sunrise. Easy money. Only a sucker wouldn't take a ride on this gravy train. Choo choo, all aboard!

This becomes the basic view of the average person.

In hindsight, everyone admits it was absurd. Economists that championed credit while the bubble inflated bemoan the unraveling. Even intelligent, conservative people are duped. They didn't buy extra houses, but took "equity" out of the home they "owned" and bought plasma TVs, hot tubs, THX jetski speakers. Or they used the "equity" for home improvements, expanding kitchens, redoing bathrooms, certain that every $1 spent on improvement would lead to $5 of resale value.

Our chimp with the Crayola business loan would note some problems with this mentality. If housing prices rise faster than income levels year after year, how will people afford mortgage payments long term? Can an entire nation earn a living flipping houses, or does someone have to produce goods & services?

Same old problem, the cars and toasters aren't reproducing like rabbits. Only the money is.

No one is interested in this contrarian drivel. Force feeding such wisdom to crazed credit hounds is futile.

The average person knows nothing of fractional reserve lending or money. If they did they might understand what was happening. Maybe. One hopes. Care to lend some?

So what was happening? Rising housing prices were caused by repeated injections of new money into the economy. Repeated inflations of the money supply.

First by the Federal Reserve, and then by commercial banks fractioning Fed deposits.

The Federal Reserve caused the housing boom by creating $229 billion over 6 years, $104 million per day on average. This is an average of $763 per American, $1,526 per American worker, for the 6 year period. Greenspan engineered the housing bubble by creating $763 out of thin air for every American!

Greenspan did not create this $229 billion all at once. It was conjured incrementally, and then inflated further by commercial banks practicing fractional reserve lending. Commercial banks created an additional $1.8 trillion over 6 years. This is an average of $6,000 per American, $12,000 per American worker, for the 6 year period.

Total money creation by Fed and commercial banks was $2.03 trillion, an average of $6,760 per American, $13,500 per American worker, for the 6 year period.

So Fed created $229 billion, which was inflated into $1.8 trillion of loans via fractional reserve lending. Millions of Americans up to their ears in debt obtained huge home loans, more than they dreamed possible. Every nickel of this money was puffed into existence out of thin air.

When you buy your house, and the seller deposits your loan check for the purchase, this is a new reserve which can be fractioned. 90% of the purchase price is lent to someone else to buy another home. More money created out of thin air. When this next person buys their home 90% of the purchase price is used to create yet another wave of new reserves. And so on, repeated with millions of home buyers...

Eventually the first money wave is petering out, the fractioned reserves growing small enough to be insignificant relative to the money supply. The pinged radar wave of rising prices is racing back to wreak havoc. A Crusoeville crash should occur, but before it does the Fed creates billions more dollars out of thin air. A new outgoing wave negates the incoming. Reserves are fractioned and expanded again, and on it goes...

How Much is a Dollar?

"That paper money has some advantages is admitted. But that its abuses also are inevitable and, by breaking up the measure of value, makes a lottery of all private property, cannot be denied."

—Thomas Jefferson

As with oranges and apples in Crusoeville, rising housing prices signify that money is worth less, not that homes are worth more. Ignorant about money and inflation, sheeple don't realize this.

Newly created money was not spent at grocery stores, go-cart tracks or bars, or the prices of food, go-cart rides, and bloody marys would have risen. 1.8 trillion computered dollars were used primarily to buy homes. Of course housing prices rose.

The scam would be easier to detect if a bloody mary increased in price from $4 to $8. Unfortunately, bar trips occur at the end of the business cycle, not the beginning. $8 bloody marys. Same vodka and tomato juice, double the price. Sheeple would catch on quick. Sadly, sheeple don't make cold calculations with houses because owning a home and raising a family in it stirs their emotions. Sheeple are more likely to pay $50,000 extra for a home than $4 extra for a bloody mary. At least we can look forward to a day when bloody marys cost $50,000.

Additional money made Crusoeville farmers think tastes had changed. They planted more apples and oranges to meet this "demand." Workers buy luxuries rather than expanding their business, but the misconception is the same. Sheeple think they are richer than they really are because they mistake an increase in the total supply of money for an increase in the supply only of theirs.

Take a $100,000 house in Crusoeville. What is it worth in terms of goods & services, rather than dollars of fluctuating value? Initially, 100,000 apples, because an apple has always been worth a dollar. Everyone knows that, even a child.

The house rises in dollar value, but perhaps not apple value, to $300,000. Those unaware that the money supply was inflated assume their $300,000 house is worth 300,000 apples. This is the tragic mistake. Apples are a metaphor for the cost of everything. Food, rent, clothes, retirement. A discrepancy of 200,000 apples is the difference between retiring and working until you drop dead.

For all housing prices to rise, only a few houses have to sell at a high price. Houses near a house that sold for $300,000 are presumed to have a similar value. They rise in value without being sold. A modest increase in money supply is amplified into a massive increase in perceived housing wealth.

$300,000 houses. Everyone assumes they have a claim to 3 times more apples because their house is worth 3 times as many dollars. But apples didn't triple in quantity when the monetary value of a house did.

This is a big, big, big problem.

Suppose we sum up Crusoeville's apparent wealth. Ask each person how many apples their house is worth, and then add up their answers to obtain the total perceived apple value of all Crusoeville houses. The total perceived apple value is much greater than the total number of apples that exist or can even be grown.

The wealth is an illusion! An appalling, mind-blowing illusion!

The illusion grows even more appalling with real-world U.S. housing bubble data. In early 2000 just before Greenspan inflated the housing bubble, total mortgage debt outstanding in America was $6.32 trillion. In early 2006 just before Greenspan popped the housing bubble, total mortgage debt outstanding was $12.4 trillion. This includes new houses, existing houses sold for higher prices, second mortgages, and equity extracted from homes by refinancing and increasing mortgages. $6.08 trillion in mortgages issued in 6 years! $1.01 trillion in new mortgages issued per year!

If Greenspan "only" created $1.8 trillion for loans, how were $6.08 trillion in mortgages issued? All mortgages weren't kept on banks' books, many were sold to Wall Street, which resold them as "Mortgage-Backed Securities" or "MBSs." Banks issued mortgages, sold them to MBSs, used money from the sale to issue additional mortgages, sold those mortgages to MBSs, used money from the sale to issue additional mortgages... Via this mechanism, $1 of newly created loan money led to a larger amount of mortgage debt.

There are roughly 130 million houses in America. The average new home sold for $207,000 in 2000, $305,000 in 2006, a $98,000 increase. Only a few million homes sold at these exorbitant market prices, but everyone who owned a home assumed it was worth about $100,000 more. 130 million homes each assumed to be worth $100,000 more is $13 trillion dollars of percieved wealth. Americans believed they possessed $13 trillion dollars in wealth which did not exist and was a mirage! That estimate is extremely rough, but even conceding significant error, it is still a stupefying sum.

In Crusoeville, people think a $300,000 house is worth 300,000 apples, but it is actually worth 100,000 apples. Apple prices should rise and housing prices fall, until the perceived value of all houses is equal to the number of apples that exist.

The dollar is the yardstick of value. Making it suddenly worth more or less than its dependable old value of 1 apple puts people at the mercy of Speculatos. Speculatos realize a dollar no longer represents a consistent amount of assets, but everyone else doesn't.

This explains the misconception which enables a bubble, but it isn't consistent with observation. In the real world, housing prices plummeted, but apple (i.e., everything else) prices didn't skyrocket. If housing prices decline, yet apple prices don't rise, what happened to newly created money that drove up housing prices?

TO SKIP THE PICTURE PAGES AFTER THIS CHAPTER, PLEASE TURN TO PAGE 68

ECONOMIC PROSPERITY REQUIRES A STABLE MONETARY UNIT

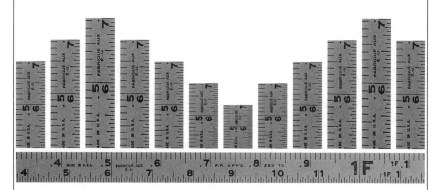

Imagine you are a carpenter. Every time you open your tape measure, the length of an inch has changed without you realizing it.

Imagine you are a baker. Every time you grab your measuring cup, the number of fluid ounces in a cup has changed without you realizing it.

Imagine you are a sucker. Every time you open your wallet and grab a dollar, the amount of goods its buys has decreased without you realizing it. The monetary unit is a measure of wealth just as the tape measure unit is a measure of length and the measuring cup unit is a measure of volume. If you don't know the dollar is being devalued, you make faulty decisions based on this misconception.

MONEY SUPPLY CHANGES CONFUSE THE MEANING OF PRICES

 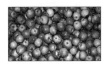 

A "Crusoe" economy with only houses, apples, and money. Apple prices have changed little over time. In people's minds, an apple is a dollar and vice versa. Apples are symbolic of food, clothes, cars, gas—everything in the economy except houses, the goods that can be bought with money from a sold house. Initially there are 50 houses, 5,000 apples, and $10,000 in circulation:

| 50 Houses
$100 Per House
$5,000 Total | 5,000 Apples
$1 Per Apple
$5,000 Total | $10,000
Money Supply |

> As an apple costs $1, people think a $100 house is worth 100 apples
> 50 houses x 100 apples per house = 5,000 perceived apples
> There are 5,000 apples.
> 1 house is worth 100 apples

An additional $1,000 is printed and spent in real estate, creating a housing bubble. 5 houses are sold for $200. As houses now sell for $200, the other 45 home owners assume their house is also worth $200, even though they didn't sell their house. People don't know more money has been printed. They think rising housing prices mean increased wealth:

| 50 Houses
$200 Per House
$10,000 Total | 5,000 Apples
$1 Per Apple
$5,000 Total | $11,000
Money Supply |

> As an apple costs $1, people think a $200 house is worth 200 apples.
> 50 houses x 200 apples per house = 10,000 perceived apples.
> There are only 5,000 apples.
> 1 house is not worth 200 apples, it is actually worth 100 apples.

The perceived apple supply is 10,000, 5,000 more apples than exist. Apple and housing price signals are incorrect. People who believe these incorrect price signals malinvest or spend wealth they don't really have. Apple prices must increase, or housing prices decrease, or a combination of both. When this happens, sheeple realize that increasing housing prices were a mirage.

ANY STABLE SUPPLY OF MONEY WILL PRODUCE PROSPERITY
THE IMPORTANT THING IS NOT TO YO-YO THE MONEY SUPPLY

Assume a Crusoeville economy with 1,000 apples. They represent the total amount of real wealth in the economy—goods & services like land, houses, cars, food, clothes. There are 100 ounces of gold money:

1,000
Apples

100
Ounces of Gold Money

The total supply of money chases the total supply of goods & services, setting prices. 1 ounce of gold buys 10 apples. Silver is worth less than gold and can be used for smaller transactions. In this simple example there is only gold. Suppose we started with 1,000 ounces of gold:

1,000
Apples

1,000
Ounces of Gold Money

1 ounce of gold buys 1 apple. Suppose we started with 10 ounces of gold:

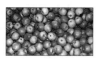

1,000
Apples

10
Ounces of Gold Money

1 ounce of gold buys 100 apples.

Which option is better? The cost of gold mining notwithstanding, the answer is none. Economic prosperity results under any of these money supplies. The important thing is that a person with an ounce of gold can always trade it for the same amount of apples, and that everyone works to obtain an ounce of gold. Prosperity is destroyed if you set one of these money supplies and suddenly change it without telling people. People think their ounce of gold buys the old amount of apples indicated by the old price, when their ounce of gold actually buys a new, different amount of apples. No one except Midas can produce gold without effort. Paper money can be created effortlessly. This is why commodity money is vital. It anchors the money supply, keeping it stable and limiting inflation.

Pop Goes the Bubble

"The way to make money is to buy when blood is running in the streets."
—John D. Rockefeller

"The paper bubble is then burst. This is what you and I, and every reasoning man, seduced by no obliquity of mind or interest, have long forseen. Yet it's disastrous effects are not the less for having been foreseen. We were laboring under a dropsical fulness of circulating medium [money]. Nearly all of it is now called in by the banks who have the regulation of the safety valves of our fortunes and who condense or explode them at their will. Lands in this state cannot now be sold for a year's rent: and unless our legislature have wisdom enough to effect a remedy by a gradual diminution only of the medium [money supply], there will be a general revolution of property in this state."
—Thomas Jefferson, during Depression v1.1819-1823

New money was computed to be loaned, so repaying the loan means the money is uncomputed. Loan principal payments vanish with the click of an enter key. Another loan can be offered if the bank hasn't fractioned all its reserves. But if people become uncertain, or so straddled with debt they can't afford additional payments, the bank can't find additional borrowers and therefore can't issue new loans. Banks can offer loans, but someone has to accept.

Eventually loans are paid off, but new ones are not issued, and the total supply of money is reduced.

How can money vanish? That's absurd, isn't it? As absurd as it magically springing into existence in the first place, no more, no less.

An ever increasing supply of money caused increasing prices. Now that this supply of money is declining, so do prices.

The party is over. Sheeple are up to their eyeballs in debt. Treading water with cinderblocks strapped to their feet. Everyone who could afford a new car bought two, plus a home with twice the square footage they needed. No 36-months-interest-free furniture sales or $2,000-cash-back car ads can convince anyone to accept any more loans.

Sheeple realize they are debt-peons, slaves to payments. The dream home that once made them smile now causes their stomach to churn. There is not enough money to drive the boat to the lake, much less gas it up or buy beer and brats.

There is no way out. This isn't suck-it-up-and-buy-hamburger-instead-of-steak-for-6-months debt. It is I'm-going-to-be-broke-the-rest-of-my-freakin'-

life-and-never-retire debt.

Selling things doesn't help because prices are plummeting, and everyone bought on the upswing. Even if buyers could be found for cars, boats and homes, prices are so low that large sums would still be owed on the loans. This might replace one of the cinderblocks with a brick, but that's it.

The average person doesn't understand fiat money, but bankers do. They knew the money supply would eventually contract and ashes, ashes, we all fall down.

Don't beat up your local bank teller. She probably has no idea what fractional reserve lending is. By bankers the author means billionaire generals, not corporals doing their bidding. The capos, the branch managers, know what fractional reserve lending is but rarely ponder its philosophical nuances. Capos went to college, and fractional reserve lending is taught at every university in America. Laundered by academia, it becomes legitimate, a gospel preached with reverence. Few students question its morality.

Soon the $100,000 house that rose to $300,000 is valued at $275,000. Then $250,000. Then $225,000.

People panic. Uncertainty grows. No one takes out new loans. This accelerates the contraction of the money supply.

Those who planned on using the "equity" in their home for retirement merely have a long term problem. Those who took "equity" out now find themselves paying a $300,000 mortgage on a $225,000 home, but they can perhaps buckle down, do little else but service their debts, and survive.

Millions signed mortgages with balloon payments due after a few years, or extremely low "subprime" interest rates that later increase. They assumed houses would rise in price forevermore, and planned on selling or refinancing in the short term. This horde of debt peons can barely pay their current mortgage, and then it doubles or a five-figure balloon payment is due.

We all know this idiot. Some of us are this idiot.

Bankers foreclose on these houses. They have now converted computered money into a physical asset. Take a $100,000 house financed at 6% with a 4% down payment. The debt peon makes payments for 3 years and then defaults. The bank has received $4,000 down, plus roughly $600 a month or $21,000. $25,000 total. A quarter of the value of the house in just three years. The bank can sell the house outright for 85% of market value and have made an easy $10,000, or remortgage it and let another debt-peon pay 25% of the value in the first three years.

A small number of foreclosures can be profitable to a bank. The downturn or bust that horrifies you makes bankers smile.

At first.

As it becomes apparent that thousands cannot pay their mortgages, even bankers worry. When a house is foreclosed upon and sold, the entire sale amount is uncomputed and vanishes with the click of an enter key. The money supply doesn't just shrink, it shrivels.

Tens of thousands of homes are soon on the foreclosure block. Each one liquidated shrinks the money supply, decreasing home prices. Those who still have mortgages see the value of their home plummet even faster, widening the "negative equity" gap between the mortgage and home's actual worth. Many decide to leave the keys under the doormat and walk away.

Those that don't walk away cut spending to service debt. Business slows everywhere. Inventories rise, profits fall, production is slashed, workers are laid off. Unemployed workers can't pay mortgages. More houses foreclosed. More money gone into the fractional reserve black hole. The money supply continues contracting, but can't be re-expanded because people have to take out loans for new money to be created.

Soon millions of houses are in foreclosure and even bankers are bankrupt. Those who understand banking but don't profit from it want to let banks fail and strip them of money creation power. Most who understand banking profit from banking, and demand bailouts. Taxpayers "donate" enough to keep the banks afloat. The Depression eventually fades from memory. Banks then resume their money creation and manufacture another Depression.

Junior High Bubblenomics

That concludes Junior High Bubblenomics. Let's digest what we've learned. If you feel overwhelmed, you're not alone. Most people learning bubblenomics for the first time feel the same.

Honest money is a commodity like wheat, wood or mammoth. Its inherent value as a commodity is why it is accepted as money in the first place. Any commodity can be used as money, but most civilizations choose gold because it is portable, divisible, durable, and scarce enough that it has high unit value.

Goldsmiths stored gold and issued promissory notes for each ounce. These notes were accepted in place of gold and became the first modern paper money. Goldsmiths created more notes than they had gold. When people demanded their gold, the goldsmith ran out. People traded goods & services for notes because they believed notes could be redeemed for gold, but were cheated.

Paper money is not wealth, it is exchanged for wealth. Paper money is not a commodity with intrinsic value and therefore entails a risk. The supply of commodity money can only be increased when people labor to produce more commodities, but mountains of paper money are created with a mere printing press or enter key.

Fractional reserve lending is a goldsmith-esque fraud. New money equal to 90% of a bank deposit can be created out of thin air and lent. When this loan is deposited, 90% of the deposit can be re-fractioned and lent. The process repeats, each new loan resulting in a purchase, but also new money created out of thin air used to make another loan. . .

Skyrocketing housing prices were a pyramid scheme driven by injections of new money. Few realized this. Rising housing prices were mistaken for an increase in the value of houses. Homes became a way to make quick money rather than a place to live. People bought houses they couldn't afford, banking on rising housing prices. The economy became a madhouse.

People thought they could sell houses at absurdly-inflated prices, and buy goods & services at current prices. That a dollar of housing value would buy an apple or 13 loaves of bread. This was the tragic miscalculation. The perceived value of all houses exceeded the actual value of all goods & services. Goods & services did not magically multiply like the money. A dollar of housing value was only worth a fraction of an apple or a single loaf of bread. Stated another way, people thought more money meant an increased amount of goods at the same old prices, rather than the same old amount of goods at increased prices.

When money is created out of thin air, any chimp can get a loan. Soon everyone is drowning in debt. Banks offer new loans. No one accepts, so no new loan money is created. No additional money drives housing prices higher.

71

As loans are paid off, money created solely to facilitate them vanishes. The money supply contracts. Housing prices decline.

People bought houses to make quick money, not payments for 30 years. They can't afford payments, so default on mortgages. Banks liquidate mortgages and mountains of computered loan money vanish. The bubble pops, housing prices plummet, millions are ruined.

Honest bankers lending pre-existing money are stingy because money is hard to obtain. Fractional reserve bankers lending computered money make unsound loans because they can always create more money.

Newly created dollars have value because wealth has been siphoned from everyone holding an existing dollar. The total supply of money claims the total supply of goods & services; if the supply of money is increased but the supply of goods & services stays the same, each unit of money claims less wealth—less goods & services. Fractional reserve bankers steal wealth when computering money, lend this stolen wealth out, and charge interest.

A house bought with a mortgage is collateral for the mortgage. If the borrower defaults, the banker owns the house. Using only computered money, the fractional reserve banker receives interest payments on the house, and can end up owning it.

Bankers overinflate bubbles and pop them. Collect interest payments on the upside, assets on the "downside." Booms and busts are not a byproduct of our monetary system, but a goal of it.

Whose goal? To answer this question we'll revisit Crusoeville, and history. History bores many, so we'll try to move quickly. The elite want you ignorant of history, so you don't realize current events are a repetition of old. Don't let them win.

Some of the claims made in the next section of the book are difficult to accept. Documentation is presented gradually, after initial claims are made, so please be patient.

Onward to High School. To Crusoeville's political system.

HIGH SCHOOL

BUBBLENOMICS

Speculatos' Lackeys

"We are governed, our minds are molded, our tastes formed, our ideas suggested, largely by men we have never heard of. Whatever attitude one chooses to take toward this condition, it remains a fact that in almost every act of our daily lives, whether in the sphere of politics or business, our social conduct or our ethical thinking, we are dominated by a relatively small number of persons who understand the mental processes and social patterns of the masses. It is they who pull the wires which control the public mind, and who harness old social forces and contrive new ways to bind and guide the world. ... The conscious and intelligent manipulation of the organized habits and opinions of the [public] is an important element in democratic society. Those who manipulate this unseen mechanism of society constitute an invisible government which is the true ruling power of our country. ... If we understand the mechanism and motives of the group mind, is it not possible to control and regiment the masses according to our will without their knowing about it? "

—Edward Bernays, Father of Propaganda

"The fact that an opinion has been widely held is no evidence that it is not utterly absurd. ... This subject [mass psychology] will make great strides when it is taken up by scientists under a scientific dictatorship ... Although this science will be diligently studied, it will be rigidly confined to the governing class. The populace will not be allowed to know how its convictions were generated. When the technique has been perfected, every government that has been in charge of education for a generation will be able to control its subjects securely."

—Bertrand Russell, Nobel Prize Winner in Literature

"History will be kind to me for I intend to write it."

—Winston Churchill

Back to Crusoeville. You are President, and more interested in doing good than enriching yourself. Crusoeville really is fictional! You realize people would be better off without Speculato and give speeches educating them about his frauds.

The granny apple viper worm is the scourge of Crusoeville. One bite from it is fatal, though such deaths are rare. Commoners take their chances, but the wealthy buy winesap apples because their acidic interior makes them inhospitable to the viper worm.

You are shrewd, and spend extra for winesap apples once you become a critic of Speculato. When you bite into a winesap apple one day and begin chewing you feel a squiggling and then agony. You spit out a viper worm. As your vision blurs and you keel over, you note an incision in the bottom of your granny apple.

After whacking you, Speculato makes political donations to control what candidates won't do. Free apple cider for retirees? Fine. The Apple-A-Day guv'ment medical plan? Sure. But a candidate who mentions Speculato or the money supply faces a well-funded opponent.

Speculato buys up newspapers to keep them from educating sheeple about him or money. Any reformer who discusses these topics is smeared by Speculato's papers. Those times inflation must be mentioned, it is obscured with terms like "liquidity," "monetization," or "cost pressures." Speculato's papers portray inflation as a price phenomenon rather than a money supply phenomenon. Sheeple focus on the effect, not the cause. As long as sheeple focus on the effect, any bogus cause can be concocted.

Soon it is as if Speculato and money supply machinations don't exist. Inflation and the business cycle are viewed as unavoidable natural occurrences like the seasons.

Your death is portrayed as a tragedy by history books, but your crusade against money is downplayed. The textbook company happens to be owned by Speculato's newspaper.

You had a life insurance policy, so your grandson was born wealthy and his time is his own. He emulates men like Thomas Jefferson and James Madison, reads 10 to 12 hours daily, and becomes enlightened.

Dusting for prints in that crime scene called history, your grandson finds that leaders who oppose Speculatos and champion honesty money are often assassinated. Bogus reasons are given, but careful research reveals Speculatos' fingerprints.

Your grandson wants to run for President to clean up the money mess. With honest money, society prospers, as history indicates.

Your grandson knows he won't be elected. Speculato is aware of his views, and will fund an attractive, slick-talking candidate. This opponent's jokes, banter, and promises will resonate with sheeple more than your grandson's deranged stories of murdered leaders and boring lectures about money.

If your grandson bucked the odds, was elected, and instituted monetary reform, he knows Speculatos would kill him. This is disheartening to him. It means Depressions and wars are doomed to continue endlessly, and history will always be an apocalypse.

Your grandson and others like him withdraw from public life, leaving Speculatos' lackeys to hold public offices. Soon it is a given that the honest and enlightened will not seek election.

Many of the enlightened withdraw from society, becoming hermits. Those that remain shut the truth out and focus on their family, friends and jobs. To the enlightened, reading the papers and observing politics is like pulling over with a bucket of popcorn and watching a roadside murder.

Exit Crusoeville, enter reality. The view of history just presented is supported by massive historical evidence, but because it is so different from what sheeple are taught, they usually dismiss it without reviewing the evidence.

Exactly what Speculatos want.

Systematic documentation of this alternative view of history would require thousands of pages. Brevity was a primary goal of this book. A quick summary of this alternative view of history is included in outlined picture pages throughout the High School degree, and additional resources are listed for those who wish to learn more.

Sheeple have a strong psychological motive for rejecting the truth; once the mask is removed, reality can be depressing. Speculatos plunder the world while sheeple regurgitate fables propagated (and propagandized) by the media. Prices are going up because productivity plateaued, says the man slaving 60 hours a week. The war was caused by Oilville, they envy our prosperity and hate our religion. A bailout is necessary to pull us out of the Depression and prevent another one. Higher taxes are the only solution, and we must all sacrifice for the greater good.

For the enlightened individual who is trying to oppose Speculatos, the greatest obstacle is not Speculatos, but sheeple. Sheeple's stupidity can be truly disheartening.

But the average person isn't stupid! Stop saying that about them! You are over-simplifying, distorting. Stop demeaning the average person!

The author is trying to help the average person, or he would not have written this book, but he refuses to sugarcoat the views of the elite. Please remember that terms like sheeple and debt-peon are views of Speculatos, not the author. These terms may anger you, but it would be dishonest not to portray the elites' perspective candidly.

The common man has demeaned himself, Speculato would say. Especially the common American, who was bequeathed a nation where none of these ills existed at first. I didn't take liberty with Americans, they gave liberty away freely.

As for the stupidity of sheeple? Speculato rarely laughs so hard. The stupidity of the common man is the one thing Speculato can always bank on. To say sheeple are not stupid is to discard rudimentary powers of observation, and makes Speculato laugh harder, as such a ridiculous statement is something only sheeple would say. To Speculato, the political and economic structure of the world is prima facie proof of the stupidity of sheeple. Speculato's view is that sheeple which are anything but stupid would deduce the fraud he perpetrates and stop the economic rape.

TO SKIP THE PICTURE PAGES AFTER THIS CHAPTER, PLEASE TURN TO PAGE 88

SPECULATOS HAVE OWNED THE MEDIA SINCE 1915

World War I was America's first major external war, and to dupe sheeple into fighting and funding it, Speculatos had to gain control of the newspapers that shape public opinion. In 1917, Representative Oscar Callaway fought Speculatos, entering the truth about their control of the media into the Congressional record where it could not be edited away:

"I insert in the record at this point a statement showing the newspaper combination ... in March, 1915, the J.P. Morgan interests, steel, shipbuilding and powder interests and their subsidiary organizations, got together 12 men high up in the newspaper world and employed them to select the most influential newspapers in the United States and sufficient number of them to control generally the policy of the daily press of the United States. These 12 men worked the problem out by selecting 170 newspapers and then began, by an elimination process, to retain only those necessary for the purpose of controlling the general policy of the daily press throughout the country. They found it was only necessary to purchase the control of 25 of the greatest newspapers. Emissaries were sent to purchase the policy of these papers; an agreement was reached; the policy of the papers was bought, to be paid for by the month; an editor was furnished for each paper to properly supervise and edit information regarding the questions of preparedness, militarism, financial policies and other things of national and international nature considered vital to the interest of the purchasers. This contract is in existence at the present time, and it accounts for the news columns of the daily press of the country."

Today Speculatos don't have to bribe the media. They bought up all large media corporations, had these buy up smaller media companies, and now own the media.

PROPAGANDA
PERPETUAL PSYCHOLOGICAL WARFARE WAGED AGAINST THE HERD

"Americans are too broadly underinformed to digest nuggets of information that seem to contradict what they know of the world ... Instead, news channels prefer to feed Americans a constant stream of simplified information, all of which fits what they already know. That way they don't have to devote more air time or newsprint space to explanations or further investigations. . . Politicians and the media have conspired to infantilize, to dumb down, the American public. At heart, politicians don't believe that Americans can handle complex truths, and the news media, especially television news, basically agrees."

—Tom Fenton, former CBS Foreign Correspondent

"Television is altering the meaning of "being informed" by creating a species of information that might properly be called disinformation. Disinformation does not mean false information. It means misleading information—misplaced, irrelevant, fragmented or superficial information—information that creates the illusion of knowing something, but which in fact leads one away from knowing."

—Neil Postman, Author and Media Theorist

"The media serve the interests of state and corporate power, which are closely interlinked, framing their reporting and analysis in a manner supportive of established privilege and limiting debate and discussion accordingly. ... The point of public relations slogans like "Support Our Troops" is that they don't mean anything. ... That's the whole point of good propaganda. You want to create a slogan that nobody's going to be against, and everybody's going to be for. Nobody knows what it means, because it doesn't mean anything. Its crucial value is that it diverts your attention from a question that does mean something."

—Noam Chomsky

"Media manipulation in the U.S. today is more efficient than it was in Nazi Germany, because here we have the pretence that we are getting all the information we want. That misconception prevents people from even looking for the truth."

—Mark Crispin Miller, Professor of Media Studies, New York University

"The media I've had a lot to do with is lazy. We fed them and they ate it every day."

—Michael Deaver, Ronald Reagan's Deputy Chief of Staff

"To play millions of minds, to watch them slowly respond to an unseen stimulus, to guide their aspirations without their knowledge—all this whether in high capacities or in humble, is a big and endless game of chess of extraordinary excitement."

—Sidney Webb, British Secretary of State (1929-1931)

"The ruling class has the schools and press under its thumb. This enables it to sway the emotions of the masses."

—Albert Einstein

"It is perfectly possible for a man to be out of prison, and yet not be free—to be under no physical constraint and yet to be a psychological captive, compelled to think, feel and act as the representatives of the national state, or of some private interest within the nation, wants him to think, feel and act. The nature of psychological compulsion is such that those who act under constraint remain under the impression that they are acting on their own initiative. The victim of mind-manipulation does not know that he is a victim. To him the walls of his prison are invisible, and he believes himself to be free. That he is not free is apparent only to other people. His servitude is strictly objective."

—Aldous Huxley, Author

"Expecting FOX News to report real news is as silly as waiting for George Bush and Dick Cheney [or Barack Obama and Joe Biden] to tell the truth. ... Americans care, but it's tough to care when you don't know what's going on. That ignorance is what the warmakers count on and what the corporate media delivers."

—Amy Goodman, Journalist

"The American propaganda system is not centrally programmed as in a totalitarian state. Instead it permeates the culture, media, and institutions. Individuals who point out unpleasant realities of current or past American behavior are often subjected to social pressures and treated as pariahs. They are disturbers of the dream."

—William H. Boyer, Author

"As political and economic freedom diminishes, sexual freedom tends to compensatingly increase and the dictator ... will do well to encourage that freedom in conjunction with the freedom to daydream under the influence of dope, movies, and radio. It will help to reconcile his subjects to the servitude which is their fate."

—Julian Huxley, Evolutionary Biologist, brother of Author Aldous Huxley

"We find few historians who have been diligent enough in their search for truth; it is their common method to take on trust what they help distribute to the public; by which means a falsehood once received from a famed writer becomes traditional to posterity."

—John Dryden

"The CIA owns everyone of any significance in the major media."

—William Cobly, Director of the Central Intelligence Agency, 1973-1976

"In the hands of the state, compulsory public education becomes a tool for political control and manipulation—a prime instrument for the thought police of the society. And precisely because every child passes through the same indoctrination process—learning the same "official history," the same "civic virtues," the same lessons of obedience and loyalty to the state—it becomes extremely difficult for the independent soul to free himself from the straightjacket of the ideology and values the political authorities wish to imprint upon the population under its jurisdiction. For the communists, it was the class struggle and obedience to the Party and Comrade Stalin; for the fascists, it was worship of the state and obedience to the Duce; for the Nazis, it was race purity and obedience to the Fuhrer. Through the institution of compulsory state education, the child is to be molded like wax into the shape desired by the state and its educational elite. We should not believe that because ours is a freer, more democratic society, the same imprinting procedure has not occurred even here, in America. Every generation of school-age children has imprinted upon it a politically correct ideology concerning America's past and the sanctity of the role of the state in society. Practically every child in the public school system learns that the "robber barons" of the 19th century exploited the common working man; that unregulated capitalism needed to be harnessed by enlightened government regulation beginning in the Progressive era at the turn of the century; that wild Wall Street speculation was a primary cause of the Great Depression; that only Franklin Roosevelt's New Deal saved America from catastrophe; and that American intervention in foreign wars has been necessary and inevitable, with the United States government required to be a global leader and an occasional world policeman."

—Richard M. Ebeling, Libertarian Author and Economist

"Why of course the people don't want war. Why should some poor slob on a farm want to risk his life in a war when the best he can get out of it is to come back to his farm in one piece? Naturally the common people don't want war neither in Russia, nor in England, nor for that matter in Germany. That is understood. But, after all, it is the leaders of the country who determine the policy and it is always a simple matter to drag the people along, whether it is a democracy, or a fascist dictatorship, or a parliament, or a communist dictatorship. Voice or no voice, the people can always be brought to the bidding of the leaders. That is easy. All you have to do is tell them they are being attacked, and denounce the peacemakers for lack of patriotism and exposing the country to danger. It works the same in any country."

—Hermann Georring, Adolf Hitler's Designated Successor

"By the skillful and sustained use of propaganda, one can make a people see even heaven as hell or an extremely wretched life as paradise."

—Adolph Hitler

OLD HICKORY TO SPECULATOS
YOU ARE A DEN OF VIPERS AND THIEVES

Andrew Jackson, 7th President of the United States (1829-1837)

"The Bank, Mr. Van Buren, is trying to kill me, but I will kill it."
—Andrew Jackson, comment made to his Vice President Martin Van Buren

"I too have been a close observer of the doings of the Bank of the United States. I have had men watching you for a long time, and am convinced that you have used the funds of the bank to speculate in the breadstuffs of the country. When you won, you divided the profits amongst you, and when you lost, you charged it to the Bank. You tell me that if I take the deposits from the Bank and annul its charter I shall ruin ten thousand families. That may be true, gentlemen, but that is your sin! Should I let you go on, you will ruin fifty thousand families, and that would be my sin! You are a den of vipers and thieves. I have determined to rout you out and, by the Eternal (slams fist) I will rout you out! If the people only understood the rank injustice of our money and banking system, there would be a revolution before morning."

—Andrew Jackson, to a delegation of bankers

President Andrew Jackson abolished America's Central Bank and instituted honest money. He was the only President in American history to pay off the federal debt. It is not coincidental that the debt was extinguished under a financial system in which money was not tethered to debt. Jackson was able to pay off the debt without contracting the money supply and inducing a Depression. Jackson also had the head of the Central Bank investigated by Congress for engineering a recession. Richard Lawrence attempted to assassinate Jackson. He fired two shots at point blank range. Both his pistols misfired. Historians believe humidity made the guns misfire. This was the first assassination attempt against a President. It was also the first time in American history Central Banking had been eradicated. Lawrence was acquitted on the grounds of insanity. Some think he pretended to be insane. Lawrence later told friends that powerful European interests promised to protect him if he was caught.

HE SHOULD HAVE RENTED MOVIES ... OR MONEY

Abraham Lincoln, 16th President of the United States (1861-1865)

"The creation of the original issue of money should be maintained as an exclusive monopoly of National Government. ... Government possessing the power to create and issue currency and credit as money and enjoying the right to withdraw both currency and credit from circulation by taxation and otherwise, need not and should not borrow capital at interest as the means of financing governmental work and public enterprise. The Government should create, issue, and circulate all the currency and credit needed to satisfy the spending power of the Government and the buying power of consumers. The privilege of creating and issuing money is not only the supreme prerogative of Government, but it is the Government's greatest creative opportunity. The taxpayers will be saved immense sums in interest, discounts, and exchanges. Money will cease to be master and become the servant of humanity. Democracy will rise superior to the money power."

—Abraham Lincoln

Nations at war usually borrowed from Speculatos. During the Civil War, Lincoln refused to do this. He had the U.S. government print paper money nicknamed "greenbacks." This denied Speculatos the ability to issue money for nothing and earn interest for free, costing them billions. Lincoln defied the money power, setting an example other leaders would follow if it went unpunished.

John Wilkes Booth assassinated Abraham Lincoln at Ford's Theatre on April 14th, 1865. Point blank gunshot to the back of the head. Booth was a famous actor with access to the theatre. He was captured and shot a few weeks later. Booth's wife claimed he was "the tool of other men."

James Garfield: Honest Money Zealot

James Garfield, 20th President of the United States (1881)

"By the experience of commercial nations in all ages it has been found that gold and silver afford the only safe foundation for a monetary system."

"The chief duty of the National Government in connection with the currency of the country is to coin money and declare its value [weight of gold or silver it contains]. Grave doubts have been entertained whether Congress is authorized by the Constitution to make any form of paper money legal tender. The present issue of United States notes [Lincoln's Greenbacks] has been sustained by the necessities of war; but such paper should depend for its value and currency upon its convenience in use and its prompt redemption in coin at the will of the holder, and not upon its compulsory circulation. These notes are not money, but promises to pay money. If the holders demand it, the promise should be kept."

"It [Greenback Party fiat money proposal] would convert the Treasury of the United States into a manufactory of paper money. It makes the House of Representatives and Senate, or the caucus of the party which happens to be in the majority, the absolute dictator of the financial and business affairs of this country. This scheme surpasses all the centralism and Caesarism that were ever charged upon the Republican party in the wildest days of the [Civil] war."

"The prosperity which now prevails is without parallel in our history. Fruitful seasons have done much to secure it, but they have not done all. The preservation of the public credit and the resumption of specie [gold and silver] payments, so successfully attained by the Administration of my predecessors, have enabled our people to secure the blessings which the seasons brought."

Garfield was elected President in 1881, shot 4 months into his Presidency by Charles Guiteau, and died 2 months later.

LOUIS T. MCFADDEN
A LONE VOICE OF TRUTH DURING THE GREAT DEPRESSION

Louis T. McFadden, U.S. Representative from Texas (1915-1935)
Chairman of the House Committee on Banking and Currency (1920-1931)

"Mr. Chairman, we have in this country one of the most corrupt institutions the world has ever known. I refer to the Federal Reserve Board and the Federal Reserve Banks. This evil institution has impoverished and ruined the people of the U.S., has bankrupted itself and has practically bankrupted our government. It has done this through the defects of the law under which it operates, through the maladministration of that law by the Fed and through the corrupt practices of the moneyed vultures who control it. Some people think the Federal Reserve banks are government institutions. They are not. They are private monopolies which prey upon the people of the U.S. for the benefit of themselves and their foreign customers; foreign and domestic speculators and swindlers; and rich and predatory money lenders. In that dark crew of financial pirates there are those who would cut a man's throat to get a dollar out of his pocket; there are those who send money into states to buy votes to control our legislatures; there are those who maintain International propaganda for the purpose of deceiving us into granting of new concessions which will permit them to cover up their past misdeeds and set again in motion their gigantic train of crime."
—Louis McFadden, speech made before Congress during the Great Depression

Representative Louis T. McFadden was Chairman of the House Banking and Currency Committee during the Stock Market Crash and Great Depression, so had an insider's view of them. He was a banker before coming to Congress, so knew how the scam worked. McFadden repeatedly (and correctly) claimed that the Fed had engineered the Great Depression, and tried to prosecute the Fed's Governors and impeach the Treasury Secretary. McFadden survived two assassination attempts, a shooting, and a poisoning that made him violently ill.

BANKSTER BANKSTER: THE DREADED C WORD

"A truth's initial commotion is directly proportional to how deeply the lie was believed. ... When a well-packaged web of lies has been sold gradually to the masses over generations, the truth will seem utterly preposterous and its speaker a raving lunatic."

—Dresden James

Jackson, Lincoln, Garfield and McFadden tried to strip Speculatos of their power to control the supply of money. All had attempts on their lives. To sheeple, this is not a pattern. Every major assassination attempt in American history was supposedly by a lone gunman. The leaders above, plus JFK, RFK, MLK... Not one Julius-Caesar scenario where a cabal assassinated someone for money or power. American history, it seems, is different than all histories before...

This accidental theory of history should strain credulity, but propaganda conditions sheeple to accept that things just happen. No one plans, much less colludes. Anyone who suggests collusion is branded with the dreaded C word: conspiracy. And demonized as a "theorist." Conspiracy theorists. Shrewd propaganda. Nuts who should take their meds and buy insurance against historical accidents. It's all a master conspiracy, right, kook? To which an indelicate "kook" might respond: it's all just random chance, right, dummy?

In your personal life, there are some accidents, but most things happen because you consciously decide they should. Everything isn't a conspiracy, but saying history is devoid of conspiracies is equally absurd. Is it really so insane to think that billionaires with massive fortunes passed down generation to generation want to preserve them, and work together towards that end?

Murders for money occur everyday. People are extinguished for their shoes, their jewelry, for $50 in their wallet. Sheeple grasp this. Yet getting them to accept that Speculatos would kill for sums a billion times greater is nearly impossible. To steal billions, you have to mug nations. And sometimes kill their leaders.

Fractional reserve lending is clever. Speculatos brilliant enough to dream such scams up aren't dumb enough to leave traceable trails or make confessions. The real world is much more ruthless than an Agatha Christie or Sue Grafton novel.

Still think its BS, eh? If you were a leader, these assassinations wouldn't give you a moment of pause? You'd champion honest money without any fear for your safety?

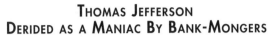

THOMAS JEFFERSON
DERIDED AS A MANIAC BY BANK-MONGERS

"I have ever been the enemy of banks; not of those discounting for cash [accepting collateral and issuing a loan of pre-existing money whose amount is less than the face value of the collateral, thereby "discounting" the collateral as a service fee for converting it to cash], but of those foisting their own paper into circulation, and thus banishing our cash. My zeal against those institutions was so warm and open at the establishment of the bank of the U.S. that I was derided as a Maniac by the tribe of bank-mongers, who were seeking to filch from the public their swindling and barren gains. ... Shall we build an altar to the old paper money of the revolution, which ruined individuals but saved the republic, and bum on that all the bank charters present and future, and their notes with them? For these are to ruin both republic and individuals. This cannot be done. The Mania is too strong. It has seized by its delusions and corruptions all the members of our governments, general, special, and individual."

—Thomas Jefferson

Today Thomas Jefferson would be derided as a conspiracy theorist.

TO LEARN MORE

Those who wish to learn more can begin with the following books. Some are difficult to find:

TRAGEDY AND HOPE: A HISTORY OF THE WORLD IN OUR TIME
BY CARROLL QUIGLEY

A dry and exhaustive 1300 page book which meticulously documents the behind-the-scenes plotting of Speculato international bankers.

THE CREATURE FROM JEKYLL ISLAND
BY EDWARD GRIFFIN

Griffin provides many primary source citations which document the machinations of Speculatos. This is the classic book in the honest-money genre. Like Ron Paul, the author Edward Griffin has fought Speculatos tirelessly for decades. He is one of the patriarchs of the honest money movement.

THE ROCKEFELLER FILE
BY GARY ALLEN

Documents the machinations and wealth of the Rockefeller family. Written decades ago, it makes many predictions which have come to pass. Some factual errors, but overall the most readable and entertaining Rockefeller book.

THE RICH AND THE SUPER RICH: A STUDY IN THE POWER OF MONEY TODAY
BY FERDINAND LUNDBERG

Documents the incestuous relationships among the rich families that constitute the American oligarchy, and shows how this ruling class exercises power. Written decades ago, some of the names have changed, but the modus operandi has not.

THE WEB OF CONSPIRACY
THE COMPLETE STORY OF THE MEN WHO MURDERED ABRAHAM LINCOLN
BY THEODORE ROSCOE

WHY WAS LINCOLN MURDERED?
BY OTTO EISENSCHIML

THIS ONE MAD ACT
THE UNKNOWN STORY OF JOHN WILKES BOOTH BY HIS GRANDDAUGHTER
BY IZOLA FORRESTER

In totality, these three books make it clear that something about the Lincoln assassination was covered up to protect someone. Definitive answers are elusive.

FIAT AIN'T JUST A CAR

"The legal tender quality [of money] is only valuable for the purposes of dishonesty."
—Salmon Chase, 6th Chief Justice of the Supreme Court

"Tender laws, of any kind, operate to destroy morality, and to dissolve, by the pretense of law, what ought to be the principle of law to support, reciprocal justice between man and man—and the punishment of a member [of Congress] who should move for such a law ought to be death."
—Thomas Paine

"With the exception only of the period of the gold standard, practically all governments of history have used their exclusive power to issue money to defraud and plunder the people."
—Friedrich von Hayek, Nobel Prize Winner in Economics

Why is Speculato allowed to print money? Step back in time. Speculato is Johnny Appleseed. Appleseed discovered apple trees, brought them to Crusoeville, and made a fortune. The apple industry was his creation. Or nature's or God's, but why split hairs. Johnny produces Johnny Applesauce, which has his face on the bottle. He is trusted. Everyone buys Johnny Applesauce.

Crusoeville's money is bottled applesauce. Bottled applesauce doesn't rot like apples yet is a commodity. It is honest money. But applesauce bottles break. And though police are diligent, hungry thieves love money, especially sprinkled with cinnamon.

Johnny issues applesauce receipts that circulate as money. Like the goldsmith. Government auditors make Johnny keep a list of receipts issued. They count applesauce in his vault to make sure there is a bottle for every receipt. If Johnny prints more receipts than he has applesauce, he goes to jail.

Like all honest governments, Crusoeville's is maintaining the integrity of contracts. No one has to enter a contract, but if you choose to, you have to honor it under penalty of law. Johnny's receipt is a contract saying your bottle of applesauce is sitting in his vault like a coat in a coat check.

Johnny's son is a bad apple. Applesauce Jr. wants to print receipts not backed by applesauce, needs guv'ment to change receipt laws so fraud is legal, so approaches the politicians. Would they like to build every county a new school? That'd get them re-elected for sure. And help the community.

We could never afford that, politicians say. Never, ever.

Not in the current flawed system, AJ (Appleseed Jr.) replies. Let me print applesauce receipts and I'll give you enough to build schools. And in a few years, more to build a bridges. And later, receipts for a statue of each of you. After that...
You can't just give us money. Looks like bribery.
We'll use bonds to make it look legit, AJ says. You print bonds and trade them to me for applesauce receipts.
That'd work. But we'd owe you interest on the bonds, right?
The people would, AJ says.
Our Founding Mothers created a limited government. Revenue is raised only from indirect taxes levied on purchases. We can't raise enough money for interest payments.
Pass an income tax that tithes assets directly, AJ says. Use that revenue to pay me interest. And fund wars and welfare.
People would never agree to that. It would make them serfs.
Tell them the income tax is a way to make rich guys like me pay their fair share, AJ says. Make the initial tax rate a small amount that won't scare them, and jack it up later.
That might work.
You can also use the income tax to engineer society, AJ says, by offering exemptions to the tax for certain behaviors and tax penalties for others. You'll control the people like puppets.
Guv'ment can print money itself, Percepticus of Orange County says. No interest payments to you are necessary. No income tax is necessary. You just want to exploit the people.
AJ laughs. You'll print so many receipts the economy crashes. No one would trust politicians with their applesauce. I'm Johnny Applesauce's namesake. They'd trust me with their children.
Can they trust you to pay the income tax? Percepticus asks. On a fortune as large as yours, the tax would be a fortune.
Be smarter to create tax-exempt foundations, AJ says. I'll place my fortune in one, and it'll be immune from taxes.
People would never go for that.
Call them charitable foundations to help the poor, AJ says. And if you don't enact this plan, I'll fund candidates who will.
This last part is all the politicians need to hear.
Percepticus warns Integritus, whose father discovered oranges. Integritus is as rich as AJ and offers receipts backed by orange juice. He keeps 100% reserves. No bogus receipts.
AJ can't compete with this honest money. Prices of things in AJ's receipts rise as he inflates their supply. This doesn't happen to OJ receipts. People favor OJ receipts to AJ receipts.
AJ has politicians make his receipts the LEGAL TENDER. Tender is com-

pensation in a contract. Legal tender is something which must be accepted as compensation in a contract, and every purchase is contract. If AJ's receipts are legal tender, all other tender is illegal. If Integritus prints OJ receipts, he goes to jail. Same for anyone who refuses AJ's receipts. Everyone in Crusoeville must use AJ's receipts and pay the inflation tax.

Integritus cries foul. But being Integritus, he won't bribe, er fund the campaigns of, politicians. AJ will, so politicians side with him. Also, when people favored OJ money over AJ's, AJ couldn't print many receipts for the politicians. With the inflation tax distributed amongst a larger herd of sheeple, more new receipts can be created, and politicians receive more of them.

Now that guv'ment enforces his money monopoly, AJ prints receipts like mad. He must keep guv'ment happy by converting their bonds into money, but he receives interest on the bonds.

Applesauce receipts soon outnumber applesauce bottles. People get suspicious and mob AJ's vault. The goldsmith was ruined by this run, but he wasn't in cahoots with guv'ment.

Guv'ment declares a "bank holiday." The system has integrity, people. Your deposits are safe. Banks can produce them at any time but will nonetheless stop doing so for a week.

Hmmm.

Nothing to see here, sir, move along.

During the "holiday," experts talk about how honest and dependable the banking system is. Everyone calms. The bank reopens. Few demand their "demand" deposits.

But what if they do? This is a constant specter hanging over AJ. Most of the applesauce which people think he has warehoused doesn't exist, after all.

AJ visits his co-conspirator, guv'ment. Having to exchange applesauce receipts for applesauce sure is pesky. Why not abandon the absurd and antiquated notion of receipts being redeemable for a fixed amount of any commodity?

Politicians hardly need a schematic. No applesauce reserves means AJ can buy oodles of guv'ment bonds. This means guv'ment can run monstrous deficits indefinitely and finance them via the inflation tax. Politicians no longer have to make real spending choices or balance the budget. Ever.

Money is no longer a promissory note. It isn't a guaranteed claim on a jar of applesauce or anything real. It has value only because of guv'ment decree, or FIAT. Remove the fiat, Integritus circulates honest money instantly.

How do you make FIAT MONEY sound legit? Try this Faustian gem: applesauce receipts can't be redeemed for applesauce, but are backed by the full faith and credit of the Crusoeville guv'ment.

Ooooh. The full faith and credit of guv'ment. Much better than a jar of applesauce. And to think I was worried.

Guv'ment economists would grit their teeth at this characterization. They would note that fiat money is backed by the goods & services which Crusoeville produces, which fiat money can buy. These economists point out that this is not nothing, and that fiat money is not "unbacked." True, but also a somewhat devious explanation which misses the point. Or perhaps conceals it. That point is inflation. When money is not defined as a specific commodity, and paper promissory notes cannot be redeemed for that commodity *at a fixed and invariant exchange rate*, sheeple are defenseless against marauding inflation. Speculatos can inflate the supply of fiat money relentlessly, so that it buys an ever decreasing amount of the goods & services it is "backed" by. Honest commodity money can always be redeemed or traded for a non-decreasing amount of the commodity it is defined as or backed by, dishonest fiat money is almost always redeemed or traded for an ever-decreasing amount of the goods & services it is "backed" by. Smarmy establishment economists who deride commodity money and the claim that fiat money is unbacked are rarely forthcoming about this monumental distinction between fiat money and commodity money.

Back to Crusoeville. AJ prints enough money to paper the Great Wall. The economy collapses. Politicians won't give up their gravy train, so the Depression is blamed on Apple Gods, a lack of liquidity, speculators. Anything and anyone but AJ, who must live to inflate another day.

AJ uses his bailout money to buy assets of citizens ruined by the crash, restoring prosperity. This cycle of inflation, Depression, bailout is repeated until the money is worthless.

Substitute gold for applesauce, and you have the monetary history of most civilizations. In ancient times there were no printing presses, so coins were DEBASED, that is, minted with ever-decreasing precious metal content. But the underlying principle remains the same. Money begins as a pure commodity, is perverted into a dilutable form, and then inflated into oblivion.

TO SKIP THE PICTURE PAGES AFTER THIS CHAPTER, PLEASE TURN TO PAGE 102

THE CORRUPTION OF AMERICA'S MONEY

Gold Dollars were last minted by America in 1889.
Each Gold Dollar contained 1.5 grams (0.05 ounces) of gold.

A 1905 $20 bill was redeemable for 20 Gold Dollars, and boasted this fact in large gold letters: "THIS CERTIFIES THAT THERE HAVE BEEN DEPOSITED IN THE TREASURY OF THE UNITED STATES OF AMERICA TWENTY DOLLARS IN GOLD COIN PAYABLE TO THE BEARER UPON DEMAND." This money was circulated by the United States Treasury as the Constitution specifies, so there is no mention of a Central Bank. This is the honest money our Founding Fathers intended, and it depicted the most honest President, George Washington.

The Federal Reserve Act created a Central Bank in 1913, and by 1914 dollar bills were circulated by the Federal Reserve, not the U.S. Treasury. Dollars bore the words "FEDERAL RESERVE NOTE" for the first time to reflect this transfer of power. Grover Cleveland was on this note. In the late 1800s, Cleveland barred the use of silver as money, leaving only gold, which was scarcer. This sudden contraction of the money supply induced a Depression and pummeled the working class. Having screwed sheeple by yo-yo-ing the money supply, Cleveland was an ideal person to appear on the first corrupt money issued by the new Central Bank. This dollar bill makes no promise of gold redemption. Speculatos were overly optimistic in releasing unbacked notes so quickly, as people were still used to honest gold certificates and didn't trust the new money. It was nonetheless important to issue such unbacked notes immediately, to establish the prerogative as a precedent.

A 1928 $20 bill could be redeemed for specie, but the "IN GOLD COIN" lettering was shrunk. Meanwhile, the supply of these paper notes grew. The Great Depression was just a year away. President Andrew Jackson, a champion of honest banking, made his debut on this $20 bill.

By 1929, on the eve of the Great Depression, Speculatos knew there would be massive redemptions of dollar bills for gold, which they could not honor. They therefore issued notes which said, "NATIONAL CURRENCY SECURED BY BONDS DEPOSITED WITH THE TREASURER OF THE UNITED STATES OF AMERICA OR BY LIKE DEPOSIT OF OTHER SECURITIES." This was a half way house to corrupt money. This note was not totally unbacked, but it was secured by paper financial instruments rather than gold.

The 1934 $20 bill changed its tune: "THE UNITED STATES OF AMERICA WILL PAY TO THE BEARER ON DEMAND TWENTY DOLLARS." No gold coin or gold ink, nor mention of bonds. This note confuses moderners. Who needs to be paid twenty dollars for a $20 bill? The fine print sheds light: "THIS NOTE IS LEGAL TENDER FOR ALL DEBTS, PUBLIC AND PRIVATE, AND IS REDEEMABLE IN LAWFUL MONEY AT THE UNITED STATES TREASURY, OR AT ANY FEDERAL RESERVE BANK." Lawful money. Is some unlawful? This was during the Great Depression. Gold certificates that made the '20s roar were being redeemed. There wasn't enough gold. FDR suspended gold redeemability, confiscated all gold, and made owning it illegal. This "deal" was new to millions of Americans whose gold was forcibly converted to these notes. Though theoretically convertible to silver, they were "redeemable" in whatever guv'ment declared "lawful money."

The 1963 $20 bill makes no promise of redeemability. Not for gold, silver, bonds, nor lawful money. No bearer must be paid anything on demand, meaning dollars can be increased in quantity virtually without limit. The "REDEEMABLE IN LAWFUL MONEY" promise which appeared on the back of previous notes is replaced by "IN GOD WE TRUST." Want honest money not being inflated? Too bad: "THIS NOTE IS LEGAL TENDER FOR ALL DEBTS, PUBLIC AND PRIVATE." As are the series 1985, 1995 and 2006 notes that followed.

Series 1963

Series 2006

Andrew Jackson spent much of his Presidency eradicating the Central Bank of his day, the Bank of the United States, and considered the re-implementation of honest commodity money one of the proudest achievements of his life. Like Thomas Jefferson with bonds (and money), Jackson would be appalled to be pictured on corrupt money issued by a Central Bank.

EXECUTIVE ORDER 6102: FDR's GOLD THEFT

POSTMASTER: PLEASE POST IN A CONSPICUOUS PLACE.—JAMES A. FARLEY, Postmaster General

UNDER EXECUTIVE ORDER OF THE PRESIDENT

Issued April 5, 1933

all persons are required to deliver

ON OR BEFORE MAY 1, 1933

all GOLD COIN, GOLD BULLION, AND GOLD CERTIFICATES now owned by them to a Federal Reserve Bank, branch or agency, or to any member bank of the Federal Reserve System.

Executive Order

FORBIDDING THE HOARDING OF GOLD COIN, GOLD BULLION AND GOLD CERTIFICATES.

By virtue of the authority vested in me by Section 5(b) of the Act of October 6, 1917, as amended by Section 2 of the Act of March 9, 1933, entitled "An Act to provide relief in the existing national emergency in banking, and for other purposes", in which amendatory Act Congress declared that a serious emergency exists, I, Franklin D. Roosevelt, President of the United States of America, do declare that said national emergency still continues to exist and pursuant to said section do hereby prohibit the hoarding of gold coin, gold bullion, and gold certificates within the continental United States by individuals, partnerships, associations and corporations and hereby prescribe the following regulations for carrying out the purpose of this order:

Section 1. For the purposes of this regulation, the term "hoarding" means the withdrawal and withholding of gold coin, gold bullion or gold certificates from the recognised and customary channels of trade. The term "person" means any individual, partnership, association or corporation.

Section 2. All persons are hereby required to deliver on or before May 1, 1933, to a Federal reserve bank or a branch or agency thereof or to any member bank of the Federal Reserve System all gold coin, gold bullion and gold certificates now owned by them or coming into their ownership on or before April 28, 1933, except the following:

(a) Such amount of gold as may be required for legitimate and customary use in industry, profession or art within a reasonable time, including gold prior to refining and stocks of gold in reasonable amounts for the usual trade requirements of owners mining and refining such gold.

(b) Gold coin and gold certificates in an amount not exceeding in the aggregate $100.00 belonging to any one person; and gold coins having a recognized special value to collectors of rare and unusual coins.

(c) Gold coin and bullion earmarked or held in trust for a recognized foreign government or foreign central bank or the Bank for International Settlements.

(d) Gold coin and bullion licensed for other proper transactions (not involving hoarding) including gold coin and bullion imported for reexport or held pending action on applications for export licenses.

Section 3. Until otherwise ordered any person becoming the owner of any gold coin, gold bullion, or gold certificates after April 28, 1933, shall, within three days after receipt thereof, deliver the same in the manner prescribed in Section 2; unless such gold coin, gold bullion or gold certificates are held for any of the purposes specified in paragraphs (a), (b) or (c) of Section 2; or unless such gold coin or gold bullion is held for the purposes specified in paragraph (d) of Section 2 and the person holding it is, with respect to such gold coin or bullion, a licensee or applicant for license pending action thereon.

Section 4. Upon receipt of gold coin, gold bullion or gold certificates delivered to it in accordance with Sections 2 or 3, the Federal reserve bank or member bank will pay therefor an equivalent amount of any other form of coin or currency coined or issued under the laws of the United States.

Section 5. Member banks shall deliver all gold coin, gold bullion and gold certificates owned or received by them (other than as exempted under the provisions of Section 2) to the Federal reserve banks of their respective districts and receive credit or payment therefor.

Section 6. The Secretary of the Treasury, out of the sum made available to the President by Section 501 of the Act of March 9, 1933, will in all proper cases pay the reasonable costs of transportation of gold coin, gold bullion or gold certificates delivered to a member bank or Federal reserve bank in accordance with Sections 2, 3, or 5 hereof, including the cost of insurance, protection, and such other incidental costs as may be necessary, upon production of satisfactory evidence of such costs. Voucher forms for this purpose may be procured from Federal reserve banks.

Section 7. In cases where the delivery of gold coin, gold bullion or gold certificates by the owners thereof within the time set forth above will involve extraordinary hardship or difficulty, the Secretary of the Treasury may, in his discretion, extend the time within which such delivery must be made. Applications for such extensions must be made in writing under oath, addressed to the Secretary of the Treasury and filed with a Federal reserve bank. Each application must state the date to which the extension is desired, the amount and location of the gold coin, gold bullion and gold certificates in respect of which application is made and the facts showing extension to be necessary to avoid extraordinary hardship or difficulty.

Section 8. The Secretary of the Treasury is hereby authorized and empowered to issue such further regulations as he may deem necessary to carry out the purposes of this order and to issue licenses thereunder, through such officers or agencies as he may designate, including licenses permitting the Federal reserve banks and member banks of the Federal Reserve System, in return for an equivalent amount of other coin, currency or credit, to deliver, earmark or hold in trust gold coin and bullion to or for persons showing the need for the same for any of the purposes specified in paragraphs (a), (c) and (d) of Section 2 of these regulations.

Section 9. Whoever wilfully violates any provision of this Executive Order or of these regulations or of any rule, regulation or license issued thereunder may be fined not more than $10,000, or, if a natural person, may be imprisoned for not more than ten years, or both; and any officer, director, or agent of any corporation who knowingly participates in any such violation may be punished by a like fine, imprisonment, or both.

This order and these regulations may be modified or revoked at any time.

THE WHITE HOUSE   FRANKLIN D ROOSEVELT
April 5, 1933.

For Further Information Consult Your Local Bank

GOLD CERTIFICATES may be identified by the words "GOLD CERTIFICATE" appearing thereon. The serial number and the Treasury seal on the face of a GOLD CERTIFICATE are printed in YELLOW. Be careful not to confuse GOLD CERTIFICATES with other issues which are redeemable in gold but which are not GOLD CERTIFICATES. Federal Reserve Notes and United States Notes are "redeemable in gold" but are not "GOLD CERTIFICATES" and are not required to be surrendered

Special attention is directed to the exceptions allowed under
Section 2 of the Executive Order

CRIMINAL PENALTIES FOR VIOLATION OF EXECUTIVE ORDER
$10,000 fine or 10 years imprisonment, or both, as
provided in Section 9 of the order

Secretary of the Treasury.

U.S. Government Printing Office: 1933 2-16064

Fort Knox: A Shrine to the Biggest Heist in History

Previous Page Executive Order 6102, issued by President Franklin Roosevelt in 1933. EO6102 should be as infamous as Watergate or Dealey Plaza. It commanded Americans to surrender gold and exchange it for paper dollars. Individuals could keep $100 in gold, anything more was illegal, punishable by 10 years in prison or $10,000. Gold became a controlled substance like marijuana or cocaine. This is an actual copy of the Executive Order that was posted in post offices around the country. FDR's gold seizure was America's first huge bank bailout.

Above Where to put 1,350 tons of confiscated gold? American gold had been privately owned, held by we the people. Government didn't need a monstrous vault because it didn't own the nation's gold. Once guv'ment had mugged the people, it needed a fortress for its loot. FDR built Fort Knox. Sheeple revere Fort Knox, unaware it is a shrine to the biggest robbery in U.S. history (prior to the bailout during Depression v9.2006-201x). Few sheeple know of FDR's gold confiscation. Those that do believe it was for the public good, as propaganda teaches.

Below Seized gold was melted into 400 troy ounce (27.5 pound) bars. Sheeple's surrendered life savings? All in all, just another brick in the wall.

FDR's BANK HOLIDAY: DEVIL'S NIGHT FOR SHEEPLE

When FDR was inaugurated in 1933, bank runs had become sprints. Banks were failing every hour. The dollar was 23.22 grains of gold. There are 480 grains in an ounce, meaning an ounce of gold was equal to $20.67. Millions were mobbing banks, handing them $20.67 and demanding an ounce of gold. Banks had issued promissory notes in excess of gold reserves and couldn't honor all promises. The rush was on. Get what you can. Anything is better than nothing.

48 hours after being sworn in as President, FDR declared a "Bank Holiday." All banks would close March 6 – 9, Monday-Thursday. To FDR the problem wasn't that banks and guv'ment had promised to redeem paper money for gold and lied, but, as he explained in the Executive Order creating the "holiday": "heavy and unwarranted withdrawals of gold and currency from our banking institutions for the purpose of hoarding ... it is in the best interests of all bank depositors that a period of respite be provided with a view to preventing further hoarding of coin, bullion, or currency."

"Unwarranted withdrawals." Ha, ha. "Best interests of all bank depositors." Ha, ha again. FDR shifted blame from Speculatos to sheeple. Sheeple were wrong for expecting banks to honor contracts. Anyone who wanted their gold was an evil hoarder.

Friday March 10th, 1933 was the day the bank "holiday" ended and banks were scheduled to face the music. If you think there are long lines for Aerosmith tickets, you should have been outside banks that morning. Where's the line end? South America. Had banks opened and been forced to honor contracts, every bank in American would've been rupted by lunch.

FDR issued Executive Order 6073, which made it illegal for banks to: "pay out any gold coin, gold bullion or gold certificates ... allow withdrawal of any currency for hoarding." Paper money couldn't be withdrawn from banks, much less gold! Banks that issued promissory notes in excess of gold were saved. Their fraud was made legal. FDR's bank holiday was Christmas, Hanukkah and New Year's rolled into one for Speculatos, a Devil's Night for sheeple.

The EO6102 gold seizure followed a few weeks later. Sheeple handed guv'ment an ounce of gold, it handed them $20.67 in paper. The exact opposite of what people tried to do running to banks and redeeming "demand" deposits for gold.

Letting banks fail would've caused short term suffering, but this is a trivial price to pay for the long term benefits of honest money. Lots of luck convincing unemployed sheeple ruled by fear.

During Depression v8.1929-1942, neither Presidents Hoover nor Roosevelt contemplated letting the free market run its course. Letting banks fail. Nor did Bush or Obama. Nor will whoever is President decades from now during the next Depression. Speculatos will never allow a President who wouldn't bail out their banks. Ever.

1933 *TIME* MAGAZINE ARTICLES ABOUT FDR's GOLD SEIZURE

JUDICIARY: GOLD INDICTMENT No. 1
OCTOBER 9, 1933

On Oct. 11, 1932 an elderly Manhattan attorney named Frederick Barber Campbell marched into Chase National Bank followed by an armed guard trundling 13 bars of gold. Mr. Campbell had just drawn this bullion from the Federal Reserve Bank in return for gold certificates. Each bar, worth approximately $5,000, had been cast by the U. S. Treasury and bore its stamp and number. Lawyer Campbell arranged for the Chase Bank to act as hired custodian for his bullion.

On Jan. 25, 1933 Mr. Campbell again appeared at Chase National with 14 more gold bars which were stowed away in the vault with the first batch. By gold standard reckoning his total deposit of metal amounted to $135,000.

On March 9 Congress passed the Emergency Banking Act which empowered the President to call all gold into the Treasury, with heavy penalties for those who disobeyed his orders. At that time $1,400,000,000 in gold [67 million troy ounces at the fixed redeemability rate of $20.67 per troy ounce, or 2,322 tons] was in circulation, most of it hoarded [legally stockpiled by its rightful owners]. In the next 30 days more than one-third of this was turned in to the Treasury [774 tons].

On April 5 President Roosevelt issued an executive order requiring holders of gold to turn it into the Treasury in exchange for paper currency under penalty of ten years imprisonment and $10,000 fine. Department of Justice agents began visiting known hoarders who, to date, have surrendered $38,901,009 in gold [1.9 million troy ounces or 65 tons]. During the same period unknown hoarders have given up more than $300,000,000 [14.5 million troy ounces or 498 tons]. Attorney General Cummings issued threat of prosecution against recalcitrants who still held $560,201,000 [27 million troy ounces or 929 tons].

[From March 9-October 9 1933, a span of 7 months, guv'ment confiscated roughly 1,350 tons of a 2,300 ton gold supply. "Recalcitrants" unwilling to give up their gold still held roughly 950 tons.]

On Aug. 28 President Roosevelt issued another order requiring every possessor of gold to register his holdings with the Treasury before Sept. 18. Those who failed to do so were also to be punished by ten years imprisonment, $10,000 fine.

On Sept. 16 Lawyer Campbell appeared at Chase National Bank, demanded his 27 bars of gold. The bank told him that under the law it could not deliver them to him but would have to surrender them to the Government in accordance with the President's orders.

On Sept. 26 Mr. Campbell started a civil suit in Manhattan Federal Court to compel the bank to release his gold deposits. In his petition he argued that the President's orders which prevented him from regaining his property were unconstitutional.

On Sept. 27 after an 18-minute session a Federal grand jury in Manhattan indicted Frederick B. Campbell for failing to register gold now valued at $200,574.34 before Sept. 18 as required by the Aug. 28 order. Also imminent was a second indictment charging actual hoarding of gold in violation of the April 5 order.

Thus last week was President Roosevelt's whole gold policy started on its winding way to the Supreme Court for a major test on constitutionality. If Defendant Campbell is convicted by a jury, and the Supreme Court sustains his conviction, the Department of Justice will be on solid legal ground to move against some 30,000 citizens who have so far defied the President's gold orders. If Defendant Campbell wins a Supreme Court appeal the Administration's whole gold program will be set at naught and President Roosevelt will have to start all over again conserving the Treasury's gold supply.

In Defendant Campbell the Government picked for this test not only the largest "gold hoarder" on its list but also a respectable lawyer whom Prosecutor Medalie called "exceedingly able." Born in Brooklyn, Mr. Campbell was graduated from Harvard Law School in 1894, is a director of U. S. and British insurance companies, belongs to such swank Manhattan clubs as Union, Metropolitan (where he lives) and Century. When he filed his civil suit against the Chase Bank, he well knew he was inviting the Government to prosecute. His argument in that suit will become his defense in the criminal action, to wit: 1) Congress has no Constitutional power to delegate its legislative authority over gold to the President; 2) the President is prevented by the 5th ("due process of law") Amendment to the Constitution from depriving him of his property. The "property" in this case is not only the gold bars in the Chase vault but his $65,000 paper profit incident to the rise in gold from $20 to $31 per oz.

Mr. Campbell, who promptly pleaded not guilty to the indictment and was released on $1,000 bail because no moral turpitude was involved in the charge, was thoroughly aware of the risks he was running in this contest with the Government. If convicted, he could be disbarred, fined $10,000, imprisoned for ten years. But he was, he intimated, making a fight for his Constitutional rights and "if I have to go to jail, I don't care."

(end of article)

Revisionists paint FDR's gold seizure as gentle and voluntary. Everyone merrily did their patriotic duty. As this primary source shows, the truth is less pleasant. Large numbers of arrests weren't necessary because government made a very public example and threatened others.

The true cost of what was lost is more than the market value of the gold confiscated. In seizing gold, FDR destroyed something priceless: honest money that defended people against the inflation tax, and kept government small and honest.

TO NEWS OF BYGONE WEEKS, HEREWITH SEQUELS FROM LAST WEEK'S NEWS
NOVEMBER 27, 1933

To the indictment of Frederick Barber Campbell. Manhattan lawyer, for failure to register with the U. S. Treasury his possession of 27 bars of gold worth $200,754.34 and for failure to exchange it for paper currency in accord with President Roosevelt's executive order (TIME, Oct. 9): decision by Federal Judge John Munro Woolsey that the Government has the constitutional right to compel hoarders to report and surrender their gold. Reason: "The right of the Government to take private property of any kind when it is deemed necessary by the appropriate authority for the public good." He ruled, nevertheless, that the order to surrender gold was technically invalid because under the Emergency Banking Act it should have been signed by the Secretary of the Treasury rather than the President, gave the Government 20 days to appeal.

(end of article)

Guv'ment rescinded the original order and issued a new one signed by the Secretary of the Treasury rather than FDR. The gold seizure was thereafter held to be legal. "The right of the Government to take private property of any kind when it is deemed necessary by the appropriate authority for the public good." Our Founding Fathers would shake their heads.

THE REAL SPECULATO

"When a government is dependent upon bankers for money, they and not the leaders of the government control the situation, since the hand that gives is above the hand that takes ... Money has no motherland; financiers are without patriotism and without decency; their sole object is gain."

—Napoleon Bonaparte

"The Rothschilds have conquered the world more thoroughly, more cunningly, and much more lastingly than all the Caesars before..."

—Frederic Morton, Rothschild Biographer

Who thought this scam up? It isn't difficult to envision a goldsmith peering into his vault and scheming a way to profit off everyone else's gold, but we don't know for sure. Money changers are as old as the Bible, and included ancient orders like the Knights Templar. In modern times, one family perfected fractional reserve lending, becoming the personification of the Speculato breed: the Rothschilds. Rothschild is a synonym for wealth and power. The Rothschilds are Europe's Rockefellers. If you do not understand the Rothchilds' historical significance, your view of history is probably mythology. They are that infamous.

The Rothschild fortune has never been publicly audited, but they may be the richest family on Earth. Billionaires guess the Rothschild worth the way sheeple do sports outcomes. It could easily be $100 billion. Some researchers think the Rothschild fortune exceeds $1 trillion. But no outsider knows for sure.

This estimate seems absurd. You're told Bill Gates is the richest man on Earth, and he is worth roughly $50 billion. How could a family 2-20 times wealthier escape public notice?

Secrecy is the Rothschild trademark. Their fortune is kept in a trust, a legal device that avoids taxation and preserves privacy. The oldest male Rothschild controls the trust, but it never becomes his property. Thus much of the Rothschild fortune is never subject to income tax, inheritance tax, or scrutiny.

Behind every great fortune is a great crime. The Rothschild fortune is large enough that you need RICO.

Mayer Amschel Bauer was born in 1743 in the Jewish Ghettos of Frankfurt, Germany, the son of a goldsmith and loan shark. Mayer became a clerk in the Oppenheimer Bank in Hanover at age 13, and in only 7 years became a junior partner of the bank.

Oppenheimer Bank cultivated relationships with nobles. This was a world of monarchies. Royalty formulated national policies. Mayer saw that lending to royals was more profitable than lending to commoners. Loans were larger, but also safer because they were guaranteed by a nation's future tax revenues.

When Mayer's father died, he returned to Frankfurt, started a money lending business and hung a red shield over his door to attract customers. In German red shield means roth (red) schild (shield). Bauer changed his name to Mayer Amschel Rothschild.

Mayer befriended German noble William IX of Hesse-Kassel by selling him rare coins below cost. William had inherited the largest fortune in Europe, $40,000,000, much of it made renting Hessian mercenary troops to nations like Britain. William was the Blackwater of the colonial world. During the American Revolution, George Washington fought Hessians employed by the British, and captured a contingent of Hessians after crossing the Delaware.

$40 million was an extraordinary sum in those times. Most readers don't know it is more than $1 billion today, which is indicative of problems created by inflation.

Beginning in 1769, Mayer collected taxes and managed estates for William. This included obtaining fees for each Hessian mercenary killed in battle. Death and war equaled profit—a lesson not lost on Mayer.

In 1805, Napoleon invaded Germany and made eradicating William's family a priority. Before he fled Europe, William entrusted roughly $3,000,000 to Mayer, and told him to invest the money in consols—British bonds.

Mayer misappropriated the money and used it to send each of his five sons to a European capital and establish a bank. Each son lent fractioned reserves, like goldsmiths, but they were careful not to issue excessive receipts. The Rothschilds were more brilliant and ruthless than their competitors and built the first international banking system. In a world without electronic communication, their collusion and synchronization was an enormous advantage.

Rothschilds became the personal bankers of many Kings, and conducted transactions for governments of England, France, Spain, Prussia, Austria, Belgium, Naples and Portugal. All the superpowers of Europe.

Europe was always fighting. Keeping armies funded was difficult. Rothschilds issued governments paper credit, charged one fee to convert it to gold, and another to smuggle that gold to armies in the field. They got the gold where it needed to be no matter what. Sneaking, cunning, lying, bribery, murder, whatever it took. The Rothschilds were large and efficient enough to make more profit than competitors while charging less. They made fortune upon fortune upon fortune. Every insider knew Rothschilds were more powerful than Kings.

Since Rothschilds funded everyone, no one wanted to anger them. Pester a Rothschild agent with the infamous "red shield" emblem and your army might not eat, a well-funded enemy army might appear, or you might find assassins or usurpers lurking. As they were the only individuals who could travel Europe with impunity, Rothschild agents smuggled materials besides gold. Cotton, yarn, tobacco, grain, coffee, sugar, dye. All for exorbitant profits. Rothschilds also smuggled information. Their intelligence network was better than any government's.

No episode illustrates the mindset and modus operandi of this Speculato species better than the battle of Waterloo, at which a British Army commanded by The Duke of Wellington defeated a French army commanded by Napoleon.

Nathan Rothschild was a prodigy, and Mayer nurtured his son's genius no matter what the cost. By 1815 Nathan had been in London less than two decades, yet was the most dominant banker in the most powerful nation on Earth. England then was like America today, an empire amassing huge debts. England borrowed heavily to fund Wellington. If Wellington lost, Napoleon would rule Europe unopposed, and British war bonds would plummet or be defaulted upon.

A Rothschild agent watched the Battle of Waterloo and then galloped to the English Channel. Savage storms had suspended sailing, but he paid £2,000— $300,000 in modern money—for a trip across. Nathan Rothschild was waiting, and became the only person in England who knew Wellington had won. Nathan went to the stock exchange, feigned distress, and sold his British consols. Everyone suspected Nathan had intel about Waterloo, assumed Wellington had lost, and sold consols. When consols were practically worthless, Nathan had agents buy them up. He acquired much of England's debt for shillings on the pound. Once word of Wellington's victory arrived, consols skyrocketed. Rothschild had multiplied his already massive wealth several times in a few days of trading.

This was the Eve of all insider trades. Rothschild engineered a crash so he could profit off it. A formula Speculatos have repeated ad nauseam ever since.

You may not be familiar with Waterloo, so let's use a modern metaphor. D-Day is underway. A storm blocks all radio communication. 100,000 Allied corpses may litter the beaches of Normandy. You learn the result, and rather than tell people the fate of their loved ones, you drive straight to the New York Stock Exchange and use the information to make millions of dollars speculating.

Speculatos care only about profit. This level of indifference to the human condition is difficult for sheeple to accept. They therefore tend to discount stories of corruption, making plunder a cake walk for Speculatos.

When Napoleon lost, French markets collapsed. The Rothschilds used their consol profits to buy up the French debt, which rose in value when the French economy recovered.

France and England were the two most powerful Empires on Earth, and the Rothschilds now owned a huge portion of their debts. This would be like owning the bulk of the debt of the U.S.S.R. and America during the Cold War.

Not a bad spot to be in. But the Rothschilds didn't simply open a Heineken and say, "I'm rich enough." Not these cats. They remained relentless. And ruthless. A $100 billion net worth is starting to sound a little less absurd, isn't it?

TO SKIP THE PICTURE PAGES AFTER THIS CHAPTER, PLEASE TURN TO PAGE 109

ROTHSCHILDS: EMPERORS OF EUROPE

"There is but one power in Europe, and that is Rothschild."

—Werner Sombart, Economist

An 1848 political cartoon. Rothschild sits on a throne made out of satchels of gold, which are piled up behind him, symbolic of his massive fortune. Kings grovel before him, begging him to favor their nation with credit and loans. In the background, the downtrodden oppressed by Kings are shown revolting. The claim that Rothschild was more powerful than nations and Kings sounds absurd to modern sheeple, but was a reality Europeans at that time understood.

Rothschild was the richest man in the world in the early 1800s. There was no close second. Rothschild amassed this fortune without creating anything. Bill Gates created Windows. Rockefeller drilled oil. Carnegie steel. Ford cars. Vanderbilt railroads. Rothschilds? Debt and war. From the beginning, Rothschilds were parasites who bled their host, humanity.

Little has changed. Substitute modern Presidents for Kings in the cartoon above, and include a small group of several dozen Speculatos rather than just Rothschild, and it would be an accurate description of the world today. Minus the revolutionaries. Sheeple today are too apathetic to rise up. Even if somehow motivated, they don't accept the reality of Speculatos. They blame politicians, not Speculatos. Sheeple swap one groveling politician for another, and are surprised when the same old problems persist.

CENTRAL BANKS
THE MOST IMPORTANT HISTORICAL DEVELOPMENT OF THE LAST 300 YEARS

"The bank hath benefit of interest on all moneys which it creates out of nothing."
—Will Paterson, Founder of the Bank of England, the 1ˢᵗ Central Bank

TOP England's Central Bank, The Bank of England, established 1694
BOTTOM America's Central Bank, The Federal Reserve, established 1913. Most Americans recognize the White House and Capitol, but few recognize the Federal Reserve. Visitors to Washington D.C. can tour the White House, Capitol and Supreme Court and learn about their operation, but they cannot tour the Federal Reserve. People can watch the Supreme Court in session and see Congress pass and debate laws. People cannot watch the Federal Reserve create billions out of thin air on a computer screen, or listen to Fed Governors debate how much money to create. Imagine a tour guide walking you through the Federal Reserve building. "On your right you'll see the computer terminal where Federal Reserve Chairman Ben Bernanke creates money out of thin air. At 2:00 he'll be monetizing the $18 billion worth of Treasury bonds that didn't sell at last week's auction. Those who wish to return can watch him create $18 billion at that time. This money creation only takes a few seconds, so please be sure to be punctual or you'll miss it."

Few sheeple understand Central Banking, and if they did, most would oppose Central Banks. In 1694, no nation on Earth had a Central Bank. Today most nations have Central Banks. The plague-like spread of Central Banks is the most important historical development of the last 300 years. Central Banks run by Speculatos have deluged the world in debt and blood, funding endless war and welfare.

ROCKEFELLERS: EMPERORS OF AMERICA

"For a Rockefeller, the Presidency of the United States would be a demotion."
—Joke in America in the 1970s, John E. Harr, *The Rockefeller Conscience*

LEFT Hillary Clinton with Laurance Rockefeller. This photo is a literal snapshot of modern politics. Hillary's expression says: "don't get too close, you wraith." But at this point her husband was President, and she nurtured Presidential aspirations. No one becomes President without groveling before Speculatos.
RIGHT President Bill Clinton in the White House with Laurance Rockefeller. No average citizen could obtain such access, Speculatos call on Presidents whenever they please.

Most candidates for high office are vetted by Speculatos. Reformers are denied the campaign contributions necessary to be elected. Speculatos do not simplistically control the world, as many "conspiracy theorists" claim. But every major leader in America knows of their power. Some insiders might disagree about the exact extent of Speculato influence, but if you speak to them off the record in a moment of honesty, none dispute the fact that Speculatos wield massive power yet conceal their influence.

Journalist Bill Moyers called David Rockefeller, "the unelected if indisputable chairman of the American Establishment ... one of the most powerful, influential and richest men in America ... [he] sits at the hub of a vast network of financiers, industrialists and politicians whose reach encircles the globe."

FORBES 2010 LIST OF THE WORLD'S BILLIONAIRES

RANK	NAME	COUNTRY	AGE	NET WORTH BILLIONS OF $
1	Carlos Slim Helu & family	Mexico	70	53.5
2	William Gates III	United States	54	53.0
3	Warren Buffett	United States	79	47.0
4	Mukesh Ambani	India	52	29.0
5	Lakshmi Mittal	India	59	28.7
6	Lawrence Ellison	United States	65	28.0
7	Bernard Arnault	France	61	27.5
8	Eike Batista	Brazil	53	27.0
9	Amancio Ortega	Spain	74	25.0
10	Karl Albrecht	Germany	90	23.5
11	Ingvar Kamprad & family	Sweden	83	23.0
12	Christy Walton & family	United States	55	22.5
13	Stefan Persson	Sweden	62	22.4
14	Li Ka-shing	Hong Kong	81	21.0
15	Jim Walton	United States	62	20.7
16	Alice Walton	United States	60	20.6
17	Liliane Bettencourt	France	87	20.0
18	S. Robson Walton	United States	66	19.8
19	Prince Alwaleed Bin Talal Alsaud	Saudi Arabia	55	19.4
20	David Thomson & family	Canada	52	19.0
21	Michael Otto & family	Germany	66	18.7
22	Lee Shau Kee	Hong Kong	82	18.5
23	Michael Bloomberg	United States	68	18.0
24	Sergey Brin	United States	36	17.5
24	Charles Koch	United States	74	17.5
154	Nicky Oppenheimer & family	South Africa	64	5.0
316	Steven Spielberg	United States	63	3.0
437	**David Rockefeller Sr.**	**United States**	**94**	**2.2**

The *Forbes* 2010 List of the World's Billionaires contained 937 billionaires worldwide. Not all billionaires will share information about their worth; *Forbes* can be forgiven for some guesstimation, but omitting family fortunes squirreled in trusts and foundations makes this list meaningless. The Rothschilds are not even on the list. *No* insider would argue that the Rothschild family is worth less than $1 billion. The Rockefeller family fortune has been estimated at more than $50 billion. In terms of known assets, there are more than 150 living heirs who are direct descendants of John D. Rockefeller, each one is a millionaire at the very least. The Rockefeller Foundation lists $3.8 billion in assets and spends $137 million in endowments per year. Rockefellers do not own the Rockefeller Foundation, but they effectively control it. No insider would seriously argue that Bill Gates or Warren Buffet are more powerful than the Rockefellers, Rothschilds, or other Speculatos, yet that is the impression sheeple have.

THE DEBT LEASH

"I care not what puppet is placed on the throne of England to rule the Empire on which the sun never sets. The man that controls Britain's money supply controls the British Empire. And I control the money supply."
— Nathan Mayer Rothschild, Speculato

"I am afraid that the ordinary citizen will not like to be told that banks can and do create money ... and they who control the credit of the nation direct the policy of Governments and hold in the hollow of their hands the destiny of the people."
— Reginald McKenna, British Chancellor of the Exchequer (1915-1916)

"There are two ways to conquer and enslave a nation. One is by the sword. The other is by debt."
— John Adams

The Rothschilds now own the bulk of the British and French national debts. One senses this is an immense power, but how do you use it to control nations?

By debt we mean bonds, promises to pay money on some future date. Guv'ments create and sell bonds for money they spend in the present, as in the first chapter of this book. They tax citizens in the future to honor these bonds.

Bonds are an asset. Bonds can be sold or borrowed against. If borrowed against, this leverage can be used to buy more bonds...

By selling a nation's bonds, Rothschild can hurt its economy. Flood markets with anything, the price declines because there is so much. If Rothschild owns 25% of a nation's bonds and sells a mere 1% of them, the price of those bonds plummets. And he still has plenty more to sell...

By depressing bond prices, Rothschild makes it hard for guv'ment to sell new bonds. Before selling bonds to their Central Bank, guv'ments sell them to private investors. Private investors spend existing money. They don't create money out of thin air and buy bonds with it. No inflation results, making this method preferable.

When Rothschild sells bonds, investors buy them. So many bonds are available that guv'ment must offer higher interest rates to sell new bonds. The cost of issuing bonds has increased—if guv'ment can sell them to private investors at all.

Honest demand is limited. When Rothschild sells bonds, he crowds guv'ment out of the market. Guv'ment has to sell more bonds to their Central Bank. The Central Bank computers money to buy bonds, creating a bubble that wouldn't exist or would have been smaller if Rothschild hadn't sold his bonds.

If Rothschild sells enough bonds, investors may begin to doubt guv'ment's ability to honor them all, and the bond market may crash rather than merely be depressed.

Corrupt nations must sell bonds to obtain money. Their bloated guv'ments can never be funded from honest taxes alone. In 2010, America ran a $4.52 billion a day deficit. Each day it spent $4.52 billion dollars it didn't have. America had to create and sell $4.52 billion in bonds daily to obtain this money. If America couldn't sell these bonds, it would have been bankrupt. Do not pass go, do not collect $200 million. If this happened, chaos would have resulted, and there would have been riots or worse. . .

Speculato can bankrupt guv'ments by dumping bonds. Guv'ment put itself at their mercy by spending more money than it had year after year, but this is why Speculato created this money system. Percepticus and Integritus would have avoided this quagmire with a limited government that rarely incurs debt.

Welfare states and military empires are ravenous creatures. Corrupt guv'ments foolish enough to create them always need to sell more bonds than investors will purchase with savings. They always resort to selling bonds to their Central Bank. But this process is accelerated when few bonds can be sold to private investors. If guv'ment sells all new bonds to their Central Bank, all money used to buy them is computered and a monstrous bubble is created. Prices shoot into the stratosphere. Money is devalued so fast that people's wages don't buy them enough to survive. Chaos ensues, and there are riots or worse. . .

When Speculato sells bonds, money is removed from circulation. He is rich enough that he doesn't spend the cash from the sale, but rather stockpiles it. The money supply is essentially reduced, contracting the bubble and producing a recession or Depression. The opposite is also true, buying bonds puts money into circulation, re-inflating the bubble or creating one.

When Speculato sells bonds and money is removed from circulation, interest rates rise. Interest is just the price of money, and is subject to supply and demand like anything else. Less money means the price of it must rise. Conversely, when Speculato buys bonds and more money circulates, interest rates drop.

Interest rates determine credit available to businesses, and the prices of loans for houses, cars, credit cards. They are the gas pedal of the economy. Rothschild can fluctuate interest rates with bond sales. His foot is on the gas pedal. He is driving the economy.

The bond market also influences the stock market, as it is the primary alternative to it. When bond prices decline, people turn to stocks. When bonds are profitable, stocks look less attractive. So Speculato is influencing the stock market too.

Speculato is paid interest on bonds, which buys more bonds, meaning he is owed ever-increasing interest payments. Much of the income tax pays interest on the debt he holds, meaning citizens are at some level serfs to him. Interest on America's federal debt was $164 billion in 2010—$1,100 per taxpayer, 18% of total personal income tax revenue.

When bonds mature, Speculato receives their face value, not just interest payments. He is paid back the money he originally loaned guv'ment. Or could be. Guv'ment will encourage him to immediately relend them the money, allowing them to immediately re-issue him a new bond without ever repaying the original loan. If he demands money rather than accepting new bonds in place of the old, guv'ment faces a cash crunch. It creates bonds on top of the $4.52 billion per day, sells them to the Central Bank, and uses computered money to pay Speculato. This massive printing of money inflates the bubble dangerously.

By selling or buying bonds, Speculato changes bond prices and the money supply, and controls the nation. Altering money supply and bond prices can limit guv'ment's ability to fund itself, fluctuate interest rates and stock prices, and create Depressions.

This threat is a knife constantly held at the nation's jugular—its credit and money, the one thing in the economy that controls everything else. Rothschild is smart and parlays his massive financial position into greater wealth. Each week he owns more debt and is more dangerous. The knife grows like Pinocchio's nose.

What can a leader do? Oppose Speculato? Educate people and institute reform? Naïve and suicidal, as we have seen and shall see. A leader must grant concessions to Speculato so he doesn't harm the economy. These concessions worsen the nation's predicament.

TO SKIP THE PICTURE PAGES AFTER THIS CHAPTER, PLEASE TURN TO PAGE 115

Observations by Bill Clinton's Mentor About Speculatos

Carroll Quigley was a renowned Georgetown University historian. He is famed as a macrohistorian, which means he studied long-term history looking for the most fundamental causalities and trends. Quigley's book *The Evolution of Civilizations* is one of the most brilliant history books ever written, and he taught the book's concepts in a history course at the Foreign Service School at Georgetown. Georgetown's Foreign Service School is nicknamed "The West Point of America's Diplomatic Corps," and its famous graduates call Quigley's course the most influential of their undergraduate careers. One such individual was Bill Clinton, who thanked Quigley for his inspiration and guidance in the speech declaring his run for the Presidency, and an inaugural address. Quigley also wrote the 1300 page tome *Tragedy and Hope: A History of the World in Our Time*, in which he meticulously documented Speculatos rise to power, and their covert exercise of that power. Conspiracy theorists tend to overemphasize the extraordinary machinations Quigley documented, while those with more mainstream views tend to underemphasize them. Quigley's instructive observations about Speculatos are included on this page and the next two:

"There does exist, and has existed for a generation, an international Anglophile network which operates, to some extent, in the way the radical Right believes the Communists act. In fact, this network, which we may identify as the Round Table Groups, has no aversion to cooperating with the Communists, or any other groups, and frequently does so. I know of this network because I have studied it for twenty years and was permitted for two years in the early 1960s to examine its papers and secret records. I have no aversion to it or to most of its aims and have, for much of my life, been close to it and to many of its instruments. I have objected, both in the past and recently, to a few of its policies ... but in general my chief difference of opinion is that it wishes to remain unknown, and

I believe its role in history is significant enough to be known."

"For the first time in its history, Western Civilization is in danger of being destroyed internally by a corrupt, criminal ruling cabal which is centered around the Rockefeller interests, which include elements from the Morgan, Brown, Rothschild, DuPont, Harriman, Kuhn-Loeb, and other groupings as well. This junta took control of the political, financial, and cultural life of America in the first two decades of the twentieth century."

"The history of the last century shows that the advice given to governments by bankers, like the advice they gave to industrialists, was consistently good for bankers, but was often disastrous for governments, businessmen, and the people generally."

"It must not be felt that these heads of the world's chief Central Banks were themselves substantive powers in world finance. They were not. Rather, they were the technicians and agents of the dominant investment bankers of their own countries, who had raised them up and were perfectly capable of throwing them down. The substantive financial powers of the world were in the hands of these international bankers who remained largely behind the scenes in their own unincorporated private banks. These formed a system of international cooperation and national dominance which was more private, more powerful, and more secret than that of their agents in the Central Banks."

"The growth of financial capitalism made possible a centralization of world economic control and use of this power for the direct benefit of financiers and the indirect injury of all other economic groups."

"The powers of financial capitalism had another far-reaching aim, nothing less than to create a world system of financial control in private hands able to dominate the political system of each country and the economy of the world as a whole. This system was to be controlled in a feudalist fashion by the Central Banks of the world acting in concert, by secret agreements arrived at in frequent meetings and conferences. The apex of the systems was to be the Bank for International Settlements in Basel, Switzerland, a private bank owned and controlled by the world's Central Banks which were themselves private corporations. Each Central Bank ... sought to dominate its government by its ability to control Treasury loans, to manipulate foreign exchanges, to influence the level of economic activity in the country, and to influence cooperative politicians by subsequent economic rewards in the business world."

"I am now quite sure that 'Tragedy and Hope' was suppressed although I do not know why or by whom."

"[Conspiracy theorists] thought I proved everything. They insist that international bankers were a single bloc, were all powerful and remain so today. I, on the contrary, stated in my book that they were much divided, often fought among themselves, had great influence but not control of political life and were sharply reduced in power about 1931-1940, when they became less influential than monopolized industry."

"[Conspiracy theorist author W. Cleon] Skousen claims that I have written of a conspiracy of the super-rich who are pro-Communist and wish to take over the world and that I'm a member of this group. But I never called it a conspiracy and don't regard it as such. I'm not an "insider" of these rich persons, although Skousen thinks so. I happen to know some of them and liked them, although I disagreed with some of the things they did before 1940."

Those critical of Speculatos and corrupt banking often brandish many of the quotes listed above, but neglect to include the last two. Conversely, many trying to debunk conspiracies include the last two quotes but not those which preceded them. The author refuses to cherry pick the quotes that help his viewpoint, and censor those that do not, so included both sets.

Speculatos' power is not absolute. No small cabal can run the world like a CEO does a company, and any claim that this is how the world operates is ludicrous. On the other hand, Speculatos wield massive power which sheeple are unaware of, and use that power to exercise influence and mold the world. It is possible to mold the world, but doing so is never an exact or easy or simplistic proposition.

It is true that monopolized industry has gained ground over the years, and the banking patriarchs lost power. It is also true that Speculatos have regained much power by buying up monopolized industry. Monopolized industry requires loans from Speculato banks, and Speculatos often placed lackeys on the Board of Directors of these corporations as a condition for credit and loans. 100 years ago most Speculatos were bankers. Today many Speculatos are bankers, but some are also corporate CEOs or individuals who sit on the Board of Directors of multiple multinational corporations—what Quigley called "monopolized industry."

This book does not claim to systematically or exhaustively document the character and modus operandi of the global establishment. This is a book about economic bubbles, those that create them, and why. Speculatos are real, they have the power to create money, and they abuse this power to create bubbles.

Establishing the Establishment

"But now the guy has got to come up with Paulie's money every week, no matter what. Business bad? Fuck you, pay me. You had a fire? Fuck you, pay me. The place got hit by lighting? Fuck you, pay me. Also, Paulie could do anything. Especially run up bills on the joint's credit. Why not? Nobody's gonna pay for it anyway. As soon as the deliveries are made in the front door, you move the stuff out the back and sell it at a discount. You take a two hundred dollar case of booze and sell it for a hundred. It doesn't matter. It's all profit. And, finally, when there's nothing left, when you can't borrow another buck from the bank or buy another case of booze, you bust the joint out. You light a match."

—Goodfellas

Pardon the profanity above, but quotes should be, well, quoted. Anyone who has seen a mob movie knows what happens next. A sucker is in debt. The gangster he owes it to exploits him. The exploitation is tougher to wrap your brain around when the sucker is a nation or the whole human race. It is also more heart wrenching. But the script is basically the same.

In mob movies, businessmen wait on gangsters before other customers without being told. Politicians do the same for Speculatos. They don't become politicians, much less stay politicians, without appeasing the people who really run things.

Speculato wants the heads of the Central Bank to be individuals he "approves." This is disastrous, but what choice does a politician or monarch have? No leader can stay in power if the economy is in shambles, and Speculato can crash it.

To run the Central Bank, Speculato selects ruthless profitmongers who have worked for him for years and make amoral decisions without any nudging. This is done discreetly. Career politicians don't need a schematic. Polite mentions of preferred appointments to Senators and Presidents at dinners or fundraisers are sufficient. The banker-owned media touts the appointee as brilliant, honest, patriotic. Once he is approved donations flood campaign coffers. Positive reinforcement for Pavlov's politicians.

The Central Bank is now run by Speculato relatives, executives from his banks, or members of academia who champion fiat money. Foxes "guard" the henhouse.

Central Banks like the Federal Reserve and Bank of England set interest rates, the supply of money, and exercise control over all the country's banks. The world waits anxiously to see if the Federal Reserve will raise or lower interest rates. Fortunes are made and lost by properly predicting such decrees. Speculato underlings now make these decisions. At worst Speculato has an inside edge predicting their actions, at best they leak information to him ahead of time.

Central Banks buy and sell bonds just like Speculato. They receive guv'ment bonds in exchange for the money they computer for guv'ment. A Central Bank could counter Speculato's actions, so influencing it is important to him. And now the Central Bank will manipulate the economy, freeing up his resources to profit off business cycles rather than create them.

This appointment modus operandi is repeated throughout guv'ment. Some senior members of the military, intelligence services, courts, and national police are Speculato approved, though not always chosen by him. These lackeys do Speculato's bidding and relay information to him. Info on a business enemy? A contact forwards records. Need some zealot who is educating people neutralized? Contacts arrange tax audits or find obscure laws to railroad him with. In rare cases where these neutralization methods fail, you whack him like a goodfella.

Eventually guv'ment balks at some request. Speculato sells bonds. Markets plummet. Politicians gulp and make the distasteful appointment Speculato wanted.

Opponents of Speculato's demands are smeared by the media, and face well-funded political rivals. Honest politicians are instant lame ducks, and out next election, except rare cases like Texas Congressman Ron Paul.

All insiders know Speculato is a fourth branch of guv'ment with a check on the powers of others. But he is a branch no insider would dare to publicly mention.

Is this explanation oversimplified? Absolutely.

Is it inaccurate? No.

There are limitations to what Rothschild could accomplish, and other Speculatos muscled their way onto the financial Olympus with him. But Speculatos wield massive power few people understand.

Eventually Rothschild had lackeys in key positions throughout guv'ment. A Central Bank exploited the people, his underlings ran it, and he owned a controlling stake in commercial banks. What next? Establish Central Banks in other nations and buy up their debt so he controlled them like England and France.

War was and is the best way to do this. In a world of Kings, it was not a tough sell. In 1694, the King of England agreed to the world's first Central Bank because he wanted a war and couldn't raise taxes. No enemy or reason had to be concocted. The King was itching to go to war, but just needed funding. War is trickier to engineer with democracies, but as history indicates, obtainable every few decades.

Nothing is more profitable to Speculatos than war. Build expensive implements, destroy them and society's infrastructure, and then rebuild both. Let people rest a few years, repeat.

Speculatos profit through ownership of Haliburtons and loans guv'ment uses to pay Haliburtons. The Rothschilds funded Napoleon and Wellington. France and England sweated Waterloo, Rothschilds just shrugged. They were winners either way. Speculatos funded both sides in modern conflicts like the World Wars.

They don't just profit off both sides of a war, but every side.

Best of all, sheeple make sacrifices during wartime they would never agree to during peace. They'll give up necessities like food, and luxuries like civil liberties—if the propaganda is effective enough. Once people have less liberty, future Depressions and wars are easier to engineer. . .

Speculatos ferment war via their lackeys in guv'ment and media. It is less a case of forcing people to do something they despise, than preying on their natural prejudices and weaknesses.

Rothschild-controlled nations warred against nations without Central Banks. Attacked nations usually accepted Central Banks to fund a defense. If they refused, Rothschilds funded enemies which devastated them. Rothschilds then bought up the nation's debt for pennies on the dollar and used this leverage to force it to adopt a Central Bank.

Speculatos worked diligently to acquire control over the money supplies of not just England and France, but Germany, Austria, Italy, and most nations in Europe. By the mid-1800s, they had completed this financial blitzkrieg. They then turned their attention to America. It took almost a century, but Speculatos instituted a Central Bank in America in 1913.

A lot has been covered, and you may be confused. Remember Crusoeville, how increasing and decreasing the money supply enriches Speculato by stealing wealth from people and collapsing the economy. Control of the money supply is the core power. Once Speculato obtains this power, he rules a nation. No ifs, no ands, no buts. Control a nation's money supply, you rule it. Period. If Speculato injects a steady stream of money, there is prosperity, if he contracts the supply, people are ruined and starve.

TO SKIP THE PICTURE PAGES AFTER THIS CHAPTER, PLEASE TURN TO PAGE 122

Checks and Balances of the 4th Branch of the United States Guv'ment

This isn't glib cynicism, but rather a candid summary of how America actually works. To try and understand the American guv'ment without appreciating the true role of the Federal Reserve and Money Power is absurd.

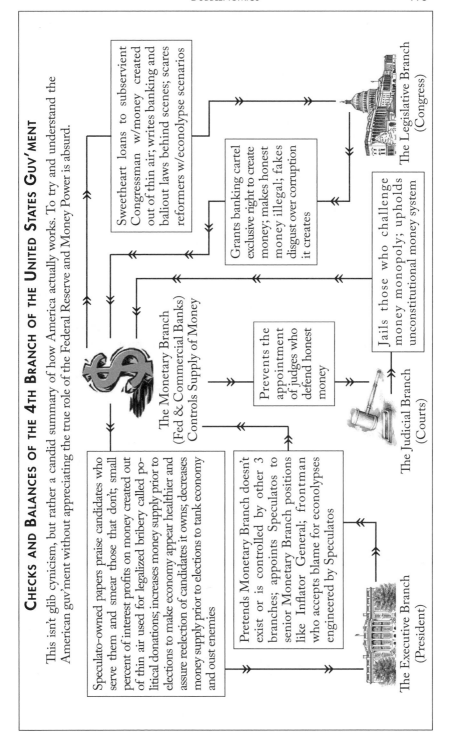

Sweetheart loans to subservient Congressman w/money created out of thin air; writes banking and bailout laws behind scenes; scares reformers w/econolypse scenarios

Grants banking cartel exclusive right to create money; makes honest money illegal; fakes disgust over corruption it creates

The Legislative Branch
(Congress)

The Monetary Branch
(Fed & Commercial Banks)
Controls Supply of Money

Jails those who challenge money monopoly; upholds unconstitutional money system

Prevents the appointment of judges who defend honest money

The Judicial Branch
(Courts)

Speculato-owned papers praise candidates who serve them and smear those that don't; small percent of interest profits on money created out of thin air used for legalized bribery called political donations; increases money supply prior to elections to make economy appear healthier and assure reelection of candidates it owns; decreases money supply prior to elections to tank economy and oust enemies

Pretends Monetary Branch doesn't exist or is controlled by other 3 branches; appoints Speculatos to senior Monetary Branch positions like Inflator General; frontman who accepts blame for econolypses engineered by Speculatos

The Executive Branch
(President)

THE MONEY POWER: A GOVERNMENT UNTO ITSELF

Calling the Money Power a 4th branch of government may seem like an exaggeration. As quotes on the following pages show, many knowledgable individuals have taken it even further, calling the Money Power a government unto itself:

"The real truth of the matter is, as you and I know, that a financial element in the large centers has owned the government of the U.S. since the days of Andrew Jackson."
—President Franklin D. Roosevelt, letter to Speculato Colonel M. House

"A power has risen up in the government greater than the people themselves, consisting of many and various powerful interests, combined in one mass, and held together by the cohesive power of the vast surplus in banks."
—John C. Calhoun, Vice President under Andrew Jackson

"The Federal Reserve Board is not a Federal agency. It is a creature and a hand maiden of the private commercial banking system of the United States, even though the Congress created them, like it did the CIA. ... The Federal Reserve has evolved into an entity in and unto itself and now believes it has no relationship to the rest of the Government."
—Henry B. Gonzalez
Chairman of the House Banking, Finance & Urban Affairs Committee (1989-1995)

"In the United States today, we have in effect two governments. We have the duly constituted government. Then we have an independent, uncontrolled and uncoordinated government in the Federal Reserve System, illegally operating the money powers which are reserved to Congress by the Constitution."
—U.S. Congressman Wright Patman,
Chairman of the House Banking and Currency Committee (1965-1975)

"The Federal Reserve is one of the most corrupt institutions the world has ever seen. There is not a man within the sound of my voice who does not know that this nation is run by the international bankers."
—U.S. Congressman Louis T. McFadden
Chairman of the House Banking and Currency Committee (1920-1931)
Spoken on the Floor of Congress

"The dirty little secret is that both houses of Congress are irrelevant. ... America's domestic policy is run by Alan Greenspan and the Federal Reserve, and America's foreign policy is now being run by the International Monetary Fund."
—Robert Reich, Secretary of Labor under Bill Clinton

"Most Americans have no real understanding of the operation of the international money lenders. The accounts of the Federal Reserve System have never been audited. It operates outside of the control of Congress and manipulates the credit of the United States."

—Barry Goldwater, U.S. Senator (1953-1965, 1969-1987)

"The real menace of our republic is this invisible government which like a giant octopus sprawls its slimy length over city, state and nation. Like the octopus of real life, it operates under cover of a self created screen. It seizes in its long and powerful tentacles our executive officers, our legislative bodies, our schools, our courts, our newspapers, and every agency created for the public protection. At the head of this octopus are the Rockefeller Standard Oil interests and a small group of powerful banking houses generally referred to as international bankers. The little coterie of powerful international bankers virtually run the United States government for their own selfish purposes. They practically control both political parties, write political platforms, make catspaws of party leaders, use the leading men of private organizations, and resort to every device to place in nomination for high public office only such candidates as will be amenable to the dictates of corrupt big business. These international bankers and Rockefeller Standard Oil interests control the majority of newspapers and magazines in this country. They use the columns of these papers to club into submission or drive out of office public officials who refuse to do the bidding of the powerful corrupt cliques which compose the invisible government."

—John F. Hylan, New York City Mayor (1918-1925)

"The super rich in America enjoy power and prerogatives unimaginable to most of us. Who can conceive of owning a private empire that includes 100 homes, 2,500 servants, untold thousands of luxuries, and untold millions of dollars? America has a royal family of finance that has known such riches for generations. It is, of course, the Rockefellers. ... Money alone is not enough to quench the thirst and lusts of the super-rich. Instead, many use their vast wealth, and the influence such riches give them, to achieve even more power. Power of a magnitude never dreamed of by the tyrants and despots of earlier ages. Power on a world wide scale. Power over people, not just products. ... the drive of the Rockefellers and their allies to create a one-world government, combining super-capitalism and Communism under the same tent, all under their control ... the Rockefellers and their allies have, for at least fifty years, been carefully following a plan to use their economic power to gain political control of first America, and then the rest of the world. Do I mean conspiracy? Yes, I do. I am convinced there is such a plot, international in scope, generations old in planning, and incredibly evil in intent."

—Larry P. McDonald, U.S. Congressman (1975-1983)
Killed in office, aboard Korean Airlines 747 when shot down by the Soviets

SPECULATOS CREATED THE FEDERAL RESERVE AT A SECRET MEETING

Frank Vanderlip, one of the "Jekyll-7" that secretly designed the Fed

"Despite my views about the value to society of greater publicity for the affairs of corporations, there was an occasion, near the close of 1910, when I was as secretive—indeed, as furtive—as any conspirator. I do not feel it is any exaggeration to speak of our secret expedition to Jekyll Island as the occasion of the actual conception of what eventually became the Federal Reserve System. We were told to leave our last names behind us. We were told, further, that we should avoid dining together on the night of our departure. We were instructed to come one at a time and as unobtrusively as possible to the railroad terminal on the New Jersey littoral of the Hudson, where Senator Aldrich's private car would be in readiness, attached to the rear end of a train for the South. Once aboard the private car we began to observe the taboo that had been fixed on last names. We addressed one another as "Ben," "Paul," "Nelson," "Abe." Davison and I adopted even deeper disguises, abandoning our first names. On the theory that we were always right, he became Wilbur and I became Orville, after those two aviation pioneers, the Wright brothers. The servants and train crew may have known the identities of one or two of us, but they did not know all, and it was the names of us printed together that would have made our mysterious journey significant in Washington, in Wall Street, even in London. Discovery, we knew, simply must not happen, or else all our time and effort would be wasted. If it were to be exposed publicly that our particular group had got together and written a banking bill, that bill would have no chance whatever of passage by Congress."

—Frank Vanderlip, from an article he wrote in the 1935 *Saturday Evening Post*

Vanderlip was 1 of 7 Speculatos at the Covert Constitutional Convention where the Fed and Income Tax were designed. As Assistant Treasury Secretary (1897-1901), Vanderlip arranged a $200 million loan from National City Bank to the U.S. Government. It was used to fight the Spanish American War, America's first major external war. After leaving guv'ment, Vanderlip became a Vice President of National City Bank. Payback for the $200 million loan he arranged. Today National City is Citigroup, the cornerstone of the Rockefeller Empire.

THE WORLD IS HIS APPLE

"Banks are an almost irresistible attraction for that element of our society which seeks unearned money."

—J Edgar Hoover

Speculato occupies a pinnacle which is the ideal place to survey and influence world events. He engineers wars and Depressions, and with tentacles at the centers of power, is apprised of new opportunities and obtains a stake in them. He is especially interested in natural resources. For example, Rothschilds helped found petroleum giant Royal Dutch Shell.

Another example is Cecil Rhodes, who exploited the diamond mines and people of South Africa, creating de Beers. Rothschilds funded Rhodes, and have a stake in de Beers. Most everyone buying a diamond is making the Rothschilds richer. De Beers has vaults overflowing with diamonds but trickles out the supply to keep prices high. A diamond monopoly is forever.

Yet another example, gold. Rothschilds own so much that for a century a Rothschild set the daily opening price at the world's largest gold market, the London Bullion Marketing Association.

Noting a pattern? Monopolies in oil, diamonds, gold and money, exorbitant profit made by controlling supply.

During the 1800s and early 1900s the world's largest natural resource deposits were discovered. The Rothschilds obtained a piece of many, making investments in America, India, Cuba, Australia, Central America, Africa. They purchased 50,000 square miles of mine land in Canada, and shares in mining consortiums Rio Tinto and Le Nickel. Rothschilds also helped finance the railways of Europe, and lent Britain money used to build the Suez Canal.

What Speculato doesn't have a vineyard and mansion? Rothschilds bought the French Bordeaux vineyards of Mouton and Lafite. When German Emperor Wilhelm I saw the Rothschild's Château de Ferrières, he gasped and said, "Kings couldn't afford this. It can only belong to a Rothschild." An Emperor said this.

It staggers the imagination. To start off as the richest family on Earth, and then obtain ground floor ownership in the world's largest diamond, oil, gold, railroad and mining companies.

Estimating the Rothschild worth is instructive, so let's try, with the caveat that it is on another level futile due to the speculation involved.

The Rothschilds obtained $3,000,000 of seed money in 1805, and increased it 20-fold after Waterloo in 1815. This is according to a Rothschild-friendly biographer. $60 million in 1815. Assume the Rothschilds earned 3.3% per year. They'd have $38 billion dollars today. As rich as Bill Gates, very roughly.

Very, very roughly, the historical average of the stock market is 10% per year. Assume the Rothschilds earned half this much, 5% per year. The $60 million grows to $737 billion today.

World Gross Domestic Product, or World GDP, is the value of all goods & services produced on Earth. World GDP was $60 trillion in 2008. $737 billion dollars would be 1/81th of the entire output of the world that year. Very roughly, the annual labor of 82 million people.

If the Rothschilds did as well as the typical stock investor and averaged 10% a year, they would now have $5.8 quadrillion. Quadrillion? Huh? That's an astronomy number. In one year, light travels 5.9 quadrillion miles. A light-year. Numbers like trillion and quadrillion used to be called astronomical numbers. Maybe they should be called economical numbers. A quadrillion dollars could be renamed a Rothschild-year.

$5.8 quadrillion is $5,800 trillion. Huh again. How much is $5,800 trillion? $5,800,000,000,000,000. $5.8 million billions. 5.8 million billionaires. Or 5.8 billion millionaires.

There are 6.7 billion humans on Earth. 5.8 billion of them, or 86%, cannot be millionaires, even if the Rothschild fortune was redistributed.

$60 trillion is one year's World GDP. The start in 1815 was roughly two centuries ago. Very roughly, $60 trillion x 200 years = $12,000 trillion dollars of GDP in two centuries. So maybe a net wealth of $5,800 trillion isn't so absurd. On one level no, on another yes, for this is almost half of everything produced by the human race in two centuries. For one family to own so much would be absurd and Pharaoh-like, but is it inaccurate?

Yes. Heinously inaccurate. GDP wasn't calculated for most of history. $60 trillion today wasn't $60 trillion then. Many items like newspapers, food, Betamax VCRs, and haircuts no longer exist or have value. A haircut was $20 of GDP, but can't be resold like an ounce of gold.

The Rothschilds are not worth $5.8 quadrillion or anything close. They didn't save and invest all their earnings, but spent some of them on castles, yachts, and servants. Though much of their wealth is squirreled in a labyrinth of tax-avoidance structures such as Rothschild Continuation Holdings, they have paid taxes. The larger a fortune grows, the tougher it becomes to manage; Rothschilds have made bad investments and lost money. Rothschild assets have been confiscated by governments, including the Nazis, and France, which nationalized their bank and Le Nickel in 1981. Families like the Rockefellers muscled their way on to the mountaintop. Electronic communication negated Rothschild intelligence advantages, and business with corporate democracies is less autocratic than with monarchs. The world remains a jungle, and the Rothschilds aren't the only smart, ruthless people. Though not as hard to influence as sheeple think, the world is not controlled as easily as these dumbed-down examples imply. These factors and others slowed the growth of the Rothschild fortune. So where does that leave us? What is the total value of everything on Earth? What percentage of it do Speculatos own? The fact that trying to estimate their wealth requires us to ask these sorts of questions is telling, isn't it? The broad trend is the point. Bankers who can create money out of thin air end up owning the world. Or a big enough percentage of the world that they effectively control (or at least greatly influence) the world. Seeing wealth accrual viewed in Earth-owning terms makes the significance of multi-generational growth apparent.

In time, most fortunes erode. Most people born rich become Paris Hiltons, not Nathan Rothschilds. Bill Gates' children probably won't found the next Microsoft. Ford's scions probably won't invent a warp drive or cure cancer. These fortunes may grow modestly, maybe even rapidly, but probably never again astronomically.

What are the odds that a family will make exorbitant profits generation after generation, consistently predicting trends and remaining on the cutting edge? No one can in an honest business environment, but if you can print money, you make the profit of Ford, Microsoft or Standard Oil without having to perfect the assembly line, invent Windows, or discover oil. It is tough not to make money making money.

Rockefeller realized oil would run out eventually. He wanted his fortune to last longer than eventually, so got into banking. Century in, century out, nothing is more profitable.

Speculatos abuse PROXY to remain secret. Rockefellers might own a quarter of the stock of Citigroup, but they hire an attorney in Switzerland who hires an attorney in London who hires an attorney in New York, who creates an investment trust that buys Citigroup stock. The trust and New York attorney are listed as the owner, not Rockefellers. Multiple trusts are created via different legal mazes to buy chunks of the same company. Or companies. A person who researches ownership of banks does not find Rockefeller, Rothschild, Morgan, Carnegie and the rest of the Speculatos that run the world. This clique of Speculatos grows ever richer and more powerful as time passes. Sheeple pay taxes. Speculato fortunes obtain tax immunity in foundations and other tax-avoidance structures. These fortunes are invested in commercial banks with a monopoly on fractional reserve money creation. Speculatos grow fabulously wealthier.

Speculatos' "charitable" foundations spend a portion of their enormous income streams on education, think tanks, and political organizations. Grants to Ivy League universities allow influence which insures that academics appointed to prestigious positions hold Speculato viewpoints—especially in education, history, politics, and economics. These prestigious Ivy League academics write textbooks which become the party line of universities nationwide. Speculato think tanks produce position papers that give their schemes credibility, and their scholars are given unfettered access to the establishment via speeches, articles, TV appearances and conferences. Tyrannical Speculato policies are painted in a proper light and propagandized as socially beneficial. Most Speculato lackeys believe in their views, and that what they are doing is good, and do not realize they have been raised up mainly because they are beneficial to Speculatos. Speculato funded organizations like the Council on Foreign Relations are the American Establishment. Only geniuses with pliable ideologies are invited to join, shills who do the wrong thing without being told so long as paid exorbitantly. Most leadership positions in the establishment are given to members of these organizations. . .

Etcetera, etcetera, ad nauseum, ad infinitum. Each Speculato has tax exempt foundations, but Speculatos collude, agreeing to a division of labor among foundations so that they function as one synchronized mechanism for control of the herd. Sheeple pay for the psychological warfare used to enslave them by granting tax exempt status to the foundations funding the PSYOP.

Back to proxy. If bank ownership were not hidden by proxy, any twit could cross reference the stock ownership lists of banks, and realize that the same few hundred families own a preponderance of shares in every major bank on Earth. The banking system would easily be identified as a form of feudalism designed to protect and enlarge the intergenerational fortunes of a clandestine oligarchy.

The power of Speculatos is not as far reaching as many who believe in conspiracies think, but it is much greater than most sheeple realize. Whether the wealth and power described is in the hands of the Rothschilds or a hundred such families is immaterial. Choosing a single allegory, Speculato, or a single family, the Rothschilds, makes teaching easier, but is not realistic. One need not believe in a simplistic, monolithic conspiracy in which the Rothschilds or Rockefellers are global Emperors to appreciate the potential for world domination inherent in the fiat money system. Those with the power to create money out of thin air will always rule everyone else.

HIGH SCHOOL BUBBLENOMICS

High School Bubblenomics taught a concept some can't accept: Speculatos are real, the source of their wealth is the power to create money, and they will go to extraordinary lengths to keep this power. Those who can't accept this truth are doomed to flounder, never identifying root causes. Sheeple blame politicians, not Speculatos. Politicians in the foreground come and go. Speculatos remain hidden in the background.

Decent-hearted people have a hard time accepting that the über-rich can be so greedy and diabolical. Speculatos can't honestly be this evil. They just can't.

To Speculatos, patriotism is primitive tribalism and sheeple are animals. They feel as much guilt killing sheeple in wars or starving them in Depressions as non-vegans do for the cow when cooking a hamburger. A Speculato is shown on the opposing page. Such kind eyes. Do you see any hint of compassion? Of a soul?

Speculatos bought control of newspapers in 1915, and have consolidated this power since then, including TV. The media which sheeple rely on for information is a Speculato propaganda machine waging psychological warfare on the herd.

Banking fraud is ancient. Goldsmiths modernized the scam in the 1600s. In 1694, when the King of England wanted to war but lacked funding, Speculatos seized a chance to nationalize the goldsmith fraud. The King granted Speculatos the sole power to create and issue money he made legal tender. This forced sheeple to use Speculato money and pay the inflation tax. Speculatos created money the King used to fight wars. Lent to him at interest, of course. The King didn't care about that. Sheeple's taxes paid interest, not him. A great deal for Kings and Speculatos, a raw deal for herds sodomized by the inflation tax and business cycle—especially sheeple who died in wars which couldn't have been fought without fiat money.

Once Speculatos have a monopoly on the power to create money, they no longer work. They create money and buy lackeys who do their bidding. Central Banking is a control mechanism as well as a profit mechanism.

Speculatos want to levy the inflation tax on every human on Earth. To do that they had to establish a Central Bank in every nation on Earth. And did. The singular historical development since 1694 is the spread of this Central Bank plague.

America typifies the outbreak. 7 Speculatos secretly designed the Federal Reserve and Income Tax, and presented them as a Congressionally-created measures to help the public.

The Income Tax and Federal Reserve are fraternal twins born in 1913. The income tax was created so guv'ment could pay interest on money it borrowed from the Federal Reserve. Our Founding Fathers' limited government did not provide enough tax revenue for interest tithes to Speculatos. Politicians agreed to the income tax because it lets them control sheeple via tax breaks for desired behaviors

126

EYES ARE THE GATEWAY TO THE SOUL OR LACK THEREOF

Speculato Paul Warburg is shown above, his wealth made him the inspiration for "Daddy Warbucks" in the play *Annie*. Warburg was nothing like Annie's kind-hearted benefactor. He chaired the Rogue Constitutional Convention of 1910, at which the Income Tax and Federal Reserve that reshaped America were secretly planned. Warburg was from Europe, where Central Banks had been shafting sheeple for centuries. The plan that emerged was Warburg's brainchild, his attempt to transplant and adapt the European Central Bank model to America. Our banking system was designed by Daddy Warbucks!

Eyes are the gateway to the soul—or lack thereof. Warburg is a predator. A heartless predator who starved sheeple in Depressions and killed them in wars to make himself Warbuckier. The Speculatos shown below are just as ruthless and remorseless.

and tax penalties for undesired behaviors.

Guv'ment could levy the inflation tax by creating money out of thin air itself. Government could also outlaw the inflation tax. Leaders that try to implement such reforms have a funny way of dying.

"Charitable" foundations were created with the income tax so Speculatos wouldn't have to pay it. Speculato fortunes grow tax-free in foundations while sheeple struggle to pay taxes.

Speculatos head financial departments of guv'ment like the Treasury, as well as the Central Bank, investment banks and commercial banks. The resulting conglomerate is essentially a fourth branch of gov'ment, the Monetary Branch. It is the most powerful of America's four branches of guv'ment.

When Speculato banks create excessive money and face runs that would rupt them, guv'ment declares a bank holiday. Propaganda makes sheeple believe that banks possess money which they don't actually have, ending the run. If confidence can't be restored, guv'ment bails banks out.

Speculatos back corrupt politicians who do their bidding, smear those that won't. No purchase pays better dividends than politicians. Speculatos fund both sides of wars, indifferent to the suffering or outcome, except as it affects their balance sheet. They use profits from wars and Depressions to buy up physical resources and energy reserves which have long-term intrinsic value. As with money, they constrict supply and jack up prices. Speculatos are great whites perpetually prowling for prey.

Speculatos are obsessed with enlarging über-fortunes handed down generation after generation after generation after generation after generation. . . Sheeple die and pay estate and inheritance taxes. Foundations and trusts are immortal, no estate or inheritance tax is paid on them. Family members control foundation funds but never own them, meaning they are not counted on tax forms and richest-dude-in-the-world surveys. This is what Speculatos like Rockefellers mean when they say, "the secret to success is to own nothing but control everything." Controllers of large trusts are so rich and powerful that the Presidency would be a demotion.

Old money makes new money by creating money. Nothing is more profitable. Speculatos own controlling interests in most major commercial banks on Earth. That is, private banks which guv'ment grants the exclusive right to create money. Speculatos use proxy and middlemen to hide this control. This keeps sheeple from realizing that a small cabal of parasites has instituted fractional-reserve feudalism.

It bears repeating that the easiest way to make money is to make money. It ain't rocket science.

The rich exploiting the poor is the oldest story in the book. Fractional reserve lending and Central Banking are the newest chapters. Our civilization has two classes of people: sheeple that must work to obtain money, and Speculatos that simply create it out of thin air.

BACHELOR'S
IN
BUBBLENOMICS

COMMON WEALTH?

"The war against illegal plunder has been fought since the beginning of the world. But how is legal plunder to be identified? Quite simply. See if the law takes from some persons what belongs to them, and gives it to other persons to whom it does not belong. See if the law benefits one citizen at the expense of another by doing what the citizen himself cannot do without committing a crime. Then abolish this law without delay. If such a law is not abolished immediately it will spread, multiply and develop into a system."

—Frédéric Bastiat

"The ultimate purpose of all income redistribution is people control."

—Leon Trotsky

Back to Crusoeville. Once Crusoeville institutes fiat money and an income tax, society declines. People are told the income tax will be minimal and tax only the super rich, but it increases and taxes everyone but the super rich. The rich pay taxes, but not the super rich. Speculato created the income tax to pay interest on his guv'ment bonds. The income tax exists to pay him, not be paid by him, or he would have opposed it and prevented its creation. His fortune is squirreled in a "charitable" foundation, immune to the taxes sheeple pay.

Speculato speculated in a war, backing Teaville, Wineville and Vodkaville, but they are losing to Schnitzelville. He is out billions of "apple" notes—unless Crusoeville tips the balance.

Crusoeville has always been peaceful. Its people consider war evil, except in self defense. Politicians who don't fight wars consider them glorious, but wars couldn't be funded by a limited government. No such restriction now. Speculato papers portray Schitzelvillians as enemies of liberty, butchers of babies, eaters of meat. Sheeple are whipped into a frenzy and agree to war.

This first world war is too huge to fund with income taxes alone, so guv'ment trades bonds for Speculato's "apple" notes, increasing interest payments to him. A Speculato lackey heads the War Purchasing Board, so military contracts go to his companies. Crusoeville wins the war, salvaging Speculato's loans to Teaville, Wineville and Vodkaville. As Schnitzelville is devastated, Speculato is able to buy its assets and debt for almost nothing. Crusoeville taxpayers pay to rebuild Teaville, Wineville and Vodkaville, and the "enemy" Schnitzelville; these contracts go to Speculato companies.

Speculato makes a killing off the war, and now has a personal debt collector—

Crusoeville's Army. If a nation refuses Speculato's demands, his papers demonize them, and Crusoeville goes to war.

Crusoeville can't always be warring. That's why there are recessions and Depressions. The income tax enables politicians to "cure" Depressions. Social programs are created to alleviate suffering and kickstart the economy. A smorgasbord of agencies arise to build dams, plant trees, fund the arts. Businesses are regulated to prevent future Depressions—except banks which create them. Sheeple need work and have no idea what causes Depressions, so don't argue.

The Depression fades, agencies don't. Especially regulatory agencies. Speculato uses these to shaft competitors. During the Depression the Apple Protection Agency is created to inspect apples for viper worms. This employs people, and is supposedly a public good, but it is hard to tell if apples contain viper worms, and people inspect apples before eating them.

It is costly to inspect apples. Small farmers are bankrupted by the requirement. This is why Speculato proposed the Apple Protection Agency, to favor big apple businesses like his.

Speculato loves guv'ment programs. He bribes politicians and obtains contracts for tasks the private sector once handled. Bids are higher than in the private sector, and projects experience "unforeseen" cost overruns which are paid by taxpayers.

To loot guv'ment, businesses need laws written or distorted, and that requires lawyers. Crusoeville is soon infested with the vermin. More graduate from law school than could ever be employed honestly, so they get creative. In the old days no one was blamed for viper worm deaths, but lawyers say apple growers are negligent. They sue, win, and apple farmers must buy viper worm insurance to protect against lawsuits. Someone allergic to oranges eats one and dies. A lawyer sues. There was no warning saying, "oranges may harm people allergic to oranges." The lawyer obtains punitive damages, increasing insurance costs, and now a warning label must be placed on each orange.

Farmers pass these costs on to consumers. Fewer people grow apples and oranges because it is a risky hassle. It is more profitable to inspect or label them. Apple and orange supplies decrease and prices rise.

A politician tries abolishing the Apple Protection Agency to save taxpayers money. People are outraged. Only a sociopath would leave them defenseless against viper worms. They don't want to abolish the APA, but create a Cinnamon Purity Bureau.

Voters feel entitled to Apple-a-Day retirement and healthcare. Those who save are mugged by guv'ment to fund the retirement and medical bills of those who don't.

Ciderfare is next. A brilliant premise: pay people not to work. Millions take guv'ment up on its generous offer.

Before the income tax, people were charitable but considered retirement, healthcare, and employment personal responsibilities. That mindset is now heretical. Moral hazards of entitlements are ignored. The collective good supersedes the liberty of any individual. Things you earn aren't yours, but ours. Or was it theirs? The enormous guv'ment must be fed. New taxes are levied on apple growing, apple transporting, apple storing. Apple everything. Universities receive grants to study why apples are red.

Sheeple jump through hoops like trained animals to obtain tax breaks, but the tax code rewards debt and consumption, not savings and frugality. The crowning irony is the Apple Retirement Account. Once upon a time, all personal income was free from taxes, now the only income exempt is in the Retirement Account.

Guv'ment is now a 40-foot tapeworm. It confiscates so much wealth people don't have enough left to live. Mothers go to work. Wealth lost to guv'ment is replenished, but children are raised by strangers and television. TV advertisers stress that you are what you own. Parental supervision immunized against the advertising Ebola, but without this vaccination children are infected. They grow into primates whose self-worth is possession-based. Education, culture and morality become unimportant. Adults live like aimless children, subsisting paycheck to paycheck, spending every nickel on the newest thingamajig.

Violence becomes commonplace. Those who can't afford luxuries steal them. People are murdered for a jar of applesauce. A single jar! Unthinkable a few decades earlier.

A nation that spends everything it earns doesn't save. With no savings, there is no investment in the future. Roads erode, bridges collapse, factories shut down. There is no money for such luxuries.

Much of the population works for guv'ment, performing activities with no economic value. More and more parasites go on Ciderfare. Fewer and fewer people produce the wealth guv'ment confiscates. Those still producing wealth work less hard and cease to innovate. Guv'ment takes most of it anyway, why bother?

The solution is to make more people grow apples and oranges, and let less collect free cider and work for guv'ment. Politicians won't shrink guv'ment because those dependent on guv'ment vote for them. People supported by guv'ment vote against anyone who tries to shrink it, and they eventually outnumber those funding it. Reform is impossible. Crusoeville is doomed. Each year there will be less workers and more parasites. . .

Crusoeville's history is now a hymn of sorrow, a cycle of endless wars and Depressions. Its citizens are trudging slaves of guv'ment. They have little time for relaxation, much less contemplation or activism. Spirituality flatlines.

Crusoeville expects to be as rich as it was when government was small and most people produced apples and oranges. It wants something for nothing. This is impossible long term, but a mirage of prosperity can be created, and the day of reckoning delayed, if Crusoeville uses its currency to enslave other nations.

TO SKIP THE PICTURE PAGES AFTER THIS CHAPTER, PLEASE TURN TO PAGE 156

AMERICA'S 1ST FEDERAL INCOME TAX FORM (1913)

"The hardest thing in the world to understand is the income tax."

—Albert Einstein

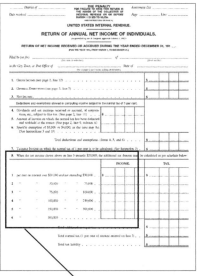

8. When the net income shown above on line 3 exceeds $20,000, the additional tax thereon mus			INCOME.			
1	per cent on amount over $20,000 and not exceeding $50,000 . .		$			
2	"	"	50,000	"	"	75,000 .
3	"	"	75,000	"	"	100,000 .
4	"	"	100,000	"	"	250,000 .
5	"	"	250,000	"	"	500,000 .
6	"	"	500,000	. . . .		

The income tax is a pitiful servitude. Sheeple giving detailed personal records to guv'ment resemble children showing report cards to parents. Lives are planned around the tax code. Sheeple jump through tax hoops like the trained animals they are. This is not liberty, and the spectacle would sicken and sadden our Founding Fathers. Colonial Americans often lived their entire life without seeing a Federal tax collector. They never saw a Federal tax form. You handed a colonial American a W-2 or 1040 form, they would have loaded their musket.

A Truth You Were Probably Never Taught in School
The Tax System Our Founding Fathers Intended

"Direct taxes will only be recurred to for great purposes."
—James Madison, Father of the U.S. Constitution

America's Founders wanted federal revenue derived primarily from indirect taxes on commerce, trade and sales. A government funded by indirect taxes is small, for if rates are raised excessively, people avoid them legally by spending less, and revenue declines.

Direct taxes like the income tax are levied against individuals' assets, and can only be avoided through criminality. History taught our framers that governments always abuse the power to directly tax citizens, and some wanted to outlaw it. Others worried indirect taxation would provide insufficient revenue during emergencies like war, and felt America might perish for lack of funding. The problem was granting government direct taxation powers only in emergencies. The solution was apportionment among the states. The U.S. Constitution says:

Article 1, Section 3: direct Taxes shall be apportioned among the several States which may be included within this Union, according to their respective Numbers

Apportion is a funky colonial term that means to divide and assign. Among who or what? The several states. How? According to their respective numbers, their population. Direct federal taxes would be levied against states, never individuals, and each state would pay an amount proportional to its population. If the federal government needs $1,000, and Virginia has 80 people and Maryland has 20 people, then Virginia pays $800, Maryland $200. Virginia and Maryland can obtain the revenue from their citizens in any way they want, the federal government cannot tell them how to raise the money, and it cannot tax individuals directly. Individuals are powerless against government, but states with militias could refuse frivolous or unconstitutional revenue requests. The federal guv'ment can raid your home easily. Raiding California or Texas is harder.

Direct taxes were one-time affairs, not perpetual income streams. If the federal government needed more emergency funds, it had to ask states again. Under the Founders' tax system, government determined revenue required from direct taxation and asked states for it; in our modern system, guv'ment takes as much as it can from individuals and then determines how to spend it.

Few sheeple can describe our original tax system. This isn't accidental. Ignorant of the past, how can they appreciate what was lost? Or understand how to regain

it? Sheeple have never known anything except an IRS which levies double-digit direct taxes, and don't realize a different revenue system is viable.
America's original tax system is one of the loftiest structures human wisdom ever erected. Indirect taxes were the primary federal revenue early in American history. The absence of direct taxes was a main reason for America's early success.

Our Founders paid a total tax rate of 6-9% outside of wartime. This was all taxes, at all levels. If our Founders had submitted to the Townshend, Sugar, Stamp and Tea taxes which precipitated the American Revolution, and chosen not to revolt, they would still have paid far lower tax rates than we do.

In 1798, a direct tax of $2 million was apportioned to pay Revolutionary War debt. In 1813 and 1815 direct taxes of $3 million and $6 million were apportioned to fund the War of 1812. In 1861, a $20 million tax was apportioned to fund the Civil War. America had existed 72 years and its people had paid a direct tax 4 times, once every 18 years on average. Apportionments had only been levied for emergencies. The system worked exactly as the Founders intended.

Imagine you paid income tax once every 18 years. It boggles the mind. The savings is enough to send a child to college or pay off a house. Few obtain as much from government as they pay—except Speculatos and parasites.

The Income Tax Act passed in 1913. It was 1% on income over $3,000, 6% on income over $500,000, and rose by 1% on incomes in between. A "minimum wage" worker earned about $450 a year then, and the average annual income was $950. The middle class didn't pay the first income tax, or they never would have agreed to it. They viewed it as a way to stick it to the rich.

In 1916, the highest rate was raised to 15%. Sheeple cheered. Shaft the rich! In 1917, the tax was 2% on income over $1,000. The money supply had been inflated relentlessly to fund World War I, so the average income was now $1,400. The creators of the income tax probably planned on this bracket creep, but did not mention it to sheeple when convincing them to support an income tax. Regardless, wealthier portions of the working class now paid. In 1918, the tax was 6% on income over $1,000, 77% on income over $1,000,000—if you hadn't squirreled your fortune in a foundation. Average income was $1,515, bracket creep made even more middle class workers pay. Sheeple weren't cheering anymore.

In 1941 America entered World War II and the lowest rate was raised to 10%. By 1944, the lowest rate was 23% on income over $500; minimum wage was 30¢ an hour or about $650 a year, and average annual income was now $2,400, so the middle class was gouged. After WWII, rates declined, but the lowest rate never dropped below 10%. Our lowest income tax rate today is 167% of the highest rate under the original income tax. The 1913 gouge-the-rich rate is paid by sheeple today.

In the 1950s, income tax rates peaked at 91% of income over $400,000. 91%! Reagan lowered rates, which today are 10% to 35%. For average working folks with incomes between $8,000-$35,000, the rate is 15%—2.5 times the highest 1913 rate. Above $370,000, you pay 35%—5.8 times the highest 1913 rate.

The first income tax code was 14 pages. Today it is 7,500 pages. The Incredible Hulk couldn't lift it. The Internal Revenue Code (IRC) is a 3.4-million-word, 24MB text file many computers can't open. A masochist who printed the IRC would empty several toners, need 15 reams of paper and end up with a 3-foot stack. Bound in books, the Internal Revenue Code resembles a set of encyclopedias. Few Americans read the tax code, much less understand it. Corporations and the rich have loopholes inserted, while the Internal Revenue "Service" railroads honest citizens who make innocent mistakes.

Few Americans believe our government is honest or that it makes wise use of tax dollars. Fewer Americans believe there is any way to lower taxes. Fear of the IRS makes sheeple pay taxes they consider unjust, and prevents political dissent.

THE WAR TO END ALL WARS
A TEXTBOOK SPECULATO MACHINATION

Speculatos didn't waste time putting the income tax and Federal Reserve to use. Just 4 years after they were created, America entered its first major external war, World War I (1914-1918). Trench warfare made World War I the most brutal conflict in history up to that point. 8.5 million dead, 37 million casualties. Soldiers leapt out of trenches and sprinted into the maws of machine guns. At the Battle of Verdun, 600,000 men died in 6 months. At the Battle of the Somme, England lost 60,000 men in the first few hours, and casualties topped 1,200,000 over 5 months.

Americans got it right and wanted nothing to do with World War I. It was a senseless war among territory-hungry European monarchies. The latest in a 6-century string of them.

Speculatos lent the Allies $1.5 billion ($24 billion today). The Allies were losing. 274 German U-boats sank 6,674 Allied ships during WWI, 24 per U-boat. Radar didn't exist. England had no way to detect U-boats. The British Isles were like a sieged city, slowly being strangled. Britain would surrender, the Allies would default on loans, and Speculatos would be out $1.5 billion. This couldn't be allowed, so Speculatos sent in their debt collection agency, the American military.

All those young Americans frittering their lives chasing fly balls. What a waste. No profit in it. Baseball has a lower mortality rate than playing trench warfare, but watching a Mediterranean sunset on your yacht, realizing you must fire your masseuse and pastry chef if Allied bonds are defaulted, you decide a few million deaths is a small price to pay to preserve a several billion dollar fortune.

The problem is convincing sheeple to fight. They are narrow minded, as people actually fighting wars often are. Reason won't work. The trick is to get sheeple angry. Then they feel rather than think and will agree to anything.

Propaganda begins with naming. You don't call this debt collection exercise "The J.P. Morgan Bailout" or "The Rothschild Repo." Certainly not "World War I of II." "The Great War" was tried. Picture Tony the Tiger selling death instead of Frosted Flakes. "This War is Gr-r-reat!" "The War to End All Wars" was chosen. This is the last war. Don't miss it! Get your glory now! A shrewd slogan, but sheeple still wouldn't enlist to sprint at machine guns.

Speculatos bought control of major newspapers, and commanded favorable war coverage in them. Germans were portrayed as enemies of liberty, butchers of babies, eaters of meat. Despite this barrage of anti-German propaganda, sheeple still got it right. They still wouldn't support the war, so a sneak attack was arranged.

Germany practiced unrestricted submarine warfare. If it floated and was British, kaput. England knew she was doomed if America didn't enter the war, especially her cunning Lord of the Admiralty (Head of the Navy), Winston Churchill. German U-boats surfaced before sinking supply ships, and allowed crews to escape to lifeboats first. Churchill ordered ships to ram U-boats, not surrender. British sailors became kamikazes. Churchill had British ships remove names from their hulls and fly American flags. When U-boats surfaced to warn the "American" ship of danger, it would fire on them. Churchill commanded British ships to fire on U-boats waving white surrender flags, and to execute captured U-boat crews rather than treating them as prisoners of war. German U-boats stopped surfacing and sank ships with all hands aboard. Churchill wasn't indifferent to the lives lost. Nor was he stupid. He wanted people killed by U-boats—American people.

The *Lusitania* was a British passenger liner that could be converted to a warship. It had strong engines and thick armor. It was massive, a mini-Titanic, and the fastest liner in the North Atlantic. *Lusitania* made regular trips from America to Britain, and transported American weapons to England. It pretended to be a passenger liner, but was a military transport.

America declared itself neutral. When George Washington was President, France and Britain warred, America declared neutrality, and didn't ship one side weapons. President Woodrow Wilson's neutrality was a bit more flexible. When sunk, *Lusitania* carried 600 tons of the explosive guncotton, 6 million rounds of ammo, and 1,248 cases of shrapnel shells. Tons of crates in cargo holds were marked as butter, cheese and oysters, but contained additional munitions. Americans travelling on *Lusitania* were not told about this contraband. They had no idea they were boarding a floating bomb which violated international neutrality treaties.

Germany knew. The German Ambassador requested a meeting with U.S. Secretary of State William Jennings Bryan, and told him that millions of rounds of ammunition were being loaded on the *Lusitania* as they were speaking. America played dumb.

Under international law, ships carrying munitions are not neutral and can be sunk. In 1913, *Lusitania* was retrofitted for armament and registered as an auxiliary battle cruiser, which made it a legal target even if not carrying munitions. Germany purchased ads in 50 newspapers to warn Americans not to travel on *Lusitania*. The U.S. State Department stopped 49 of the ads from running.

Lusitania neared Britain, and was supposed to meet its escort, the British Destroyer *Juno*. There was no *Juno*. Britain had recalled it. *Lusitania* had been ordered to shut down one of its four boilers, supposedly to conserve fuel. It entered sub-infested waters at ¾ speed without any protection. A U-boat turkey shoot. If Hellen Keller commanded a U-boat, she could have sunk the *Lusitania*.

England had deciphered German communication codes, and knew German U-boat names and patrol locations. In the British high command's map room, a large circle showed the patrol area of German U-boat U-20, two smaller circles within the large circle showed where two British ships were torpedoed by U-20 the day before, and a 4th *Lusitania*-circle moved steadily eastward towards these 3 circles. While British commanders crossed their fingers waiting for *Lusitania* to be sunk, President Wilson's liaison Colonel House met with England's King George V to discuss America's response to the sinking.

When U-20 torpedoed the *Lusitania* there was a modest initial explosion, and then a second explosion which *Lusitania* Captain William Turner called "an unusually heavy detonation." The munitions exploding. The Titanic was 42,000 tons and sank in 160 minutes. *Lusitania* was 32,000 tons and sank in 18 minutes.

1,198 of *Lusitania's* 1,959 passengers died, 100 children and babies, and 128 Americans. The *Titanic* was 550 miles from land when it lost 1,517 passengers, but *Lusitania* was sunk 8 miles off the coast of Ireland. Civilian boats could have rescued survivors, but the British Navy threatened to attack any boat that offered aid. Britain wanted to maximize the casualty rate.

Lord John Mersey, the Crown's official investigator of the Titanic sinking, headed the *Lusitania* "investigation." It was a British Warren Report. Mersey was instructed to blame *Lusitania's* Captain and make no mention of munitions. He followed orders. Mersey accepted pay for his Titanic investigation, but refused pay for *Lusitania*. Two days after submitting his *Lusitania* report, he wrote the British

Prime Minister: "I must request that henceforth I be excused from administering His Majesty's Justice." Mersey's only public comment was made years later: "The *Lusitania* case was a damn dirty business."

For decades, the U.S. and British guv'ments and media smeared anyone claiming that *Lusitania* carried munitions. Britain declared the wreck a "protective site," denying divers access. The Royal Navy dropped depth charges on the wreck, destroying evidence and making it risky for divers. The British Secret Service tried to buy *Lusitania's* salvage rights but failed. The *Lusitania* wreck was explored in 2006, and millions of rounds of American-made Remington .303 ammunition were found.

Woodrow Wilson's Secretary of State William Jennings Bryan knew the American government had let its citizens die to engineer a war, and resigned in disgust. Bryan was willing to lie to Germany about supplying Britain, but drew the line at killing Americans.

Lusitania tipped the scales of American public opinion. In asking Congress for a declaration of war against Germany, Woodrow Wilson said America had to "make the world safe for democracy." America declared war on Germany in April 1917. Congress immediately gave $1 billion to the Allies which was transferred to Speculatos like Morgan and Rothschild. A billion didn't put a dent in costs. The newly-created Fed levied the inflation tax to provide revenue—and never stopped. A century later, the Energizer Fed Bunny is still inflating...

Speculatos played every financial end. They issued bonds that financed the Allied and Central Powers, had themselves appointed purchasing agents for America, Britain, Russia, Italy, Canada, Germany, Austria-Hungary and Turkey, and owned munitions companies. They earned interest on war loans, double commissions buying and selling munitions as guv'ment purchasing agents, and profits from manufacturing munitions.

American purchasing was monopolized by the War Industries Board, a smorgasbord of insiders who bled government dry. Profitable cost-plus contracts were steered to Speculato companies such as General Electric, DuPont and U.S. Steel. Cost-plus means government pays a company's costs plus profit that is a percentage of those costs, no matter how high costs run. The War Industries Board looked the other way when Speculato companies fraudulently overstated costs The same sweetheart deal Dick Cheney secured for Haliburton. Taxpayers ignorant of history are doomed to be bilked repeatedly, and all that...

The U.S. guv'ment spent $35.5 billion on World War I, $320 billion in today's dollars. Corporate profits were $38 billion, $340 billion in today's dollars. WWI was a wealth transferal from sheeple to Speculato corporations.

J.P. Morgan Jr. made a half billion of today's dollars on WWI, and testified to Congress that he hated war. With a straight face. In 1915, lone gunman Frank Holt tried to assassinate Morgan Jr. to stop the profiteering fueling WWI. This is why Speculatos keep low profiles, use fronts and bagmen, and brainwash sheeple. If sheeple understood the truth, Speculatos would face mobs of gunmen.

From 1915 to 1919, America's money supply doubled from $20.6 billion to $39.8 billion. In just four years, a dollar bought half as much. Sheeple paid recycled taxes like the income tax, "invested" in Liberty Bonds, and then were raped by the inflation tax. Excessive money creation also caused a Depression in 1919.

Before WWI, America's federal budget was $750 million, by the end of war it was $18.5 billion. 70% of this budget was debt, and 77% of this debt was "monetized" by Fed. 55% of the money spent during WWI was created out of thin air by Fed!

Fed was hailed as indispensable to the victory effort. This perverse reckoning failed to account what was lost. Lives, but also monetary integrity. Inflation was no longer fraud, but a patriotic necessity. The dimmest politician realized Fed could levy a hidden tax by monetizing T-debt. Deficit spending was institutionalized.

All U.S. wars after "The War to End All Wars" followed its blueprint. Planned "sneak" attacks. Orchestrated propaganda. Lies. Profit as the primary motive. Research these wars carefully, you find a soup of sin as sickening as World War I's.

Summarizing the ceaseless carnage of the 20th century would be a tangent, and hack at branches rather than chop roots. Perpetual war was certain once a Central Bank and income tax were created. This is the result every time in history such a system was instituted. Central Banks create a "war cycle" as well as a "business cycle."

Abolish Central Banks and the inflation tax, every war in modern history isn't possible or is smaller. Sheeple want big guv'ment to fund social programs, but not war. Like asking for a pet T-Rex to eat your enemies, and being shocked when it devours your friends. Human nature is the cause of war. But wars need funding, and Central Banks provide a limitless supply. As long as Speculatos and politicians can levy inflation and income taxes, there will be war.

President Woodrow Wilson had mixed emotions about World War I, but justified the collective good. A slippery slope. Anything can be rationalized using similar reasoning. And has been. Do modern leaders feel similar ambiguity about Pearl Harbor, Gulf of Tonkin and 9-11?

THE NEW YORK TIMES MISLED SHEEPLE
ABOUT THE LUSITANIA FALSE FLAG OPERATION

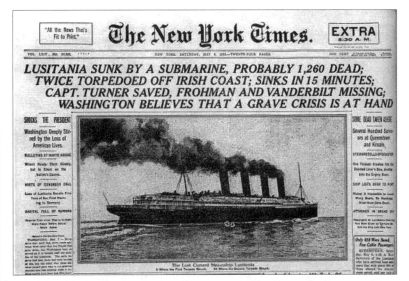

In his ship log, U-20 Captain Walther Schwieger noted: "It looks as if the ship will stay afloat only for a very short time. … I couldn't have fired another torpedo into this mass of humans desperately trying to save themselves." One shot, one kill. In German naval logs anyway. In U.S. papers, one torpedo became two. The exploding munitions were blamed on a torpedo that was never fired.

"The first casualty when war comes is truth."
—U.S. Senator Hiram Johnson, 1917.

This is an oft quoted proverb, which Johnson made in reference to World War I and the *Lusitania* sinking. Insiders knew the story fed to sheeple was a lie.

"The *Lusitania* was sent at considerably reduced speed into an area where a U-boat was known to be waiting and with her escorts withdrawn."
—Royal Navy Lt. Commander Joseph Kenworthy
First-hand witness of the *Lusitania* false flag operation
In British command center while British admiralty waited for *Lusitania* to be sunk

"Germany has a right to prevent contraband going to the Allies, and a ship carrying contraband should not rely upon passengers to protect her from attack—it would be like putting women and children in front of an army."
—U.S. Secretary of State Williams Jennings Bryan
3 weeks before resigning

After several close calls with German submarines, *Lusitania* Captain Daniel Dow resigned, saying that he was unwilling "to carry the responsibility of mixing passengers with munitions or contraband." Two months later *Lusitania* was sunk.

ABOVE The *Lusitania* sinking. Speculatos had no problem killing 1,260 unsuspecting ship passengers to salvage their bad investments. Nor the millions of combatants and civilians who died in World War I.

THE WINSTON CHURCHILL HISTORY BOOKS RARELY TELL YOU ABOUT

"The first British countermove, made on my responsibility was to deter the Germans from surface attack. The submerged U-boat had to rely increasingly on underwater attack and thus ran the greater risk of mistaking neutral for British ships and of drowning neutral crews and thus embroiling Germany with other Great Powers. ... There are many kinds of maneuvers in war. The maneuver which brings an ally into the field is as serviceable as that which wins a great battle. ... [German U-boat] survivors should be taken prisoner or shot, whichever is the most convenient ... In all actions, white flags should be fired upon with promptitude."

—Winston Churchill,
Lord of the Admiralty during World War I
Until fired for planning the Gallipoli massacre at which 44,000 Allied troops died

GERMANY TRIED TO AVOID WAR WITH US

JOHN BULL USES THE AMERICAN FLAG FOR PROTECTION.— From the *American* (New York)

CUNARD
Established 1840
EUROPE VIA LIVERPOOL
LUSITANIA
Fastest and Largest Steamer
now in Atlantic Service Sails
SATURDAY, MAY 1, 10 A.M.
Transylvania..Fri., May 7, 5 P.M.
Orduna.....Tues., May 18,10 A.M
Tuscania.....Fri., May 21; 5 P.M
LUSITANIA..Sat., May 29, 10 A.M
Transylvania..Fri., June 4, 5 P.M

Gibraltar—Genoa—Naples—Piraeus
S.S. Carpathia, Thur., May 13, Noon

ROUND THE WORLD TOURS
Through bookings to all principal Port
of the World.
COMPANY'S OFFICE. 21-94 State St.. N. Y

NOTICE!
TRAVELLERS intending to
embark on the Atlantic voyage
are reminded that a state of
war exists between Germany
and her allies and Great Britain
and her allies; that the zone of
war includes the waters adjacent to the British Isles; that,
in accordance with formal notice given by the Imperial German Government, vessels flying the flag of Great Britain, or
of any of her allies, are liable to
destruction in those waters and
that travellers sailing in the war
zone on ships of Great Britain
or her allies do so at their own
risk.

IMPERIAL GERMAN EMBASSY
WASHINGTON, D. C., APRIL 22, 1915.

LEFT Churchill's attempts to draw the U.S. into the WWI were well known. This cartoon appeared in the *American* in March 1915, two months before *Lusitania* was sunk. John Bull is the British Uncle Sam. The *Lusitania* flies a U.S. flag even though it is British. *Lusitania's* Captain says, "Cawn't you see 'Im a bloomin' Yankee!!" Yankee is British slang for American. The confused German sub commander responds, "Who iss it Vat boat?"

RIGHT Germany ran this ad in 50 U.S. newspapers. The U.S. State Department blocked it in 49 papers. The Des Moines Register ran it so a copy survived. The text: "NOTICE! TRAVELLERS intending to embark on the Atlantic voyage are reminded that a state of war exists between Germany and her allies and Great Britain and her allies; that the zone of war includes the waters adjacent to the British Isles; that, in accordance with formal notice given by the Imperial German Government, vessels flying the flag of Great Britain, or any of her allies, are liable to destruction in those waters and that travellers sailing in the war zone on the ships of Great Britain or her allies do so at their own risk. IMPERIAL GERMAN EMBASSY, Washington, D.C. 22nd April 1915"

BOTTOM A post-*Lusitania* recruitment poster. The sinking was so infamous no explanation was even necessary. Sheeple finally volunteered to play trench warfare and sprint into the maws of machine guns.

Marine Major General Smedley Butler: War Is A Racket

At the time of his death in 1940, Butler was the most decorated Marine in U.S. history. He is one of 19 people twice awarded the Medal of Honor, one of 3 awarded both the Marine Corps Brevet Medal and the Medal of Honor, and the only person to be awarded the Brevet Medal and two Medals of Honor, all for separate actions. As a Major General, Butler was also privy to war planning at the most senior levels. He is one of the few individuals with first-hand knowledge of Speculato machinations who revealed what he knew and opposed them. Butler travelled America giving a famous speech entitled *War is a Racket* and published a book with the same name. *War is a Racket* is one of the most succinct, visceral criticisms of war ever written. Some excerpts:

"War is a racket. It always has been. It is possibly the oldest, easily the most profitable, surely the most vicious. It is the only one international in scope. It is the only one in which the profits are reckoned in dollars and the losses in lives.

A racket is best described, I believe, as something that is not what it seems to the majority of the people. Only a small "inside" group knows what it is about. It is conducted for the benefit of the very few, at the expense of the very many. Out of war a few people make huge fortunes.

In the World War [I] a mere handful garnered the profits of the conflict. At least 21,000 new millionaires and billionaires were made in the United States during the World War. That many admitted their huge blood gains in their income tax returns. How many other war millionaires falsified their tax returns no one knows.

How many of these war millionaires shouldered a rifle? How many dug a trench? How many knew what it meant to go hungry in a rat-infested dug-out? How many spent sleepless, frightened nights, ducking shells and shrapnel and machine gun bullets? How many parried a bayonet thrust of an enemy? How many were wounded or killed in battle?

Out of war nations acquire additional territory, if they are victorious. They just take it. This newly acquired territory promptly is exploited by the few—the self-same few who wrung dollars out of blood in the war. The general public shoulders the bill. And what is this bill?

This bill renders a horrible accounting. Newly placed gravestones. Mangled bodies. Shattered minds. Broken hearts and homes. Economic instability. Depression and all its attendant miseries. Back-breaking taxation for generations.

... Now that I see the international war clouds gathering, as they are today, I must face it and speak out. ... There are 40,000,000 men under arms in the world today, and our statesmen and diplomats have the temerity to say that war is not in the making. Hell's bells! Are these 40,000,000 men being trained to be dancers? [Butler gave this speech in the 1930s. Hitler invaded Poland in 1939, beginning World War II, the bloodiest war in history.] ... we [will] be all stirred up to hate Japan and go to war—a war that might well cost us tens of billions of dollars, hundreds of thousands of lives of Americans, and many more hundreds of thousands of physically maimed and mentally unbalanced men.

Of course, for this loss, there would be a compensating profit—fortunes would be made. Millions and billions of dollars would be piled up. By a few. Munitions makers. Bankers. Ship builders. Manufacturers. Meat packers. Speculators. They would fare well. Yes, they are getting ready for another war. Why shouldn't they? It pays high dividends.

But what does it profit the men who are killed? What does it profit their mothers, sisters, wives and sweethearts? What does it profit their children? What does it profit anyone except the very few to whom war means huge profits?

Take our own case. Until 1898 we didn't own a bit of territory outside the mainland of North America. At that time our national debt was a little more than $1,000,000,000. Then we became "internationally minded." We forgot, or shunted aside, the advice of the Father of our country. We forgot George Washington's warning about "entangling alliances." We went to war. We acquired outside territory. At the end of the World War [I] period, as a direct result of our fiddling in international affairs, our national debt had jumped to over $25,000,000,000.

It would have been far cheaper (not to say safer) for the average American who pays the bills to stay out of foreign entanglements. For a very few this racket, like bootlegging and other underworld rackets, brings fancy profits, but the cost of operations is always transferred to the people—who do not profit.

The World War, rather our brief participation in it, cost the United States some $52,000,000,000. Figure it out. That means $400 to every American man, woman, and child. And we haven't paid the debt yet. We are paying it, our children will pay it, and our children's children probably still will be paying the cost of that war.

The normal profits of a business concern in the U.S. are six, eight, ten, and sometimes twelve percent. But war-time profits—ah! that is another matter—twenty, sixty, one hundred, three hundred, and even eighteen hundred per cent—the sky is the limit. All that traffic will bear. Uncle Sam has the money. Let's get it. Of course, it isn't put that crudely in war time. It is dressed into speeches about patriotism, love of country, and "we must all put our shoulders to the wheel," but the profits jump and leap and skyrocket—and are safely pocketed.

Listen to Senate Document No. 259. The Sixty-Fifth Congress, reporting on corporate earnings and government revenues. Considering the profits of 122 meat packers, 153 cotton manufacturers, 299 garment makers, 49 steel plants, and 340 coal producers during the war. Profits under 25 per cent were exceptional. For instance the coal companies made between 100 per cent and 7,856 per cent on their capital stock during the war. The Chicago packers doubled and tripled their earnings.

And let us not forget the bankers who financed the great war. If anyone had the cream of the profits it was the bankers. Being partnerships rather than incorporated organizations, they do not have to report to stockholders. And their profits were as secret as they were immense. How the bankers made their millions and their billions I do not know, because those little secrets never become public—even before a Senate investigatory body.

It has been estimated by statisticians and economists and researchers that the war cost your Uncle Sam $52,000,000,000. Of this sum, $39,000,000,000 was expended in the actual war itself. This expenditure yielded $16,000,000,000 in profits. That is how the 21,000 billionaires and millionaires got that way. This $16,000,000,000 profits is not to be sneezed at. It is quite a tidy sum. And it went to a very few.

Who provides the profits—these nice little profits of 20, 100, 300, 1,500 and 1,800 per cent? We all pay them—in taxation. We paid bankers their profits when we bought Liberty Bonds at $100.00 and sold them back at $84 or $86 to the bankers. Bankers collected $100 plus. It was a simple manipulation. The bankers control the security marts. It was easy for them to depress the price of these bonds. Then all of us—the people—got frightened and sold the bonds at $84 or $86. Bankers bought them. Then these bankers stimulated a boom and government bonds went to par—and above. Then the bankers collected their profits.

But the soldier pays the biggest part of the bill.

If you don't believe this, visit the American cemeteries on the battlefields abroad. Or visit any of the veteran's hospitals in the United States. On a tour of the country, in the midst of which I am at the time of this writing, I have visited eighteen government hospitals for veterans. In them are a total of about 50,000 destroyed men—men who were the pick of the nation eighteen years ago. ...

Boys with a normal viewpoint were taken out of the fields and offices and factories and classrooms and put into the ranks. There they were remolded; they were made over; they were made to "about face"; to regard murder as the order of the day. They were put shoulder to shoulder and, through mass psychology, they were entirely changed. We used them for a couple of years and trained them to think nothing at all of killing or of being killed.

Then, suddenly, we discharged them and told them to make another "about face"! This time they had to do their own readjustment, sans mass psychology, sans officers' aid and advice and sans nation-wide propaganda. We didn't need them any more. So we scattered them about without any "three-minute" or "Liberty Loan" speeches or parades. Many, too many, of these fine young boys are eventually destroyed, mentally, because they could not make that final "about face" alone... These [boys] already have been mentally destroyed. These boys don't even look like human beings. Oh, the looks on their faces! Physically, they are in good shape; mentally, they are gone.

There are thousands and thousands of these cases, and more and more are coming in all the time. The tremendous excitement of the war, the sudden cutting off of that excitement—the young boys couldn't stand it.

That's a part of the bill. So much for the dead—they have paid their part of the war profits. So much for the mentally and physically wounded—they are paying now their share of the war profits. But the others paid, too—they paid with heartbreaks when they tore themselves away from their firesides and their families to don the uniform of Uncle Sam—on which a profit had been made. They paid another part in the training camps where they were regimented and drilled while others took their jobs and their places in the lives of their communities. The paid for it in the trenches where they shot and were shot; where they were hungry for days at a time; where they slept in the mud and the cold and in the rain—with the moans and shrieks of the dying for a horrible lullaby.

But don't forget—the soldier paid part of the dollars and cents bill too.

Napoleon once said, "All men are enamored of decorations ... they positively hunger for them." By developing the Napoleonic system—the medal business—the government learned it could get soldiers for less money, because the boys liked to be decorated. Until the Civil War there were no medals. Then the Congressional Medal of Honor was handed out. It made enlistments easier. After the Civil War no new medals were issued until the Spanish-American War.

In the World War, we used propaganda to make the boys accept conscription. They were made to feel ashamed if they didn't join the army. So vicious was this war propaganda that even God was brought into it. With few exceptions our clergymen joined in the clamor to kill, kill, kill. To kill the Germans. God is on our side... it is His will that the Germans be killed. And in Germany, the good pastors called upon the Germans to kill the allies... to please the same God. That was a part of the general propaganda, built up to make people war conscious and murder conscious.

Beautiful ideals were painted for our boys who were sent out to die. This was the "war to end all wars." This was the "war to make the world safe for democracy."

No one mentioned to them, as they marched away, that their going and their dying would mean huge war profits. No one told these American soldiers that they might be shot down by bullets made by their own brothers here. No one told them that the ships on which they were going to cross might be torpedoed by submarines built with United States patents. They were just told it was to be a "glorious adventure."

Thus, having stuffed patriotism down their throats, it was decided to make them help pay for the war, too. So, we gave them the large salary of $30 a month. All they had to do for this munificent sum was to leave their dear ones behind, give up their jobs, lie in swampy trenches, eat canned willy (when they could get it) and kill and kill and kill... and be killed.

But wait!

Half of that wage (just a little more than a riveter in a shipyard or a laborer in a munitions factory safe at home made in a day) was promptly taken from him to support his dependents, so that they would not become a charge upon his community. Then we made him pay what amounted to accident insurance — something the employer pays for in an enlightened state—and that cost him $6 a month. He had less than $9 a month left.

Then, the most crowning insolence of all—he was virtually blackjacked into paying for his own ammunition, clothing, and food by being made to buy Liberty Bonds. Most soldiers got no money at all on pay days. We made them buy Liberty Bonds at $100 and then we bought them back—when they came back from the war and couldn't find work—at $84 and $86. And the soldiers bought about $2,000,000,000 worth of these bonds!

Yes, the soldier pays the greater part of the bill. His family pays too. They pay it in the same heart-break that he does. As he suffers, they suffer. At nights, as he lay in the trenches and watched shrapnel burst about him, they lay home in their beds and tossed sleeplessly—his father, his mother, his wife, his sisters, his brothers, his sons, and his daughters.

When he returned home minus an eye, or minus a leg or with his mind broken, they suffered too—as much as and even sometimes more than he. Yes, and they, too, contributed their dollars to the profits of the munitions makers and bankers and shipbuilders and the manufacturers and the speculators made. They, too, bought Liberty Bonds and contributed to the profit of the bankers after the Armistice in the hocus-pocus of manipulated Liberty Bond prices.

And even now the families of the wounded men and of the mentally broken and those who never were able to readjust themselves are still suffering and paying.

Well, it's a racket, all right. A few profit—and the many pay. But there is a way to stop it. You can't end it by disarmament conferences. You can't eliminate it by peace parleys at Geneva. Well-meaning but impractical groups can't wipe it out by resolutions. It can be smashed effectively only by taking the profit out of war. ... Capital won't permit the taking of the profit out of war until the people—those who do the suffering and still pay the price—make up their minds that those they elect to office shall do their bidding, and not that of the profiteers.

The swivel-chair admirals of Washington (and there are always a lot of them) are very adroit lobbyists. And they are smart. They don't shout that "We need a lot of battleships to war on this nation or that nation." Oh no. First of all, they let it be known that America is menaced by a great naval power. Almost any day, these admirals will tell you, the great fleet of this supposed enemy will strike suddenly and annihilate 125,000,000 people. Just like that. Then they begin to cry for a larger navy. For what? To fight the enemy? Oh my, no. Oh, no. For defense purposes only. ...

I am not a fool as to believe that war is a thing of the past. I know the people do not want war, but there is no use in saying we cannot be pushed into another war. Looking back, Woodrow Wilson was re-elected president in 1916 on a platform that he had "kept us out of war" and on the implied promise that he would "keep us out of war." Yet, five months later he asked Congress to declare war on Germany. In that five-month interval the people had not been asked whether they had changed their minds. The 4,000,000 young men who put on uniforms and marched or sailed away were not asked whether they wanted to go forth to suffer and die.

Then what caused our government to change its mind so suddenly? Money. An allied commission, it may be recalled, came over shortly before the war declaration and called on the President. The President summoned a group of advisers. The head of the commission spoke. Stripped of its diplomatic language, this is what he told the President and his group: "There is no use kidding ourselves any longer. The cause of the allies is lost. We now owe you (American bankers, American munitions makers, American manufacturers, American speculators, American exporters) five or six billion dollars. If we lose (and without the help of the United States we must lose) we, England, France and Italy, cannot pay back this money... and Germany won't. So..."

Had secrecy been outlawed as far as war negotiations were concerned, and had the press been invited to be present at that conference, or had radio been available to broadcast the proceedings, America never would have entered the World War. But this conference, like all war discussions, was shrouded in utmost secrecy. When our boys were sent off to war they were told it was a "war to make the world safe for democracy" and a "war to end all wars."

Well, eighteen years after, the world has less of democracy than it had then. ... And very little, if anything, has been accomplished to assure us that the World War was really the war to end all wars. The professional soldiers and sailors don't want to disarm. No admiral wants to be without a ship. No general wants to be without a command. Both mean men without jobs. They are not for disarmament. They cannot be for limitations of arms."

General Butler penned this roughly 75 years ago. Nothing has changed.

ALL WARS IN U.S. HISTORY WERE FUNDED
BY INFLATING THE MONEY SUPPLY

"I do not think it is an exaggeration to say history is largely a history of inflation, usually inflations engineered by governments for the gain of governments."
—Friedrich von Hayek, Nobel Prize Winner in Economics

INFLATION ANNUAL PERCENTAGE CHANGE 1774-2007

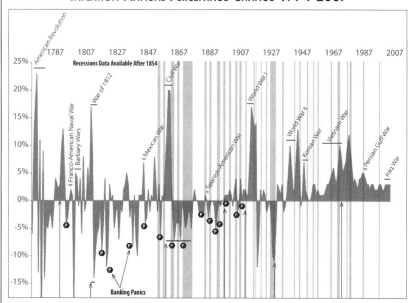

The graph above shows the inflation rate throughout American history expressed as a percentage. If the money supply is $100 in 1892, and the graph shows a 5% inflation rate, the money supply was increased by 5%, to $105. Huge spikes in the inflation rate coincide with all major wars in American history. Major wars coincide with all huge spikes in the inflation rate, the lone exception being the "stagflation" and oil embargo of the 1970s. Since the 1980s, government has shiatsued statistics to understate actual inflation rates, which is why our Middle Eastern adventures haven't spiked the right side of the chart. People would never pay the conventional taxes necessary to support wars. Politicians *always* resort to the inflation tax to fund wars. If there is no ability to levy an inflation tax, there are few wars. If a nation is faced with war and has no ability to levy an inflation tax, it finds a way to levy an inflation tax. Speculatos force nations with honest money to adopt Central Banks by creating wars. If a nation is not at war but institutes an inflation tax, politicians use inflation tax revenue to start wars. One of the biggest benefits of honest money is that is chains the human lust for war. Where there is inflation, there is war. Where there is war, there is inflation. Always.

FOR A FEW CASUALTIES MORE

"Military men are dumb, stupid animals to be used as pawns for foreign policy."
—Henry Kissinger

Peace was foremost in our Founders' minds, even the warrior Washington, who counseled, "The great rule of conduct for us, in regard to foreign nations, is in extending our commercial relations, to have with them as little political connection as possible." Franklin felt, "There never was a good war or a bad peace." Jefferson advocated, "Peace, commerce, and honest friendship with all nations, entangling alliances with none." Until Fed was created, America remained true to this ideal. From its creation in 1789 until 1913, America was in 3 major wars. The War of 1812 and Spanish American War were minor compared to modern wars like World Wars I and II. The only major American war prior to 1913 was the Civil War, and it was internal. 125 years, 1 war every 41 years on average, none of them major external conflicts. Decades of peace between wars. From 1913-2009, America fought 7 major wars. 97 years, 1 war every 14 years on average, all of them major external conflicts. The longest period of peace since Fed was created was the 22 years between World War I and II, and 11 of those years were the Fed-engineered Great Depression. The longest period of peace since Fed was created was the 16 years between Vietnam and Iraq I. No American born since 1913 has grown to adulthood without enduring a Depression or war. Peace. Precious peace. America gave up all hope of peace when it created the Federal Reserve.

CENTRAL BANKS CREATE A WAR CYCLE

America founded (1789)

23 years

War of 1812 (1812-1815)

46 years

Civil War (1861-1865)

33 years

Spanish American War (1898)

15 years

Federal Reserve created (1913)

4 years

World War I (1917-1919)

10 years

Great Depression (1929-1943)
World War II (1941-1945)

5 years

Korean War (1950-1953)

10 years

Vietnam War (1963-1975)

15 years

Iraq I (1990-1991)

12 years

Iraq II/Afghanistan (2003-20xx?)

**BF-BEFORE FED
(1789-1913)**
125 years, 3 wars
1 war per 41 years on average
No major external conflicts

**AF-AFTER FED
(1913-2009)**
97 years, 7 wars
1 war per 14 years on average
All major external conflicts

AMERICA'S FOUNDING FATHERS KNEW THE DANGERS OF DIRECT TAXES, CORRUPT MONEY AND NATIONAL DEBT

"To preserve independence, we must not let our rulers load us with perpetual debt. We must make our election between economy and liberty, or profusion and servitude. If we run into such debts as that we must be taxed in our meat and in our drink, in our necessaries and our comforts, in our labors and our amusements, for our callings and our creeds, as the people of England are, our people, like them, must come to labor sixteen hours in the twenty-four, give the earnings of fifteen of these to the government for their debts and daily expenses, and the sixteenth being insufficient to afford us bread, we must live, as they now do, on oatmeal and potatoes, have no time to think, no means of calling the mismanagers to account, but be glad to obtain subsistence by hiring ourselves to rivet their chains on the necks of our fellow-sufferers."

—Thomas Jefferson

"No earthly consideration could induce my consent to contract such a debt as England has by her wars for commerce, to reduce our citizens by taxes to such wretchedness ... And all this to feed the avidity of a few millinary merchants and to keep up one thousand ships of war for the protection of their commercial speculations."

—Thomas Jefferson

Technology has allowed us to labor half as much as colonials, to work 8 hours per day instead of 16. Flight changed the naval dynamic. America's 11 carrier strike groups are the modern equivalent of "one thousand ships of war." No other nation has more than 3 carrier groups. Americans are hardly starving, but most of what Jefferson feared came to pass.

TO LEARN MORE

THE REAL ABRAHAM LINCOLN
A NEW LOOK AT LINCOLN, HIS AGENDA, AND HIS UNNECESSARY WAR
BY THOMAS DILORENZO

Lincoln subverted the U.S. Constitution, trampled states' rights, and launched an unnecessary Civil War, murdering our Founders' republic and destroying the limited government they cherished.

LUSITANIA
BY COLIN SIMPSON

Documents the planning of the sinking of *Lusitania*, and the lies used to engineer American entry into World War I.

YOUR COUNTRY AT WAR
BY CHARLES A LINDBERGH, SR.

The truth about World War I, told by the famous anti-war, anti-Fed Congressman who had an insider's view.

WALL STREET AND THE BOLSHEVIK REVOLUTION
BY ANTHONY SUTTON

Trotsky and Lenin were backed by Speculatos who engineered the Russian revolution.

TRADING WITH THE ENEMY: THE NAZI-AMERICAN MONEY PLOT 1933-1949
BY CHARLES HIGHAM

American Speculatos financed Nazi Germany. A readable non-academic summary. Some knockoffs that followed are better written, this was the first.

FDR MY EXPLOITED FATHER IN LAW
BY CURTIS B. DALL

First-hand insider's view of FDR's collusion with Speculatos. Dall's conclusion that FDR was exploited may be wishful thinking.

DAY OF DECEIT: THE TRUTH ABOUT FDR AND PEARL HARBOR
BY ROBERT STINNETT

Some errors, but overall an intriguing circumstantial case that FDR had advanced knowledge about Pearl Harbor and let it happen so America could enter WWII.

THE BEST ENEMY MONEY CAN BUY
BY ANTHONY SUTTON

America built much of the U.S.S.R.'s military industrial complex.

Exploiting Hutville

"You Americans, you treat the Third World the way an Iraqi peasant treats his new bride. Three days of honeymoon, and then it's off to the fields."

—Saddam Hussein

"How do I respond when I see that in some countries there is vitriolic hatred for America? I'm amazed. I'm amazed that there's such misunderstanding of what our country is about that people would hate us. I am—like most Americans, I just can't believe it because I know how good we are."

—George W. Bush

"The gulf between our [America's] dream and the realities that we live with is something we do not understand and do not want to admit. It is almost as though we were asking that others look at what we want and turn their eyes, as we do, away from what we are. This rigid refusal to look at ourselves may well destroy us."

—James Baldwin, Author

Back to Appleseed Junior. His fiat notes aren't backed by applesauce, and are legal tender, Crusoeville's sole money.

Before Speculato, there were no Depressions. Businesses failed, and bigger failures caused rare recessions, but the entire economy didn't flop at once. With Speculato inflating the money supply, Depressions occur every few decades. All businesses rise and fall together. The economic ship rides monetary waves.

Speculato rules Crusoeville, but wants to conquer other countries. He could have Crusoeville invade them, but is a student of history. Even if you conquer the world militarily, you can't hold it, as Alexander the Great and empires such as the Roman, Ottoman and British learned. The conquered know they are enslaved, hate their oppressors, and overthrow them eventually. Speculato decides to conquer the world using credit. Then the conquered won't realize they are enslaved.

Crusoeville's malignant guv'ment is short cash, and won't cut spending or raise taxes, so it prints bonds to stay afloat. The mountains of new money created to buy bonds will cause skyrocketing prices and collapse the Crusoeville economy—if the money only circulates in Crusoeville.

Hutville produces straw and huts, commodities less valuable than apples. Hutville is poor, weak, and exploited by other nations. It inflates "straw-backed" money similar to Crusoeville's "apple" notes.

Speculato makes Hutville's President Mobutu an offer. Hutville will abandon straw money and use Crusoeville's apple notes. If Mobutu accepts, Speculato will give Mobutu enough apple notes to make him rich. Implicit in this "offer" is the unstated threat of a Crusoeville-engineered revolution which replaces Mobutu. Crusoeville could also conquer Hutville, as they did Buffaloville.

Mobutu knows switching to apple notes is bad for Hutville. But if he says no, the next leader will say yes. He will die, forsake a fortune, and Speculato will still get his way. Mobutu makes apple notes Hutville's legal tender. No other money is allowed. Anyone who refuses apple notes as payment is arrested.

Straw notes are not accepted worldwide, but apple notes are, which helps Hutville. Hutville also doesn't have to worry about other nations harassing it. Crusoeville tells other nations to butt out. No one is going to exploit Hutville but Crusoeville!

Speculato can print more notes out of thin air because they circulate in Crusoeville and Hutville. He can tax every resident of Crusoeville and Hutville with the inflation tax. As apple notes cannot be refused in Hutville, Speculato prints them and lends them to Crusoeville residents who use them to buy straw.

Hutville can't print apple notes. To obtain apples it must produce straw, sell it for apple notes, and use these to buy apples. Crusoeville doesn't have to produce apples to buy straw. It simply prints more "apple" notes, which residents of Hutville have to accept because they are legal tender. Crusoevillers receive something (straw) for nothing (worthless paper money). Crusoevillers have become Speculatos, scamming straw by levying an inflation tax on Hutville's citizens.

Crusoevillains sleeping in straw beds and lounging on straw couches don't understand this mechanism. To them, Hutvillers are backwards idiots. How else can they tolerate such corrupt guv'ments, and grow poorer year after year? Crusoeville does fine, why is it so hard for Hutville?

Hutvillers riot and Crusoeville crushes the rebellion. Mobutu helps. He has more loyalty to Speculato than Hutville, as Speculato is the source of his wealth. The Crusoeville media lies about the cause of the riots. Hutville resents Crusoeville's prosperity. It hates Crusoeville's religion. Viper worms flourish in Crusoeville's warm climate, and this pisses Hutvillers off. Anything except the truth: Crusoeville exploits Hutvillers, and they are angry about it.

An apple note business cycle arises in Hutville. If Crusoeville provides apple notes, there is prosperity in Hutville. If Crusoeville contracts the apple note supply, Hutville suffers a Depression. A monetary umbilical cord also exists between Hutville and Crusoeville. If Crusoeville inflates apple notes recklessly, the economies of Hutville and Crusoeville crash together.

These crashes are inevitable, and Speculato profits off them in Hutville as in Crusoeville. He knows a crash is coming, cashes out, and buys up assets once prices plummet. Using only the power to create money, he soon owns much of Hutville and Crusoeville.

Hutvillers are broker than Crusoevillains and desperate for loans, but their primitive economy makes issuing personal loans impractical and risky. Still, it'd be nice to shackle Hutvillers with debt. Screw their sheeple with the inflation tax and massive loan payments, just like Crusoevillers. They can't eat their cake, so why let them have it?

Speculato lends money to Hutville. No dithering with millions of personal loans, just one massive loan to the guv'ment. Hutville is impoverished by the high inflation tax, so Mobutu is desperate. As Speculato computers 28 gajillion apple notes out of thin air and loans them to Hutville, he can't help chuckling.

This is a trap, of course. A debt trap. Why would Mobutu agree to it? Same old reason. He is corrupt, and if he refuses he will be replaced by a yes man.

Hutville could use its loan to modernize straw farming or build a couch and mattress factory. Then Hutville could pay off the loan and pull itself out of poverty. Instead Mobutu buys palaces around the world, builds a military, and buys a few apples to pacify Hutvillers.

Mobutu uses Hutville's straw fields as collateral for its loan. Speculato contracts the supply of apple notes, crashes the Hutville economy, and claims the straw fields. He modernizes straw farming and builds a couch and mattress factory. Hutvillers no longer own fields to grow straw on, and the minority that get jobs at the straw plantation or couch factory live like slaves. Any movement for a minimum wage or other progressive rights is quashed by Mobutu using his shiny new military. Complain, you vanish. Crusoevillains want cheap straw, so they can't give Hutvillers the same rights they have.

Hutville can survive only with another loan from Speculato. It puts up its lakes as collateral. Speculato crashes the economy, confiscates the lakes, and charges Hutvillers for drinking water.

The process is repeated until Speculato owns much of Hutville. Mobutu wants another loan, but there is no collateral. Speculato can't give Hutville something for nothing, but really wants more easy money. Why not have Crusoevillers guarantee the loan?

This would rile Crusoeville up—if sheeple figured fiat money out, had time to contemplate and be informed, and an interest in either even if they had time. The Apple Bowl or Fiona Apple concert is more important to sheeple than economics or politics.

Hutville's loans become so large the principal can never be repaid, so it stops trying. Which is fine with Speculato. He didn't lend his wealth, so he's only concerned with interest payments. Would Mr. Dictator like a 50 year mortgage, 100 year mortgage, or prefer to pay only the interest and never own his country?

Why, never own his country, of course.

Interest payments gobble up half of Hutville's national output. There isn't enough wealth left to buy necessities, much less invest in improvements that generate wealth. Hutville can never dig itself out. It is a minimum wage worker with 20 maxed credit cards.

Individuals with 20 maxxed credit cards can declare bankruptcy, but not Hutvilles. If Mobutu tries to default on Speculato loans, he is overthrown or assassinated, and replaced by a leader who will pay the Speculato tithe.

There was no bankruptcy in colonial America; if you couldn't pay a debt, you were jailed in a "Debtor's Prison." Prominent colonial Americans spent time in debtor's prison, including Revolutionary War hero General Light-Horse Harry Lee, and two signers of the *Declaration of Independence*, James Wilson and Robert Morris. Morris' fate is instructive. In today's dollars Morris was a billionaire, and he was nicknamed "The Financier of the Revolution." During the American Revolution, Morris was the second most powerful man in America next to George Washington. At some of the Revolution's darkest moments, when General Washington was more desperate than normal (his army was destitute for the entire war so it was always a relative proposition) and could not obtain funding elsewhere, Morris sent caches of his personal gold to him. It is not an exaggeration to say that the revolution might have been lost without Morris' largesse. Yet Morris was also a Speculato who made exorbitant profits off the war, and Washington was horrified when he learned of such speculations years later. Late in life Morris over-speculated in land, went broke, and spent 3 years in debtor's prison. America's first bankruptcy law was passed in part to free Morris, but his incarceration is a telling indication of the spirit of financial accountability which prevailed at the time. People were jailed for less than $1 of debt—though a dollar then is worth much more today. Small wonder that our Founding Fathers created a minimalist government; they truly believed that everyone should pay their bills, and that no one was exempt from this responsibility, no matter how high their station. Morris did not receive a bailout, he went to jail. If today's global financial crisis had occurred when George Washington was President (which would have been impossible under the honest money system the Constitution specifies and which prevailed then), thousands of Speculatos and the CEOs of every major bank would be sitting in debtor's prison, as would the irresponsible, greedy, fools who bought McMansions they couldn't afford. It is fascinating to ponder how differently Americans today might treat their finances if there were no bankruptcy and debtor's prisons existed. If a person who racked up 20 credit cards had to pay them off or rot in jail, period. There would at least be moral consistency, as Americans would be held to the same standard they apply to Hutvilles.

Pardon the digression, back to Hutville. When Hutville defaults on payments, Crusoeville tax revenues make up the difference. Speculato gets paid no matter what because the Crusoeville and Hutville economies are at the mercy of his monetary waves.

Destitute Hutvillers have only straw. But a Hutviller who wraps himself in straw and lights himself on fire can cause major damage. Crusoevillians cannot comprehend such desperation. How can people be driven to such lunacy, they wonder, as they adjust the cushions on the bargain straw couch purchased with credit?

TO SKIP THE PICTURE PAGES AFTER THIS CHAPTER, PLEASE TURN TO PAGE 164

CAN'T WE ALL JUST GET ALONG

World GDP in 2008 was $60.1 trillion. This is the total value of all goods & services produced by all humans on Earth in 2008. There were roughly 6.7 billion humans on Earth at the end of 2008. If distributed equally, there were enough resources for each human to have $8,970.

We are the world, we are the children, we are the ones who make a brighter day, so lets start giving. There are people dying and it's time to lend a hand, i—screw that, let the children starve to death, I'm not giving up my SUV, plasma TV and 3,000 square foot home. I need $150 Raybans for that brighter day...

Are you willing to live on $8,970 next year? Maybe you're the next Gandhi and answered yes, but for most Americans and 1st worlders, the answer is hell no. This is why America exploits Hutvilles.

The World Bank defines extreme poverty as living on less than $1.25 a day, moderate poverty as living on less than $2.00 a day. 1.4 billion people live on less than $1.25 per day, 1.6 billion people live on $1.25-$2.00 per day. 3 billion people live on less than $2.00 per day—45% of the human race. In America, the poverty line is $10,500 per year. No double standard. What the third world needs is fast food value menu for that $1.25 or $2.00 per day. No supersizing.

Yes, prices are lower in Hutvilles, so $2 per day buys much more in Hutvilles than in America. But $2 a day does not provide a prosperous existence anywhere on Earth.

Imagine an alien suddenly flew here from another civilization, and cruised over the whole of the Earth. On one region of Earth billions starve, on the other the obese population waddles around like walruses. The alien would want to populate the universe with this highly evolved life form, right?

The author is not a socialist advocating totally equal resource distribution, but these stats do illustrate a point. Having third worlders living on $730 a year frees up the $8,240 in resources they might have used. U.S. GDP is an average of $45,000 per person. On average, each American must keep 4 third worlders starving to maintain their standard of living.

Oversimplified? Yes. Inaccurate? No.

Why not just grow the economic "pie." If every human had $45,000 a year to live on, world GDP would be $301 trillion, 6 times larger. Earth is already running out of resources. There are not enough resources to double world GDP, much less sextuple it. Everyone on Earth can't live like Americans.

Speculatos acknowledge this pillage candidly, and perform the wealth transfusion. They look starving 3rd worlders in the eyes, rob them blind, and sleep like babies. The American sheeple gripe about the foreign policy that provides their luxurious lifestyle, yet refuse to live frugally so that the global plantation system can be abolished. American sheeple demand minimum wages and whine about the smallest reduction in their lifestyle, but have no problem with the workers who produce their wares earning nickels per hour.

GOT MILK?

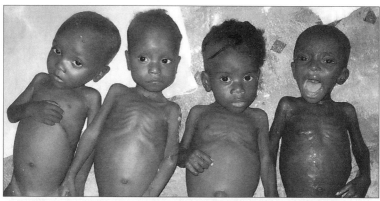

"He who passively accepts evil is as much involved in it as he who helps to perpetrate it. He who accepts evil without protesting against it is really cooperating with it."

—Martin Luther King, Jr.

THE WORLD BANK AND IMF
THE OVERSEER AND WHIP OF THE GLOBAL PLANTATION

The World Bank and International Monetary Fund (IMF) were created at the Bretton Woods Monetary Conference at the end of World War II. At this conference, the dollar was made the world reserve currency, in part because of America's dominant position after World War II.

The World Bank has more than 175 member countries, and lends money to Hutvilles, supposedly to aid their development. The actual goal is impoverishment of Hutvilles, and wealth transferals to Speculatos' multinational corporations, especially banks. The World Bank arranges loans to Hutvilles by acting as a middleman for the commercial and investment banks of 1st world nations.

When Hutvilles inevitably default on massive World Bank loans, the IMF arranges bailouts. Loan defaults and the need for bailouts are not an accidental consequence. Hutvilles are purposefully offered larger loans than they can repay to maximize interest payments to Speculatos. Speculatos would never make such insane loans if they were not certain they would be bailed out. Ye same old bailout game we have seen within nations is applied between nations, on an international and supranational scale.

Each 1st world nation who joined the IMF—and most have—donates money to the IMF which it then loans for bailouts. This donated money is either taken directly from recycled-tax revenues, or is created by the central and commercial banks and is an inflation tax; regardless, IMF funds are obtained by siphoning wealth from the sheeple of 1st world nations. Ye same old formula, Speculatos keep profit on loans, and make sheeple pay losses.

As a precondition for bailout loans, the IMF demands its infamous "austerity" measures, which force Hutvilles to slash government budgets, especially funding for social services. "Austerity" measures are policies favorable to 1st-world corporations that manufacture in Hutvilles: no minimum wage, a low maximum wage, no OSHA, no overtime pay, no limitation on hours worked per day or week, no unions, no health insurance or benefits, no unemployment insurance, no child labor laws, no environmental regulations or limitations on pollution, etc. Social protections 1st-world sheeple take for granted and would be indignant if denied, are denied to Hutvillers who manufacture their cheap clothes, electronics, and appliances.

Hutville natural resources are either used as collateral for loans, or direct payments of natural resources are arranged as loan payments. Natural resources are either seized when loans are defaulted, or transferred as loan payments. Speculatos obtain them well below market value, and then sell them to 1st world nations at normal market value, earning massive profit. These resources enable the luxurious 1st-world standard of living that its sheeple expect as a birthright and take for granted, never realizing its true cost. 1st-world sheeple vociferously refute any claim that their prosperity is created by anything but their own hard work, and remain blissfully ignorant of the exploitation which provides their prosperity.

As a precondition for bailout loans, The IMF also demands "free market" reforms in which ownership of Hutville utilities and infrastructure are transferred to Speculato corporations for pennies on the dollar. Speculatos then charge exorbitant prices for utilities and use of infrastructure, impoverishingHutvillers further. Hutvilles must also give lucrative construction and development contracts to Speculato corporations, rather than local businesses which would keep wealth in the Hutville and provide its citizens with better paying jobs.

IMF, World Bank, BIS (Bank for International Settlements), and Central Bank executives interlock with 1st-world military-industrial complexes and oil conglomerates., so that they act with synchronization. International treaties like the General Agreement on Tariffs and Trade (GATT) and organizations like the World Trade Organization (WTO) empower these multinational cartels, superseding national sovereignty, legalizing the exploitative practices described above.

Additional, more stringent austerity measures are also demanded as preconditions for future loans. The noose is gradually but inexorably tightened.

These "austerity" measures lead to "IMF Riots" by impoverished Hutvillers. Speculatos expect these IMF riots, they are part of their business plan as surely as bailouts are. Dictators which 1st-world intelligence agencies clandestinely prop up are expected to quash such rebellions mercilessly, and discreetly. If they do not, they are replaced by a Dictator that will.

Propaganda gives a more flowery and altruistic summary of World Bank and IMF activities, but their actual purpose is to get Hutvilles get massively into debt to Speculato commercial and investment banks. When Hutvilles can't pay those loans, the IMF functions as the collection agency. Most collection agencies try to make those who owe pay, the IMF tries to make someone else pay. That someone else is first world sheeple, via recycled or inflation taxes.

The system is a modern plantation in which 6 billion second and third world sheeple are field slaves who live in abject poverty, 1 billion first world sheeple are house slaves allowed some luxury, and 1 million Speculatos are Masters who control the slaves and live a life of fabulous opulence.

CRUSOEVILLE CURRENCY BLOC

"The first panacea for a misguided nation is inflation of the currency; the second is war. Both bring a temporary prosperity; both bring a permanent ruin. But both are the refuge of political and economic opportunists."

—Ernest Hemingway

"The enormous gap between what U.S. leaders do in the world and what Americans think their leaders are doing is one of the great propaganda accomplishments of the dominant political mythology."

—Michael Parenti, Historian

Crusoeville repeats the Hutville formula with Bananaville, Coffeeville and Margaritaville. Apple notes become their currency. Speculato lends computered money to Crusoevillains, who buy bananas, coffee, and margaritas. They obtain these goods without giving up apples.

Crusoeville has created a CURRENCY BLOC. An entire group, or bloc, of countries use its currency.

Everyone in Crusoeville borrows. Endless credit is taken for granted. Crusoevillain arrogance grows. Margaritas, coffee and bananas are viewed as a birthright.

For every banana, cup of coffee or margarita Crusoeville obtains, an inflation tax is levied on a distant peasant. The world becomes a fiefdom of haves and have-nots, of Crusoeville and Hutvilles. Speculatos engineering the fiefdom grow fabulously rich.

Hutvilles near Crusoeville join its currency bloc and are flooded with apple notes. These new balloons fill up fast. If Crusoeville keeps printing apple notes, hyperinflation will result, apple notes will be rejected, and economies collapse. If Crusoeville stops printing apple notes, returning price waves will create a massive Depression in all nations in the bloc. The day of reckoning is unavoidable, but it can be delayed if Crusoeville expands relentlessly and finds new nations to pay the inflation tax.

Crusoe starts wars to force nations to join its currency bloc or keep them from abandoning it. This enriches Speculatos and perpetuates the credit Crusoevillains are addicted to.

Crusoevillains don't realize how their prosperity is created and oppose these wars. Oil is primarily found in one place. You guessed it, Oilville. Crusoeville invades Oilville to obtain oil. Crusoevillains oppose the invasion, yet gripe about high oil prices.

What is a Speculato to do with sheeple? You can not invade Oilville, and pay high oil prices. Or invade Oilville, and obtain lower oil prices. You cannot not invade Oilville, and maintain lower oil prices. Simple, right?

Other villes hate hypocritical Crusoevillains. The Crusoeville media never reports its abuse of other villes, but the rest of the world knows of them. Confident in the accuracy of their delusional worldview, Crusoevillains assume that all other villes are nuts or stupid. Crusoeville banks, corporations, and armies are on a pilgrimage to better less fortunate villes, yet the ignorant brutes hate us. The ingratitude!

More nations must be forced to join the apple currency bloc, but there are no more wimps. Cornville and Lobsterville are not Hutvilles. They have their own militaries and Speculatos. Crusoeville's currency bloc gives it the power to make trouble for Cornville and Lobsterville, but Cornville and Lobsterville could team up and create problems for Crusoeville. Cornville and Lobsterville are willing to negotiate, but Cornville won't be cornholed, and Lobsterville isn't getting tossed in the pot. No way are they giving control of their money to another ville.

Speculato proposes a compromise. Cornville prints corn notes, but backs them with apple notes instead of corn. Corn notes were backed by an ear of corn. A corn note could always be exchanged for an ear. Now a corn note would only redeemable for an apple note. Cornville would PEG corn notes to apple notes.

"Apple" notes aren't backed by apples. Crusoeville could print gajillions, exchange them for corn notes, buy up corn, and bleed Cornville dry. Cornville would have to defend its currency by printing as many corn notes as Crusoeville did apple notes, but it can't disperse inflation over several villes the way Crusoeville can and would lose this economic war when its prices were hyperinflated but Crusoeville's weren't. Cornville won't peg corn notes to apple notes unless Crusoeville is on an apple standard. Then apple notes can't be inflated and pegging makes sense.

Pegging keeps Crusoeville from attacking Cornville. Crusoeville is the most prosperous nation on Earth, and riding its currency coattails gives Cornville clout. If everyone knows corn notes can be redeemed for apple notes, they become as good as apple notes. Corn notes are accepted in villes that rejected them or charged outrageous exchange rates previously. Pegging benefits Cornville—as long as Crusoeville doesn't print bogus apple notes.

Problem is, Crusoeville can't go back on an apple standard in which each apple note can always be redeemed for an apple. There aren't enough apples on the whole planet for all the notes it has printed, and its prosperity depends on the inflation tax. Crusoeville does what all Speculatos do. It lies. It agrees to back its notes with apples, even though it has no intention of honoring its promise.

Now Cornville has to redeem a corn note for an apple note anytime anyone asks. Cornville's Central Bank has to keep tons of apple notes on hand as reserves, the way the goldsmith had to gold.

Crusoeville isn't giving apple notes away. Cornville has to trade corn for them.

Crusoeville has another bubble to fill, and obtains corn without giving up apples. Cornville gets cornholed, but not as bad as Hutvilles. It still has a currency it controls, and could stop redeeming corn notes for apple notes if Crusoeville prints too many.

Cornville would love to be in Crusoeville's position and tax the world by printing money, but they aren't large or powerful enough. Only the most dominant nations have a WORLD RESERVE CURRENCY that is universally stockpiled, and which other nations use to back their currency.

Cornville, Lobsterville, Cattleville and Sushiville back their currencies with apple notes. More bubbles to inflate. Crusoevillains get corn, lobster, steaks and sushi by printing money out of thin air.

And the press prints on. . . until villes realize "apple" notes aren't really backed by apples, and that Crusoeville has no intention of honoring its commitments.

OIL STANDARD

"Elite money managers, with especially strong support from U.S. authorities, struck an agreement with OPEC to price oil in U.S. dollars exclusively for all worldwide transactions. This gave the dollar a special place among world currencies and in essence "backed" the dollar with oil. In return, the U.S. promised to protect the various oil-rich kingdoms in the Persian Gulf against threat of invasion or domestic coup. The agreement with OPEC in the 1970s to price oil in dollars has provided tremendous artificial strength to the dollar as the preeminent reserve currency. This has created a universal demand for the dollar, and soaks up the huge number of new dollars generated each year. Last year alone [2005] M3 [the M3 money supply] increased over $700 billion. Most importantly, the dollar/oil relationship has to be maintained to keep the dollar as a preeminent currency. Any attack on this relationship will be forcefully challenged—as it already has been."

—Ron Paul

Why doesn't Crusoeville produce more apples and honor its commitments? Crusoevillains lost interest in work long ago. Breaking a sweat is for the peasants of Hutvilles.

Crusoeville's internal bureaucracy and external empire gobble up what little Crusoevillains do produce, but the guv'ment is still short cash. It prints apple notes like paper's going to be outlawed. Cornville and Lobsterville call Crusoeville's bluff and demand apples for apple notes. Other villes do the same. Crusoeville gives them a mile-high middle finger by suspending redemption of apple notes for apples. This fraud infuriates villes, but what can they do? Crusoeville's army is as invincible as its "apple" notes are worthless.

Villes traded goods for "apple" notes, and have to obtain something for them. Or try. If they sell a large quantity of apple notes, those they still hold become worthless. Their only option is to gradually spend "apple" notes on the few apples Crusoeville produces. It could take centuries to get rid of all their apple notes.

Now that its fraud is discovered, Crusoeville can't circulate additional apple notes. No new money gushes into Hutville to buy straw, Margaritaville to buy drinks, Cornville to buy corn. Or any other ville. This is the bubble we first saw in Crusoeville, but on a massive scale. The economies of Hutville, Bananaville, Coffeeville, Margaritaville, Cornville, Lobsterville, Cattleville and Sushiville implode. A Great Depression engulfs these villes.

Crusoevillains have no idea what caused the Great Depression. The sheeple of other villes realize it is related to the shortage of "apple" notes. They can't figure out the specifics, but realize Crusoeville abused its "apple" note power somehow. The Depression ends, distrust of Crusoeville remains. No threats or promises can make villes accept "apple" notes again.

Or so it seems...

Oil becomes indispensable. Villes can do without apples, straw, lobster, in a crisis maybe even margaritas, but not oil. Crusoeville offers to protect Oilville, keep its leaders in power, let them limit oil production to jack-up prices, and suppress alternative energy that would free villes from oil dependence. In exchange, Oilville makes villes buy oil with apple notes. No other currency or commodity will be accepted as payment. You want oil, you buy it with "apple" notes. Period. Oilville agrees. Now all villes need mountains of "apple" notes to buy oil. Crusoeville doesn't have to redeem apple notes for apples. Apple notes will be inflated, all villes know it, but they must use them if they want oil. Fire up the "apple" note presses and build some new ones!

Crusoeville is even richer. All villes trade real goods & services to obtain "apple" notes. This includes old apple bloc countries like Hutville and Margaritaville, and new ones like Carville, Clothesville and Diamondville. Crusoevillains purchase cars, clothes, and diamonds using "apple" notes printed out of thin air. No apples surrendered.

The world is now one large ship riding the "apple" note wave. When Crusoevillains have gorged themselves into oblivion, this bubble will pop too, resulting in a Greater Depression which engulfs every ville in the world.

Substitute dollars for apple notes, and this trite allegory bears more than a passing resemblance to the real world. Exit Crusoeville, enter reality. If you create money and circulate it in the general economy where it chases goods, then prices increase quickly. Speculatos don't want this. They want to print as much money as possible, and that means newly created money must be placed in a bubble where it doesn't chase goods and drive up general prices.

In a house, for example. The house price can increase, but until the owner tries to convert the house to goods & services in the general economy, prices of everyday goods like groceries and clothes don't increase. As shown, this is how the misconception that everybody is richer arises. As long as most people are simply watching their house rise in value and not trying to convert it to physical goods & services, the disparity between the perceived wealth (housing prices) and actual wealth (goods & services houses can claim when sold) can grow to awesome proportions.

An economy can have many bubbles. A stock-market bubble. A housing bubble. A T-debt bubble. A commercial-real-estate bubble. A credit-card bubble. The same basic concept applied to different repositories of money.

Take stocks. Millions invest in the stock market. Prices often rise not because companies are worth more, but because more money was pumped in. Earnings don't grow, companies aren't more profitable, but prices of stocks nonetheless rise.

As with houses, a few stocks sold for an obscene price cause everyone assume that their unsold stock will fetch the same obscene price. This amplifies the money injection.

Money can be shifted from one place in the economy to another, causing prices to rise, but when this is done prices decline where money is removed from. A company may rise in price, or a beautiful house, or even a single commodity, but when they all do, monetary inflation is the cause.

The Dow was 400 in 1929, 10,000 75 years later in 2004. If a person from 1929 time travelled to 2004 and checked the Dow, they would think their portfolio was 32 times more valuable. Until they realized that the money supply was increased from $73 billion to $9,000 billion—a 125 fold increase. Dividends aside, they lost wealth.

Bubbles are a mirage. Once a large number of people try to convert their supposed wealth into real goods & services, bubble prices plummet, general prices rise, or both, and the illusion is shattered. The wealth never existed. The printing press does not produce goods & services, just paper money.

Inflator Generals stop creating money and pop bubbles because newly created money is no longer being diverted into the bubble. When newly created money is no longer driving up bubble prices, but rather begins chasing goods & services, then general prices of everyday purchases begin rising. At this point additional money creation will ravage the economy. There are many reasons why Inflator Generals halt money creation and pop bubbles, but this is one reason.

Speculatos engineer bubbles and fill them with ever-increasing sums of money. The more bubbles, the more money that can be created, the bigger the boom, but also the bigger the bust.

There don't seem to be any more bubbles for "apple" notes. Crusoevillains are drowning in debt, and every ville has vaults full of "apple" notes. But Speculatos are more creative than Edison when it comes to inventing new scams. Fraud is 99% obfuscation, 1% perspiration—but only if you're prosecuted! There is always another bubble, if one is ingenious and dishonest enough. . .

TO SKIP THE PICTURE PAGES AFTER THIS CHAPTER, PLEASE TURN TO PAGE 171

A 1 PAGE MONETARY HISTORY OF AMERICA

From 1789 until 1933, America was on a "gold standard" in which the dollar was a fixed weight of gold. Though not perfect, the gold standard protected people from marauding inflation. Very roughly, prices decreased 50% from 1789-1913. A loaf of bread that cost $1 in 1789 cost 50¢ in 1913. Technology and invention allowed the same worker to produce twice as much, so prices gradually decreased.

The Fed inflation clockwork was created in 1913. America immediately abused the inflation tax to fund World War I. After WWI, Fed kept inflating, creating the "Roaring 20s" boom and stock market bubble. Fed popped the stock market bubble by halting inflation. The Great Depression resulted. In 1933, FDR seized privately owned gold to bailout banks. They had issued more money than gold, faced depositor runs, and would have been rupted otherwise. As today, the solution wasn't to hold banks accountable but to defraud we the people to bail banks out.

In 1945, the United Nations Bretton Woods Money Conference made the dollar the world reserve currency. The dollar was backed by gold, currencies of other nations were backed by dollars. This allowed America to print dollars, spend them overseas, and obtain foreign goods without surrendering any American goods. This inflation funded the Cold, Korean and Vietnam Wars, and Lyndon Johnson's budget-busting "Great Society" of Medicare and Medicaid.

The world accepted dollars because they believed they were backed by gold. America created so many dollars nations realized that few dollars could actually be redeemed for gold. In 1971, France and Germany tried to redeem billions of dollars for gold. This would have emptied Fort Knox. Nixon "closed the gold window," refusing to redeem dollars for gold. America defrauded the world.

Nations now had Alps of worthless dollars. They couldn't buy U.S. goods with them. America didn't—and doesn't—produce enough goods to honor all the dollars it creates. The only way to get something for dollars is to invest them in T-debts which pay more dollars. If nations with Himalayas of dollars stop buying T-debts, America must resort to hyperinflation to fund deficits, and dollars nations hold become worthless. A $3 trillion catch-22. Small wonder the world hates US.

In closing the gold window, America declared bankruptcy. Liquidating America is difficult for creditors, as it has the hugest army in history. America agreed to protect Saudi Arabia if it made OPEC sell oil *only* in dollars. Nations exchange goods for computed dollars to buy OPEC oil. Dollars are backed by OPEC oil. America uses force to keep OPEC oil from being sold in euros, yen or yuan. If this were allowed, the dollar would collapse and so would the U.S. economy.

FUTURES

"We must avoid the temptation to demonize derivatives, which are a vital tool in modern financial markets. They are so useful in managing risk that if they didn't exist, we would surely have to invent them."
—Arthur Levitt, 25th Chairman of the Securities & Exchange Commission

Back to Crusoeville in its pre-crash bliss. $1 per apple. Until a drought hits one year. Much of my apple crop is lost. Many go appleless. They don't like it but know it wasn't anyone's fault. Such things happen. It is an uncertain world.

Johnny Appleseed wants to make sure he has apples next year. He'll pay $1.25 an apple to have 1,000 apples a week sold to him before anyone else buys. He doesn't want his applesauce plant shut down again because of apple shortages. Assume his motivation isn't sinister. He isn't trying to speculate, just produce applesauce.

This agreement is called a FUTURES CONTRACT, or in investment lingo an apple FUTURE. It is a binding contract to buy or sell a commodity at a future date. No matter how much the price of apples rises or falls, I have to sell 1,000 apples a week to Johnny for $1.25 each. I can project future income better and face less uncertainty—especially about plummeting apple prices. Johnny knows he'll have apples this year. He is less profitable because he pays more for apples, but less profit is better than no profit like during the drought.

Johnny and I both took a risk. Apples sold for $1.50 during the drought, and if it happens again, I'm still bound by law to sell Johnny his apples at $1.25. If there is no drought, Johnny could buy apples for $1.00, but must still pay me $1.25 for them.

The apple future is an honest contract. Johnny and I both gave something, and we both got something.

A futures contract is a type of DERIVATIVE. A derivative is called a derivative because its value is derived from something real but it is not that real something. It is lesser, secondary, derivative.

Take the apple future. Johnny Appleseed doesn't own apples yet, he merely has an agreement to receive them at a specified future time. I don't have Johnny's money yet, just an agreement to obtain it.

Johnny and I could have created a riskier contract in which I agree to sell him apples next year at market price, or 10¢ above market price, no matter what the price. This is a more complicated—and more realistic—example. In this case apple prices are the fluctuating price which will determine the derivative contract value.

Institutions that borrow and lend money can end up with money shortages similar to the applesauce producer's apple shortage, so derivatives are also created for financial instruments like stocks and bonds, and fluctuate in value according to currency values, stock prices, or interest rates.

When I buy stock I own a piece of a corporation. There might be a lot of shares and mine might only equate to a doorknob or beam in a factory, but it is nonetheless something physical, tangible, real. Not a derivative. It is a contract specifying terms under which something physical, tangible, and real will be exchanged at a future time.

This can be a confusing concept, so let's examine it further. Suppose the drought eroded the topsoil on some of my land. I must buy more land, but don't have the money. A loan is possible, but it is so large it makes my wife nervous. Another drought would bankrupt us, and she doesn't want our kids living like Hutvillers.

I form a corporation, Appleachian. People buy shares. I obtain the money to buy land from shareholders, but they now own Appleachian, and get a portion of my apple income every year. The incorporation agreement gave me enough shares that I control the corporation. Now I never have to use a broken wheelbarrow or skimp. If I need a new wheelbarrow, I check with my shareholders, issue more shares, sell them, and raise money. My shareholders don't want me abusing this power—giving myself a million shares as a bonus, for example—because new shares dilute old ones just like money. But when a true need arises they don't mind issuing stock. Stocks are useful because they make my business more efficient and productive. I have the funding to make improvements rapidly, and shareholders earn more income than they would have otherwise, as they aren't clever or inventive enough to start and run an apple business.

I need a cart loan. My son is turning 16, I want him to drive. I go to First Fraud Bank and bring Appleachian stock to use as collateral. First Fraud Bank knows Appleachian has real assets and that the stock is a claim on them, and therefore agrees. The stock has a market value of $10,000 but First Fraud Bank will only loan me $2,500 against it, in case the price drops. If I default on the loan, First Fraud Bank can sell the stock. If Appleachian goes broke and its assets are sold at firesale prices, First Fraud Bank still gets its money back.

The stock is an asset, but one with limitations due to the difficulty and uncertainty one encounters converting it to a spendable form of wealth.

In the real world, no one uses stock as collateral for a car loan, but this example illustrates a point.

My daughter marries a slacker and next year they need help buying a house. I try to use my future contract with Johnny as collateral for the mortgage. First Fraud Bank refuses. Johnny Appleseed will pay me $1,250 a week, I say. My derivative contract is an asset.

Suppose a viper worm kills you, the banker says. Rare, but it happens. Or what if the drought is so bad this year there are no apples? If that happens I can sell your land and wheelbarrows to liquidate the Appleachian stock. But I can't do that with the apple future. It is not a direct claim to an asset the way your stock is. It cannot be used as collateral for a loan.

A single apple has a single real value. The apple exists somewhere physically, can be sold at a current price, and this is its real worth. Yet each person with an apple future has a piece of paper, a derivative contract, that requires them to buy or sell an apple. You wouldn't sum up all future contracts and conclude that this many apples exists. This would be many times the actual number of apples that exist, an illusory wealth total which far exceeds the actual value of all physical apples. The physical apples are the wealth, not the futures contracts.

In an honest economy, there is at most one futures contract per apple, usually far less, as most apples are sold on the open market at fluctuating prices.

Who would create more futures contracts than there are apples? You can guess the answer, and as you can imagine, you and I get bamboozled when Speculatos abuse futures to enrich themselves.

BACK TO THE FUTURES

"There are two times in a man's life when he should not speculate: when he can't afford it, and when he can."

—Mark Twain

The future between Johnny Appleseed and I solved actual physical problems. It is a tool for honest businessmen. Speculatos pervert this honest dynamic. They create futures contracts solely to generate paper profits. What's wrong with this? Isn't the point of business profit?

Profit isn't evil, but honest businesses offer something of value and sell it for profit. In honest societies, everyone produces something. That something can be a service, even lending or investing money, but Speculatos siphon wealth without producing wealth. They violate the societal compact that you produce something to get something. Speculatos are parasites.

Johnny Appleseed buys an apple future from me, and others follow suit. Apple vendors, the jelly producer, even the cider maker. Everyone wants to be sure they have a supply of apples.

Next year there is a more severe drought. More people are appleless. Apples jump to $1.75. The $1.25 apple future is a bargain, and is exchanged like money. Not quite as easily, but futures are traded like stocks. A market for them arises.

Appleseed's future contract lets him buy apples for $1.25. He sells them at the market price of $1.75 and "earns" 50¢ an apple. Way more profitable than using apples to make applesauce!

Apple futures become a craze. Some sheeple think the drought could be a regular occurrence. Apples might be $3.00 next year. Sheeple pay $2.50 per apple future in anticipation of selling it for $3.00. As with the housing bubble or stock market, greed makes any risk seem reasonable. No matter how much you pay, another fool will always pay more.

Johnny Appleseed sells his $1.25 future contract for $2.50. He "earns" $1.25 of profit per paper-shuffled apple. My profit is 50¢ per apple and I grow them.

I agreed to the future contract, so a deal's a deal, but I refuse to renew the agreement. Johnny Appleseed is bummed. After earning easy money selling futures, making applesauce sucks. It wasn't just the money, but the power, watching everyone scurry around in a frenzy while he stood above the fray like a God.

Johnny is rich from futures. Everyone knows it. Does he need a contract to buy apples in order to sell them? Can't he sell apples he doesn't have? Or buy apples no one has sold?

John Q. Sucker wants to buy 1,000 apple futures at $2.50 per apple. At a future date he must buy 1,000 apples for $2.50 each. He can't change his mind, and if he doesn't have the money he can be sued and assets like his house sold to obtain it. Sucker isn't worried. Everyone knows apples will soon cost $3.00. What sucker wouldn't buy a $2.50 apple and sell it for $3.00? It's a gravy train. Choo choo, all aboard.

Everyone knows Johnny Appleseed had a futures contract with Appleachian. When he sells a future for $2.50, no one worries about his ability to cough up the apples. Apples themselves are an afterthought. No one plans on getting stuck with physical apples. They're going to flip futures until they're filthy stinking rich!

Johnny Appleseed sells an apple future to John Q. Sucker. Futures prices are increasing. Suckers don't just want futures, they have to have them. Appleseed draws up a contract: he'll sell Sucker 1,000 apples at $2.75 per apple August 1st next year. More than the Sucker wanted to pay, but he'll still make a pile when the drought that couldn't possibly not happen drives apple prices up to $3.00 or $4.00 or $5.00 or more.

Johnny Appleseed must cough up 1,000 apples he doesn't have. He plants apple trees, right?

You knew that was a joke.

Johnny approaches Jane R. Gullible. What if the drought that couldn't possibly not happen isn't as severe as everyone thinks? Gullible's eyes bulge. She owns 10,000 apple futures. Hedge your bets, Appleseed says. I'll buy 1,000 apples from you for $2.60, 10¢ more than you paid. She bites. Johnny creates another contract: he'll buy 1,000 of Gullible's apples for $2.60 on August 1st next year.

Johnny has two futures contracts due on the same date, one buying 1,000 apples for $2.60, another selling them for $2.75. He doesn't need apples! Gullible has to come up with apples and give them to Sucker. And Johnny made $150. Not a fortune, but he can repeat this process again and again and again. And he will.

Johnny buys and sells solely to exploit price differences. This is ARBITRAGE. Johnny has no interest in the physical apples. He might as well be peddling unicorn futures.

If Johnny can't balance out his buys and sells, he must honor them, and will go bankrupt fast. He assumes a risk, and some say he should be rewarded. But at a deeper level Johnny never created anything of value like honest members of society. In manipulating futures, he obtained something for nothing.

With no one concerned about physical apples, futures in them proliferate. Any two citizens can create a futures contract. All you need is a paper and a pen. It's like printing money.

Soon there are more futures contracts than apples. To honor all futures contracts, each physical apple must be bought and sold numerous times. This is why the banker would not accept my apple future, or derivative, as collateral. Everyone might bring in such an agreement and claim it was an asset. A single physical apple might be borrowed against numerous times, even though it only exists once. When Speculatos obtain something for nothing, sheeple give up something for nothing. Parasite A has a future with a farmer and buys an apple for $1.25. Parasite A honors a future with Parasite B, and sells the apple to him for $1.75. Parasite B honors a future with Parasite C, and sells the apple to him for $2.50. Parasite C raises the price to $3.75 and sells the apple to. . . the poor sucker who actually just wants to eat an apple, not use it to get rich, and now pays 3 times more for it.

In 2008, 81% of oil futures were held by speculators who didn't produce or use oil. Oil skyrocketed above $100 a barrel. Every time you pumped a $4.00 gallon of gas, you put at least $2.00 into the pocket of some Speculato. Speculatos lounging on yachts producing nothing were making billions buying and selling futures. They weren't just profiting off rising oil prices, they were the cause of rising oil prices.

Excessive amounts of futures also deny profit to those producing commodities. In a marketplace with few futures or derivatives, a farmer growing corn might sell corn for a little less some years, a little more some years. Futures speculators can drive the price of corn up or down before it is ever produced, siphoning wealth that should go to the producer of the actual commodity. The corn grower ends up having to sell his corn for less, for reasons that have nothing to do with the physical supply of, or demand for, corn.

In the real world, only the rich buy futures. Futures are like the high-roller room in a casino. They are so risky that massive credit is required to trade them, and only the rich have it. Futures exist for all major commodities, allowing a small cabal of billionaire traders to amass fabulous fortunes by driving up prices.

Futures can increase market instability. When markets are rising, everyone tends to bet the same way, so contracts don't balance. Suppose there is 1 apple in the world. 10 futures contracts are created, 9 selling apples, 1 buying, all at $1 per apple. The apple is bought to satisfy the buy contract, and sold to satisfy one of the sell contracts, then what? 8 more people are bound by law to sell an apple, but there aren't 8 apple buy contracts, much less 8 apples.

Those purchasing apple futures for legitimate business use don't end up in this pinch because they can't pay a ridiculous price. If each jar of applesauce requires one apple and sells for $2.50, Johnny can't pay $3.50 an apple. He'll never agree to such a contract. Only a Speculato will. Futures contracts used for honest purposes usually don't cause skyrocketing prices.

Shouldn't you have to grow or own apples to sell apple futures? Have some real use for apples to buy future contracts? Don't be ridiculous. What do you expect billionaire Speculatos to do? Work for a living?

Mortgaging the Futures

"Years earlier, as a cashier at McDonald's, I had been trained in the art of 'suggestive selling.' If a customer ordered a cheeseburger and fries, I knew to ask 'Would you like an apple pie with that?' That strategy worked at Morgan Stanley. If a customer ordered a simple treasury bond, you asked 'Would you like a leveraged derivative with that?'"

—Frank Partnoy
Former Derivatives Structurer at Investment Bank Morgan Stanley

Soon people have bought all the apple futures they can. Frost wiped out an orange crop, and now orange futures exist too. Futures are soon traded for every commodity.

Speculatos want more profit, so they trade futures on MARGIN. That is, buy futures contracts for a percentage of face value. Say 10%. They can buy $10 worth of contracts for every $1 they have, or 10 times more contracts. The fractional reserve lending fraud is applied to futures, which can now be flipped in massive quantities for arbitrage.

Speculatos want more paper profit, so STOCK OPTIONS are created. A share of Appleachian stock sells for $50. For $1, you purchase the option to buy a share at a future date. You aren't obligated to buy the share, you merely have the option, but you pay the $1 even if you don't exercise it. Option prices above or below current prices are bets that prices will rise or fall. Buy options are CALLS, because stock is called for from the seller. Sell options are PUTS, which put stocks to the buyer.

A person buys Appleachian at $50 thinking it will go up in price, or to obtain dividend payments from profits. But what if the price drops to $5, like it did during the last drought? If you buy a $25 put for $1, you can sell your share for $25 rather than $5 and limit your loss. You HEDGE your stock bet with the option, using it as a form of insurance.

You can also use the $25 put to speculate. If Appleachian prices drop to $5, you buy a share, exercise your put and sell it for $25. $20 profit, and you didn't have to own a share of Appleachian stock initially. A 20 to 1 jackpot on the $1 you paid for the put. Credit isn't required to spin the options wheel, meaning options can be sold to sheeple who fancy themselves Speculatos. Few of these slot machines pay out, and the house makes easy money.

You may have heard the term "Hedge Fund." Hedge funds are super risky mutual funds created by Speculatos. Normal mutual funds buy stocks and bonds and therefore own assets which limit their risk. Hedge Funds can return spectacular profits which dwarf those of normal mutual funds. They do so by not buying stocks or bonds with intrinsic value, but rather by buying "hedges"—short sale or derivative bets. This is not investing, it is gambling. Hedge Funds have no assets, only bets. They are famous for generating massive profits and going instantly bankrupt.

As with futures, Speculatos selling options don't own the stocks being bought or sold, or have the assets to honor all options. They run a shell game to obtain easy profits. Speculatos try to balance out positions, or sell options for events that won't happen. But if imbalances arise or they guess wrong, they have no options, and must cough up dough they don't have.

Speculatos want more profit, so they sell futures and options for the money of all the villes. Corn note futures, lobster note futures, margarita note futures, even apple note futures. And options. These futures gamble on the prices—that is, interest rates—of currencies. They also gamble on the exchange rates of currencies, the number of dollars it takes to obtain a pound or yen as nations expand and contract their money supplies.

You can bet money on the price of money! As with commodity futures, currency futures are sold on margin, and Speculatos don't have enough money to cover all their positions.

Welcome to Vegas. Step right up and place your bet. We've got commodity futures, currency futures and stock options. Ten'll getya twenty, five can getcha fifty, and if you throw the House & Senate enough action we'll comp you a bailout.

Sheeple embrace the misconception that the purpose of investing is to provide investment. Everyone wants profit, but in the old days it was generated by investing money in businesses producing real goods & services. Shouldn't you buy a stock, or not buy a stock? Only buy futures for goods you actually need? Aren't commitments to sell things you don't have and can't afford just fraud? If not, shouldn't this "investing" be called gambling?

Don't be naive. The purpose of stocks, options, and futures is to generate massive speculative profits for financial high priests. Their derivative deity is an angry God, and to keep it appeased, sheeple must constantly be sacrificed at the altar of finance.

New sacrificial sheeple are rounded up by concocting new frauds. Suppose the banker accepted your derivative as collateral. Suppose everyone holding an apple future or other derivative could suddenly call it an asset like a stock or wheelbarrow or land, or, God forbid, an apple. Borrow against it, spend it, make it part of the value used in computing a company's stock price. My, what a bubble you'd have.

MARKETY MARK ACCOUNTING

"Blaming fair-value [mark-to-market] accounting for the credit crisis is a lot like going to a doctor for a diagnosis and then blaming him for telling you that you are sick."
—Dane Motte, Senior Equity Analyst at Investment Bank JP Morgan Chase

"Suspending mark-to-market accounting, in essence, suspends reality."
—Beth Brooke, Global Vice Chair of Accounting Firm Ernst and Young

Derivatives are financial instruments which require a payment to be made at a future date. The payment amount is determined by fluctuating reference items such as commodity prices, stock prices or interest rates. These reference items fluctuate before the derivative contract is settled, meaning the value of the derivative fluctuates before it is settled. Payments on a derivative are only made when it comes due and is settled, but holders of derivatives record profits and losses long before this, without paying each other.

Businesses keep ledgers. The ledgers of honest businesses reflect their actual financial state. Honest businesses don't make themselves look richer or poorer with accounting gimmicks. This is like saying "politicians shouldn't lie." Everyone knows they do. But is it a little lie like, "Great to be here with you all," or a whopper like, "I'm not a crook." Most businesses shiatsu the books a little, we're concerned with mongo frauds.

How do you value a derivative for bookkeeping purposes? You don't know what it will be worth when settled, so estimates of its current value differ from this final value.

You could admit you have no idea what the derivative will be worth, and pencil a question mark into your ledger. A year from now we owe Speculato a huge amount of money we can't determine. Cool, man. Let's see what happens. Maybe it'll bankrupt us, maybe it won't. Wanna start an office pool?

A CEO would want an estimate of the amount to plan for it. An expert in apple markets could forecast prices, but forecasts are speculative, and forecasters can be bribed. The current price of apples is inarguable, so one could value an apple future this way. Or value any derivative based on the current market value of the reference item that determines its price.

This is an imperfect solution. Take an honest accountant, Bob. Speculation might drive apple prices to $3.00, but Bob knows that large numbers of them can't ever sell for this much. Bob wouldn't claim that each apple is worth $3.00, but would choose a lower and more conservative value, the BOOK VALUE.

Bob's coworker Fudger would happily MARK-TO-MARKET. Mark: pencil the value in the books. To market: at current market value. Mark-to-market: to

179

pencil something in the books at its current market value, rather than book value. Mark-to-market originated with futures trading. Futures traders buy risky contracts with 10% down, but if they bet wrong they can owe a fortune. For example, you agree to buy 1,000 apples a year from now no matter what the price; if the current price of an apple rises from $1 to $10, your liability has increased from $1,000 to $10,000. To keep traders from ending up with debts they can't pay, futures exchanges mark-to-market. At the end of each day, outstanding contracts are marked-to-market, and traders must keep funds equal to the market-marked value.

In futures trading, mark-to-market avoids credit abuses, but Speculatos transplant it elsewhere, and abuse it to defraud people.

Why not use mark-to-market to value everything, not just futures?

Take Appleachian. If apples are marked at $3.00 instead of $1.00, and Appleachian has 1 million unpicked apples, its value increased by $2 million. On paper. Money doesn't grow on trees, but it grows on ledgers if your bookkeeper has a green thumb.

This apparent wealth drives Appleachian's stock price into the stratosphere and makes it look wealthier than it really is. The CEO is hailed as a genius, and the stock he receives as a yearly bonus is more valuable. $3.00 apples give Appleachian more collateral to obtain larger loans, which it uses to buy more land, plant more trees, and grow more "$3" apples.

Another bubble is created, just like in Crusoeville, but the perceived wealth is conjured by marking-to-market rather than a printing press. To those buying stocks and issuing loans based on inflated values, this wealth is as real as paper money.

When the bubble pops and apples return to their normal price of $1, $2 million in wealth evaporates. Poof! Gone! Stock prices tumble. Sheeple who invested in Appleachian need a change of underwear. Creditors holding Appleachian's loans get nervous, as collateral vanished. If Appleachian's CEO was shady, he took out huge loans which require income from $3 apples. When apples sell at $1, Appleachian cannot make loan payments and is bankrupt.

This is immoral, but is it illegal? Not usually. Money isn't being embezzled, inflated values are being penciled into ledgers. All a CEO has to do is say, "I thought apples were worth $3.00. Convict me of stupidity or incompetence, but I didn't steal."

There are infinite ways to abuse mark-to-market accounting. New apple trees are planted. Most trees produce 50 apples per year, but rare studs produce 100 apples. A "random" sampling of young trees indicates they will produce 100 apples. $3 apples, of course. Next year's apple crop doubled—on paper. 2 million apples instead of 1 million. $3 million of net worth conjured out of thin air. If you're buying land, you estimate its value by the number of apples it can produce. Usually 100 trees can be planted per acre, but "random" sampling indicates that has jumped to 150, and this is included in long term income estimates. Millions more dollars conjured out of thin air...

And so forth. This basic fraud can be applied to anything penciled in a ledger. Wildly overstate the value of anything, you create another form of inflation. The human tendency for optimism is partially responsible, but there are incentives to cheat.

Especially for derivatives traders whose commissions are determined by "earnings" computed marking-to-market. They create trillions of dollars of derivatives out of thin air, transmute them into assets by marking them into books at market value, and then collect fat commissions based on those inflated values.

On the upside, Speculatos mark-to-market and pocket piles of loot. On the downside, they sing the same old bailout song. The problem isn't their fraud or mismanagement, it is mark-to-market accounting. If they weren't required to mark plummeting asset prices at market value, they wouldn't be going bankrupt.

Another seductive lie that is part truth. Mark-to-market accounting shouldn't be abused in the first place, and long term, should be restricted. Innocent workers are hurt when companies go bankrupt, and this can be avoided by allowing them to mark assets down over time rather than all at once. But it is unjust to let Speculatos mark-to-market on the upswing when book values are below market values, and then switch to book values when market prices plummet below book values. Speculatos shouldn't be allowed to create a business cycle, profit off it, and then leave sheeple holding the bag. That doesn't mean they won't be allowed.

Banks lobbiests forced changes in accounting rules. It is now legal to mark-to-market at maximum value during booms and suspend the practice during busts. Count the $1 apple (book value) as $3 (market value) during a boom, but avoid counting it as 25¢ (market value) during a bust and instead pencil it in at $1 (book value). Try this with a house. Value a $100,000 house (book value) as $300,000 (market value) during the boom, and count the increased "equity" as an asset which allows issuance of additional loans. When the housing market collapses the house price drops to $50,000 (market value). The bank lost $250,000 of "equity" ($300,000 - $50,000 = $250,000), but their exposure is greater because this "equity" was the backing for additional loans. When the $250,000 in "equity" vanishes, the backing for loans vanishes, and banks plummet below legal limits which specify the small percentage of assets or capital which must back outstanding loans. Banks are then bankrupt, and should be shut down by regulators. Unless they cook the books. Banks pencil a $50,000 mortgage into the books at $100,000 (book value). If they hadn't used their increased "equity" to issue loans, this re-marking would save them, but they are so exposed even this fraud isn't sufficient. They pencil the $50,000 mortgage in their books at $200,000 and call this a book value.

When banks are allowed to perform such machinations with millions of mortgages worth trillions of dollars, the distortions and misrepresentations rapidly become gargantuan. Ledgers which once provided an accurate snapshot of a company's health are now meaningless to everyone but guru insiders. Suspending mark-to-market accounting, in essence, suspends reality.

Mark-to-market can hurt companies unfairly. Speculatos can crash prices, bankrupting companies forced to mark-to-market at crashed prices. Speculatos crash prices by SHORT SELLING.

TO SKIP THE PICTURE PAGES AFTER THIS CHAPTER, PLEASE TURN TO PAGE 183

FEDERAL ACCOUNTING STANDARDS BOARD CHAIRMAN
DENOUNCES POLITICIZATION OF MARK-TO-MARKET ACCOUNTING

DOW JONES NEWSWIRE
JUNE 26, 2009

The head of the board that sets U.S. accounting standards on Friday took a stab at financial-services lobbyists who earlier this year pressured the board to ease mark-to-market accounting standards. ... Financial Accounting Standards Board Chairman Robert Herz said he had major concerns about how the "politicization" of accounting can harm investor confidence. "Unfortunately, there have been certain major companies—including ones that subsequently failed and had to be rescued by the government—and industry trade groups that have sought political intervention into accounting standard setting," Herz said. "While that is their right, and while we certainly welcome active dialogue with lawmakers, politicization of accounting standard setting by special interests risks undermining public confidence in the integrity of financial reporting."

Herz's comments come just a few months after he faced angry lawmakers in a March hearing who accused him of acting too slowly in responding to industry concerns that mark-to-market accounting rules were having a detrimental impact on bank balance sheets. Mark-to-market rules require banks and other companies to assign a value to an asset such as a mortgage security based on the current market price.

Big trade groups like the American Bankers Association and the U.S. Chamber of Commerce lobbied for more lax standards, saying the rules were forcing banks to write down billions on their books and therefore making it hard to meet certain regulatory capital requirements. Following intense pressure from Congress, FASB accelerated its approval process to ease the standards, which now allow companies to exercise greater judgment in determining the fair value of their assets.

Herz didn't drop the names of those groups or companies that pressured FASB to take action, but pressed by reporters in a question-and-answer session, he offered an example. "A three-letter insurance company that begins with A," he said, referring to American International Group (AIG). He said about a year ago, AIG's former CEO, Martin Sullivan "spent a fair amount of time here in Washington and on Capitol Hill trying to convince lawmakers there were no problems with the credit-default swaps they had entered into—it was all bogus fair value accounting." In truth, he said, the accounting actually represented the "first signs" that alerted people of real problems.

Short Selling

"As a former Treasury official, I am amazed that the U.S. government, in the midst of one the worst financial crises ever, is content for short-selling to drive down the asset prices that the government is trying to support. ... No bailout or stimulus plan has any hope until the uptick rule is reinstated. ... If we add to my simple menu of remedies a ban, punishable by instant death, for short selling any national currency, the world can be rescued from the current crisis without years of suffering."

—Paul Craig Roberts,
United States Assistant Secretary of the Treasury (1981-1982)

When you buy a stock or bond or other asset, you bet the price will increase. For example, you buy shares of IBM at $10 and sell them at $30. What if IBM is selling at $30 and you think it will drop to $10? How do you bet on that?

In an honest economy, you don't. Stocks aren't created to facilitate betting, but fund companies and reward investors. If IBM is $30 and you think it'll drop to $10, you place a bet by selling it. If you don't own IBM, you can't bet on its decline, except by not buying it.

Speculatos hate this honest system. Why should they have to own a stock to sell it? Or own anything to sell it? Short selling is selling something you don't have. Something you are short of.

Short selling can be confusing if you're new to investing. Normal investing is long selling. In long selling, an asset is bought, the price increases, and then it is sold. In short selling the process is reversed. The asset is sold, the price decreases, and then it is bought.

If IBM is $30 and you think it'll drop to $10, why not short sell a share you don't have for $30? When the price drops to $10, you buy it and made $20. Assuming someone lends you a share to SHORT. Do Avis or Hertz have stock rentals? Rent-a-share?

A short sale is a future contract involving a stock rather than an apple. You sold someone a stock you don't have, and must obtain that stock by a specified date. If the stock price increases rather than decreases, you bet wrong. You must buy a share of stock at a higher price. You lost money.

Short selling is risky. Short sellers bet on short term market fluctuations. This is riskier than making a long term investment in a company you believe is making a good product. Who always predicts market fluctuations accurately? No one.

Few will lend stocks for risky parlor bets, but this doesn't stop Speculatos.

When you buy stock, you don't take physical possession of it. The broker keeps the stock. You think the stock sits unused like a coat in a coat check, but the stock is lent to short sellers without you being told. As with fractioned bank deposits which are lent to borrowers but still exist in depositor accounts, the share of stock now exists twice.

When a second virtual copy of a stock is created and lent, the stock is HY-POTHECATED. Rent-a-share charges a fee to short sellers who "borrow" the "hypothecated" stock, but doesn't give the actual owner a portion of the rental fee. When short sold stock is bought at a lower price, the short position is "closed" and the stock is "un-hypothecated." Similar to money whisked in and out of existence by banks. Money is computered and lent, pays interest, is repaid and uncomputered. Stock is hypothecated and sold, reduced in price, bought back and unhypothecated.

As with fraudulent fractional reserve lending, short selling is legal. The fine print of brokerage contracts gives brokers and banks permission to hypothecate.

In selling stock shares which were not obtained from the pool of existing shares, Speculatos create new phantom shares of stock. Short selling hypothecated stock is counterfeiting. Hypothecating results in faulty price signals that Speculatos exploit. Same inflation scam, different bells and whistles.

The traders you see shouting and waving on exchange floors set stock prices by balancing buy and sell orders. An increase in sell orders drops prices. If the increase in sell orders is monstrous, the stock price collapses. When millions of shares of stock can be hypothecated, it is not hard to collapse a stock price. The stock is bought for pennies on the dollar once the price plummets. Short selling is a self-fulfilling prophecy. A way to not just profit off declining prices, but cause them.

Short selling worsened the Great Depression. Speculatos short sold stocks for years as the market nosedived. Every time the market stabilized, Speculatos moved in, short sold, and nosedived it again. Vultures picking the carcass clean. This vulturing was repeated during Depression v9.2006-201x.

The UPTICK RULE was instituted in 1938 during the Great Depression to limit short selling. If a stock didn't increase in price the previous day, it couldn't be short sold. Speculatos couldn't gang up on a stock day after day and short sell it into oblivion. Lobbyists had the uptick rule repealed in 2007.

NAKED SHORT SELLING is selling stock (or other assets) without borrowing the stock (or other assets). The pretense of "lending" stock is abandoned.

The practical limit to naked shorting is credit and regulators. Speculatos could bet wrong, so the bet size allowed is proportional to their assets or credit. Of course, innermost Speculatos obtain unlimited credit from banks that fraction money out of thin air. Excessive short selling attracts regulators, so if you haven't bribed them or don't have political connections, you can't manipulate prices too overtly. If a company has 10 million shares and you naked short 5 million shares, the fraud is obvious. Shorting 50,000 shares is smarter. Naked short selling is illegal in most nations. By trading offshore from places like the Caymans, Pirates of the Caribbean escape regulations, and naked short sell anyway.

Speculatos make trillions of dollars each year short selling. Healthy companies are collapsed to enrich billionaires looking for a quick score. Low stock prices indicate weakness. When strong companies are made to look weak by short selling abuses, stock prices no longer reflect reality. Faulty price signals result in malinvestment. Markets become a craps table rather than a way to allocate resources to companies creating goods & services.

Speculatos isolate assets via multiple corporations. Their short selling corporation may go broke, but other assets can't be confiscated. Money used for short sale bets is created by banks. When banks go broke, taxpayers bail them out. The usual formula. Speculatos keep profit and make others pay losses.

MARKET MAKERS on exchanges are allowed to naked short sell to keep markets flowing. If there are 20 buyers and 15 sellers of Appleachian stock, a market maker is allowed to short sell 5 shares so that every seller has a buyer and markets keep moving. Sounds good in theory, but market makers abuse their power to short sell. If a grocery store runs out of steaks, it doesn't short sell you them. Why should stocks any different?

The most frequently shorted item is currency. Fractional reserve lending makes currency easier to counterfeit than stocks. Less risk of regulators nailing you, as naked shorts can be clothed quickly. Money claims the entire economy, so profit potentials in currency shorting are maximized. More than 100 national currencies exist, none backed by a commodity at a fixed rate, each fluctuating relative to the other, with inaccurate price signals that have not corrected. Infinite betting opportunities. Speculatos have a bank fraction them a loan of newly created money, and use it to short some other money. . .

Shorting currencies is sinister. Sheeple can refuse to invest in stocks, but guv'ments make money legal tender, and residents of a country can't survive without using it. Sheeple are forced to use currencies which Speculatos then sack.

Speculatos make short selling sound natural, the yang to the yin of long selling, an indispensable part of a modern economy.

Lies, as usual. While it is reasonable to occasionally pre-pay for something a store does not possess but orders, this could never be a widespread business practice. If everyone sold items they didn't possess, the economy would have no basis in reality. Imagine a "short selling" Wal-Mart or Sears with nothing on its shelves.

In an honest economy, most shorting would be criminalized. Only assets owned or legitimately surrendered would be sold.

INSIDE THE DEN OF VIPERS

"I did subprime first. I lived with the worst first. These guys lied to infinity. What I learned from that experience was that Wall Street didn't give a shit what it sold."
—Steve Eisman, Former employee of former investment bank Lehman Brothers

Welcome to G-Sax, King of the Investment Banks. No insider calls it Goldman Sachs, its G-Sax. You'll be working under me for your first few months. If you want to make it here, scuttle all the ethics garbage you learned in college. We live on commissions. If we can't concoct something to sell, there's no more Maseratis, trophy mistresses, or caviar cat food.

Facilitate investment that creates goods & services? Hell no, investment takes too long and isn't profitable enough. We're the middlemost middlemen. We resell what already exists.

Start with mortgages. Let's borrow $100 million, buy 1,000 mortgages, bundle them, and call it a "Mortgage Backed Security" or MBS. We've "securitized" mortgages. Converted them into a security like a stock or bond. The assets that constitute the value of the security are mortgages. The security is "mortgage-backed." We sell the MBS like stock and collect a 1% commission. $100 million value, 1% is $1 million.

Who'll lend us $100 million? No one, if loans came from savings and had to be surrendered by those who earned them. A commercial bank like Citi or B-of-A will create money for us.

Mortgage payments now go to the MBS, not the bank that originally issued the mortgage. These payments are earnings, profit which MBS investors expect. No one trusts stocks since the dot.com crash. Bonds are safe, but don't pay enough. We'll market MBSs as safer than stocks, more profitable than bonds. What about defaults on mortgages? A few mortgages might fail, but we bundled 1,000. That reduces risk.

MBSs prices are skyrocketing with the housing bubble. Mongo commissions! Investors' appetite for MBSs is infinite. We need more minimum wage workers to buy mansions so we have additional mortgage product to repackage and peddle.

Of course the housing market will crash. That doesn't pay a commission, so why bring it up? Maybe M-BSs are junk, maybe they aren't. That's for buyers to decide, not me, and once my commission check cashes, I could care less.

We've securitized all the mortgages we can. Damn I want a Ferrari. Let's repeat the process with bonds. Obtain a loan, buy up low-quality BBB bonds, bundle and resell them. We need a trustworthy name for this dodgy debt. Collateralized debt?

Debt obligation? Stop laughing, I know all debt should be collateralized. What debt isn't an obligation? Ours, once taxpayers bail us out.

Oh yes they will. The best investment is politicians, and we have a strong position in that market. Our ex-CEO Uncle Hank is Treasury Secretary. G-Sax alumni run Citigroup, Merrill Lynch, AIG, Wachovia, and the New York Stock Exchange. G-Sax alumni spend billions lobbying and wield prodigious influence. We'll get a lion's share of the bailout. And then some.

No, G-Sax isn't a subsidiary of the U.S. Treasury. The U.S. Treasury is a subsidiary of G-Sax. No, we won't etch the G-Sax logo on the Capitol building or change our name to Guv'ment Sachs. Call ourselves G-Saxons? That I like. We sacked government.

How about "Collateralized Debt Obligation"? Perfect. Sounds like something Mother Teresa'd sell. Let's up the ante and peddle $1 billion worth of BBB bonds. A $10 million commission.

That Ferrari's a rocket with wheels. I want a yacht. Let's jam $10 billion in CDOs. $100 million commission. No, that isn't a lot. There's oceans of bonds: local governments, state governments, federal guv'ment, corporations, foreign guv'ments. And thousands of retirement funds with trillions to invest.

Yacht's great, but I need a jet. Let's borrow money short term at low interest, lend it long term at high interest, and pocket the difference. Borrow 1 year at 3%, lend 10 years at 5%. 2% profit on a $1 billion loan is $20 million. I know we're lending 10 years but must repay in 1 year. If we can't borrow more money in a year, another ex-CEO Uncle Rubin will have Citi fraction reserves for us. What if interest rates exceed 5% by then and we have to pay higher rates than we're charging? Caveat emptor, buyer beware. Caveat taxpayor, actually. We're not taking people for a ride, if they don't examine what they're buying it's not my probl— ride, ride, hey, let's call them "Structured Investment Vehicles." SIVs. No, HIVs wouldn't be a better name. Nor would Structured Investment Jalopies.

What am I gonna do with all my money? Retire before 40 worth 9-figures and do charity work. No, not soup kitchens. Not the Peace Corps. The War Corps. War, what is it good for? Profit, say it again. Sorry, I'm laughing too hard to sing the rest. G-Saxons in guv'ment helped me make my fortune, I'll help the next generation do the same. You have to give something back.

We have an Initial Public Offing. No, they aren't Public Offerings. They're Public Offings. Made my 10th million off IPOs during the dot.com bubble. I was 28. And to think I almost studied engineering and became a working schmuck. Listen and learn while I make some calls.

Hey, Jerry. Got a hot IPO. Mygallons.com. Tomorrow's gas at today's prices. Lets sheeple pre-purchase fuel. Yes, gas prices will keep rising. Yes, I'm sure. We buy the futures that drive oil prices up. Mygallons is going public for lemmings at $20. 100 million shares. I'll cut you in for 100,000 shares at $15, you buy 30,000 shares at $25 once the price takes off. You in? Good.

Hey, Meg. Still have the Jaws ringtone set for my number? Good, good. Got a scorchin' IPO. Mygallons.com. It's been profitable at least 90 days. Don't worry, the CEO is on the pony circuit schmoozing investors. And we resurrected Hemingway to write the financials. I'll cut you in for 100,000 shares at $15, you buy 28,000 shares at $30 once the price takes off. . .

Hey, Ken. Got a smokin' IPO called mygallons.com. I'll cut you in for 100,000 shares at $15, you buy 6,000 shares at $85 once the price takes off. Spinning? I jog. Laddering? Don't climb either. Don't worry about the Securities and Exchange Commission. After the dot.com bubble, the SEC prosecuted us for spinning IPOs to insiders and laddering IPO prices. No one went to jail, we paid a $100 million fine on $10 billion in profit, about 1%. The SEC tax. They'll prosecute us for MBSs too, and we'll pay back 1%. Business as usual. Sure, I could do 200,000 shares, if you buy 13,000 shares at $88. . .

G-Sax gets 7% of every IPO share sold. 100 million shares sold at $20 is a $140 million commission. If shares sell for an average of $40, that's a $280 million commission. That's why we ladder the prices. I'll also buy shares through my Cayman accounts. Untraceable. Buy 100,000 shares at $20, sell at $70 before the bottom drops out. Quick $5 million. Day traders without an inside track aren't my problem. Lemmings find the cliff eventually.

Bought a condo in Monaco with the mygallons loot, but now investors are nervous about MBSs, CDOs and SIVs. Say we lied and should be prosecuted. Cry me a river, suckers. Still, there has to be a way to profit off th—one sec, gotta take this call.

Hey, Barthalamou. Don't swear. I didn't lie about MBSs. No, MBS doesn't mean More-of-my-BS. No, we shouldn't call them M-BSs. I never said the mortgages weren't subprime. Then don't buy anymore. I don't care about sheeple's lost life savings, and you're making millions too, so spare me the sermon. Let's do dinner at Harris Ranch this weekend and concoct a solution. You fly us out in your Gulfstream, rest of the trip's on me. All right, see you then.

Frantic banks are begging us to buy more mortgages. If banks didn't think we'd buy bogus mortgages, they wouldn't issue them. They can't let toxic mortgages sit on their books, it'd bankrupt them. Banks drop turds in our lap, we smear them on investors. Well, we were smearing them on investors. Investors are noticing the smell. They aren't buying the M-BS. Meaning we can't buy more mortgages. Meaning banks are screwed. They've got toxic mortgages they can't get rid of.

What to do? What to do? What the hell do we d—let's sell insurance on the MBSs, CDOs and HIVs. We'll earn commissions on Credit Default Swap insurance and Barthalamou can prop his bogus paper up. Everyone will believe in the system again. I know a guy at AIG. They've got a mountain of money from life, home and car insurance policies. Let's call him.

Hey, Ralfo. I need to insure a $100 million M-BS. No, the mortgages aren't subprime. They're safer tha—don't laugh so loud. Why do you care, Ralfo. Good or bad, commission's the same, right? Taxpayers'll foot the bill. Caveat taxpayor. Course I'm sure. We grease political skids till they're frictionless. My man. Knew I could count on you. No, I don't wanna hedge the moon. You're an even greedier prick than me. And I love it. CDSs on CDOs, where the M-BS stops, nobody knows! G-Sax will purchase some additional M-BS hedges. Not for a client, for us. You gotta lower the laugh a few decibels, Ralfo. And watch the cynicism. I'd never short sell M-BSs just to trigger insurance payouts.

Don't worry, Ralfo. If you get canned, I'll get you in on the next scam, carbon credits. Cap and trade. Guv'ment limits on "greenhouse" gas emissions. Anyone exceeds cap limits, they have to buy carbon credits. A Chicago Climate Exchange exists. Market'll be trillions. Guv'ment will lower the cap supply to supposedly help the environment, skyrocketing prices. We'll make a killing. Carbon credits will be shorted, borrowed, bundled, insured—the housing bubble all over again. I care about the environment. I drove gas prices up to $4 a gallon. That curbed greenhouse gas emissions. Thanks Ralfo, and take care.

No, I don't have a morsel of guilt. Yep, we're selling investors bogus M-BSs, then selling them bogus insurance on those bogus M-BSs, then making personal side bets that those M-BSs will implode. I don't know if this is the definition of securities fraud, I don't have a dictionary. Moral hazard? We're the Dukes of Moral Hazard. Yee-haw!

Of course AIG can't pay. But no one will question its ability to pay because it is the largest insurance company on Earth. Confidence in M-BSs will be restored so we earn more commissions before the economy implodes.

I know it's hard to believe that taxpayers will agree to such a monstrous bailout once the economy implodes. Never underestimate the stupidity of sheeple.

It's a zero sum game. Cliché grande, but true. G-Sax paid out $4.7 billion in bonuses last quarter, more than half a million per employee. We produced nothing. For us to gain, many must lose. If you can't deal with that, get an engineering degree. Guys with consciences don't last long around here.

Party tonight. Black tie. G-Sax made millions off the Africa starvations in the news, we're throwing a shindig to celebrate. Let's write up the Credit Default Swaps with Ralfo and get out of here early. Should we use a pen, or a crayon?

TO SKIP THE PICTURE PAGES AFTER THIS CHAPTER, PLEASE TURN TO PAGE 191

TV BABBLEHEAD AND EX-G-SAXON JIM CRAMER
IT'S ALL ABOUT THE COMMISSION!

"The commissions on structured products are so huge let's jam it. It's all about the 'commish'. The commission on structured product is gigantic. I could make a fortune jamming that crummy paper but I had a degree of conscience. Shocker. But listen, the commission in structured product is so gigantic! The customer has no idea what the product really is because it is invented. You assume the customer is really stupid. Like we used to say about the German bankers, 'The German banks are just bozos. Throw them anything.' Or the Australians. Morons. Or the Florida Fund. 'They're so stupid let's give them Triple B [junk-grade bonds].' Then we'd just laugh and laugh at the customers and jam them with the commission. That's what happened. Remember, this is about commissions, about how much money you can make by jamming stupid customers. I've seen it all my life. You jam stupid customers."

—Jim Cramer, ex-Goldman-Sachs Broker, host of *Mad Money* TV Show

Cramer claims that he was the only G-Saxon with a conscience who didn't plunder. Please pardon the author's skepticism, but such lies are beyond cliche, an accepted ruse. Like inmates in a prison who are all "innocent." It is easy to develop a "conscience" and talk smack after you've plundered millions and are set for life.

CREDIT DEFAULT SWINDLES

"Derivatives don't kill companies. People kill companies."

—Wall Street saying

"The new impetus for us as investors is to be balance-sheet suppliers. We've detected a rise in the pricing of total-return swaps in which we provide a balance-sheet rental. The trade is simple: We buy an asset and then transfer all of the credit risk of the asset back to the bank that sold us the asset. For the counterparty, it's a way for it to take the risk of an asset but not have to fund it."

—Carl Schuman, Managing Director for Credit Derivatives
Westdeutsche Landesbank

Credit Default Swaps (CDSs) are insurance taken out on financial instruments. In banker-ese, "credit default" means screwed. Someone who was issued credit (a loan) has defaulted (stopped making payments on the loan). The buyer of a CDS makes payments to a seller, who pays him if there is credit default on the insured financial instrument. "Credit default swap" is a fancy term that means insurance for investments. Mortgage insurance is a credit default swap. If you can't pay your mortgage, the insurer does. You purchase this protection.

You only insure assets you own, but a credit default swap can be purchased for assets someone else owns. If you had a $1 million life insurance policy, you might worry about your spouse killing you. Imagine if your neighbor could take out a $10 million life insurance policy on you.

A CDS can be issued for anything. A company, a loan, a credit card, a bond, an interest rate, a person, a sick goldfish. You can't insure a car or home for more than its worth, but there are no such restrictions with CDSs. You tan take out a $10 billion CDS on a sick goldfish. All you need is one party willing to make regular payments in expectation of event A, and another willing to agree to a payout if event A happens.

Your neighbor takes out a life insurance policy on your spouse and children. Then a fire insurance policy on your house. You notice gas cans near his garage. . .

The insurance industry is regulated to try and limit such abuses, as are futures exchanges and stock markets. Derivatives like MBSs, CDOs, SIVs, ABSs, CLOs and CDSs are unregulated. You can't look up derivative prices in your local paper the way you can stock prices. This alphabet soup of structured investments is not traded on any public exchange, has no set of universal standards, and is created and traded solely by private agreements. A license to steal. A lack of license, technically.

CDSs are used to insure risky investments. Why insure safe investments? And

191

what's riskier than MBSs, CDOs, and SIVs which you suddenly realize are worthless? Take the $100 million M-BS which Barthalamou bought. He manages pension funds, the retirement savings of sheeple, and used their money for the M-BS. Barthalamou knows the housing bubble is going to pop. When it does, the M-BS will go bankrupt, workers won't be able to retire, and he won't be a pension fund manager anymore. Unless he insures the M-BS.

Barthalamou purchases a credit default swap which pays out $100 million if his M-BS goes under. This costs him $1 million a year. Barthalamou sleeps like a baby now. His butt is covered. The risk of default has been transferred to the CDS seller.

Even if the M-BS doesn't go rupt, it squanders 1% of its value on insurance. Be nice if Barthalamou made sound investments that don't require insurance.

Holders of bogus M-BSs, CDOs, SIVs, ABSs, and CLOs purchase insurance as Barthalamou did. Speculatos who created these scams double their money insuring them. Trillions of dollars of CDSs are created. Nervous fund managers sleep like babies again, confident that they have dumped risk in someone else's lap. If anyone examines their portfolio and expresses concern about the high risk and low quality of the "investments" it contains, they are told not to worry. Everything is insured. When insurance is factored in, these BBB junk investments are actually AAA.

Selling credit default swaps is ridiculously profitable if the economy is booming. Imagine you're a Speculato. You sell CDSs to everyone who wants them. Purchasers make monthly payments for protection against failures that will of course never happen, and you guarantee monstrous payments you'll never have to make for those events that will of course never happen. If you issue $100 billion in CDSs which pay 1% per year, that is $1 billion in income per year. For doing nothing.

Speculatos didn't actually issue that many CDSs, did they? More than that, actually. Much more. But let's not get ahead o—

Wait a second. What if the insurer on the hook for all those CDS payments is asked to make them? If the events that will of course never happen do in fact happen? Does the insurer have enough money to make all its CDS payments? Does any company? And if they don't have the money, isn't this "insurance" a fraud?

Not when sheeple are hoofing the bill. Remember, these thieves bank on salvation from taxpayers.

Imagine thieves at AIG, the largest insurance company on Earth, sitting around scheming a way to earn more premiums. Everybody who needs car and home insurance has pretty much bought it. But what if AIG could start selling insurance on every stock, bond, mutual fund and loan on Earth? Such CDS agreements were structured just like normal insurance policies, except the payout was in the event of a bond default, stock decline, or loan foreclosure.

Normal insurance companies don't have enough money to back all policies, why should CDS insurers? Every house in America doesn't catch fire at once. Hurricane Katrina doesn't hit all of America at once. Half of Americans don't keel over from a heart attack or get hit by a car all at once. Conventional insurance is based on rare events. As the entire economy is at the mercy of monetary waves, every business in America can decline at once, resulting in massive bond defaults. Millions of mortgages can be defaulted on at once. Sellers of CDSs can suddenly be asked to payout claims on most of their "policies" all at once.

Barthalamou eventually worries about his insurer's ability to pay. He faces the music and admits that he made bad investments, right? Wrong. The original CDS was issued by AIG. Barthalamou approaches First Fraud Bank, and purchases a CDS on his CDS. He buys insurance for his insurance! More easy money for CDS issuers.

This is so opposite to the real world and common sense that it makes sheeple recoil. Who buys insurance on their insurance? Someone who cares only about making easy paper profits at the expense of the rest of society.

This progression of re-insuring CDS insurance occurred as many as a dozen times. Insurance was bought on the insurance for the insurance. Then insurance was bought on the insurance for the insurance for the insurance. And so forth, until there were a dozen or more nested layers of bogus CDSs, each bought to protect against the default of the previous CDS.

You hurt your knee chasing supermodels around the deck of your yacht, can't scuba dive, but still want to see undersea life. You need a submersible sub for the yacht. You're already a member of the mile high club, time to try the mile low.

Problem is, all the bogus alphabet-soup structured investments have been insured. People are starting to think the economy might be overextended, so peddling bogus paper is getting more difficult. You sell CDSs and derivatives not as insurance, but as ways to speculate. To bet on the decline everyone's expecting.

A bond buyer "bets" that the bond will be repaid. They "bet" that it won't be repaid by selling it. In an honest economy, people who don't own a bond can't bet that it will default. Derivatives allow two parties to write up a contract saying that one will pay the other if a bond is defaulted. The derivative is essentially a form of short selling.

Your neighbor is planning to kill you and collect millions in insurance. Why not sell insurance policies on you to all his neighbors who realize what he is planning? Now the whole block has life insurance policies on you, your family, and house. Damn, nothing left to sell. Wait, why not sell policies on the neighbor planning the murder. Your brother will probably kill him. . .

CDSs do the same things, but with businesses, becoming just another way to gamble on market outcomes. The person receiving the insurance payment doesn't have to own anything or suffer any loss. This creates perverse incentives. When those who don't own a company place massive bets which are paid only if it fails, they find a way to make it fail. Such bets serve no useful business function, and are merely another way for parasites to suck more blood from the host.

Where does it end? When do these thieves stop cooking up ways to rip everyone else off? As long as sheeple allow the fraud and hoof the bill for it, the answer is never.

To skip the picture pages after this chapter, please turn to page 195

SECURITIES AND EXCHANGE COMMISSION CHAIRMAN
CDS BUYERS CAN NAKED SHORT DEBT WITHOUT RESTRICTION

CHRISTOPHER COX, SECURITIES AND EXCHANGE COMMISSION CHAIRMAN
U.S. SENATE COMMITTEE ON BANKING, HOUSING, AND URBAN AFFAIRS
SEPTEMBER 23, 2008

Last week, the SEC took temporary emergency action to ban short selling in financial securities. We took this action in close coordination with regulators around the world. The Commission also approved two additional measures to ease the crisis of confidence in the markets The second requires weekly reporting to the SEC by hedge funds and other large investment managers of their daily short positions. The Commission's recent actions followed on the heels of new market-wide SEC rules that more strictly enforce the ban on abusive naked short selling.

Last month, the Enforcement Division entered into agreements that when finalized will be the largest settlements in the history of the SEC, on behalf of investors who bought auction rate securities from Merrill Lynch, Wachovia, UBS and Citigroup. The terms of these agreements would provide complete recovery for individual investors. Our Enforcement Division is continuing to investigate other firms.

Recently the Commission brought enforcement actions against two portfolio managers of Bear Stearns Asset Management, whose hedge funds collapsed in June of last year. We allege that they deceived their investors and institutional counterparties about the financial state of the hedge funds, and in particular the hedge funds' over-exposure to subprime mortgage-backed securities. ...

The $58 trillion notional market in credit default swaps—double the amount outstanding in 2006—is regulated by no one. Neither the SEC nor any regulator has authority over the CDS market, even to require minimal disclosure to the market. This is an area that our Enforcement Division is focused on using our antifraud authority, even though swaps are not defined as securities, because of concerns that CDS offer outsized incentives to market participants to see an issuer referenced in a CDS default or experience another credit event.

Economically, a CDS buyer is tantamount to a short seller of the bond underlying the CDS. Whereas a person who owns a bond profits when its issuer is in a position to repay the bond, a short seller profits when, among other things, the bond goes into default. Importantly, CDS buyers do not have to own the bond or other debt instrument upon which a CDS contract is based. This means CDS buyers can "naked short" the debt of companies without restriction. This potential for unfettered naked shorting and the lack of regulation in this market are cause for great concern.

THE WORLD IS NOT ENOUGH

"It is difficult not to marvel at the imagination which was implicit in this gargantuan insanity. If there must be madness, something may be said for having it on a heroic scale."

—John Kenneth Galbraith, Economist

Galbraith was referring to the Great Depression in the quote above, but it is also an apt summary of the derivative madness of Depression v9.2006.201x. The Bank of International Settlements, the King bank, the one Central Banks bank at, estimated $1.2 quadrillion in outstanding derivatives worldwide in mid-2008. This was just before the U.S. economy collapsed and bank bailouts began. $1.2 quadrillion! Astronomy numbers again. $1.2 quadrillion is $1,200 trillion, or $170,000 for every human on Earth. World GDP, the value of everything produced by the world in 2008, was $60 trillion, or roughly $9,000 per person. Outstanding derivatives were 18 times greater than world GDP!

A very, very, very, very rough estimate of the value of everything on Earth is $400 trillion. Every acre of land. Every car, house, boat, business, stock, bond, goat, chicken, fish, futon and backpack. If you auctioned the entire planet and sold everything on it except people, you'd pay off one third of the derivatives that exist. We can't auction Earth, meaning the wealth available to salvage derivatives is smaller. It is impossible to pay them all, or even a fraction. Derivatives are a scam.

How on Earth it is possible to create so many liabilities that they dwarf all existing assets? Derivatives are not assets, but bets on what will happen to assets. They are not investment, but a form of gambling, and the banking casino's rules allow Speculatos to place as many bets as they want without having their credit checked.

Wall Street manufactures paper profits. Derivatives don't invest in businesses or create real goods & services. Derivatives create nothing, but creators of derivatives receive something: commissions. Tens of thousands of parasites hustle on Wall Street, siphoning billions in commissions out of the economy. So many ticks the dog is dizzy.

In the real world there is variation in derivative commissions, 1% was chosen to keep math simple. If Wall Street parasites receive $1 billion in commissions, then they created or sold $100 billion of securities or derivatives to earn that 1%. Read that sentence several times if you need to, it is the key to understanding this mess.

Bush Treasury Secretary Henry "Hank" Paulson was CEO of Goldman Sachs and is worth $700 million. Robert Rubin, Clinton's Secretary of Treasury, amassed $100 million as CEO of Goldman Sachs, and earned $126 million as a Director and CEO of Citigroup. Paulson and Rubin are worth almost $1 billion. Two guys. Most Wall Streeters aren't worth hundreds of millions, but this tribe of ticks are collectively worth hundreds of billions. Let's say $100 billion. To obtain $100 billion in commissions, they had to generate paper transactions totaling $10 trillion. Bill Gates created Windows. John D. Rockefeller created oil wells. Henry Ford created cars. What did Paulson create? Or Rubin? Nothing.

Paulson and Rubin would argue that even though they didn't directly create anything, they facilitated the creation of useful businesses and public works by securing funding for them. Paulson didn't make his fortune by speculating with his personal funds, he was paid about $100 million in salary and received about 4 millions of shares of G-Sax stock which he sold for roughly $600 million. Paulson was CEO of G-Sax from 1999-2006, until he was appointed Treasury Secretary by President George W. Bush. Very roughly, Paulson's CEO pay averaged $100 million a year. He was the highest paid CEO on Wall Street, which had the highest CEO salaries in America, which has the highest CEO salaries in the world. As G-Sax's CEO, Paulson channeled billions of investment dollars to useful business enterprises and public works, but he was also a major creator—perhaps the major creator—of the derivatives bubble. The profits which G-Sax made off derivatives paid some of Paulson's exorbitant salary and contributed to the value of his stock.

$1.2 quadrillion in derivatives were created by G-Saxons like Paulson. 1% of $1.2 quadrillion is $12 trillion—a very, very, very rough estimate of the commissions siphoned by Speculatos worldwide in the derivatives boondoggle. $12 trillion taken from honest workers who produce real goods & services. That is a lot of yachts, jacuzzis, mansions and jets. Gaggles of Wall Street parasites who probably didn't make as much as Paulson, but made millions of dollars each.

In March 2008, JP Morgan Chase Bank held $90 trillion in derivatives, Citibank $41 trillion, Bank of America $39 trillion. U.S. commercial banks held $180 trillion total. There are thousands of commercial banks in America, but these 3 behemoth banks held 92% of derivatives. The next largest holder of derivatives was Wachovia, with $5 trillion, but it was acquired by Wells Fargo to prevent bankruptcy when its derivatives came due. Wachovia was the fourth largest bank in America.

America's 2008 GDP was $14 trillion. JP Morgan held potential liabilities equal to 6 times the annual output of America. Bank of America and Citibank each held 2 to 3 times. Total derivative positions of all banks were 13 times U.S. GDP.

If the derivative positions of these big banks weakened, they would collapse, and take the entire banking system and U.S. economy with them. To earn quick, easy profit, Speculatos put the entire U.S. economy at risk.

All $1.2 quadrillion in derivatives worldwide won't default. But with banks so overextended, it doesn't take much to sink the U.S.S. Economy. And the UK's economy, and Japan's, and Russia's, and Germany's. . .

In mid 2008, JP Morgan Chase had $741 billion in deposits, Bank of America $806 billion, Citicorp $826 billion—$2.37 trillion total, 30.4% of the $7.80 trillion M2 money supply. These are your deposits. The checking and savings accounts of Americans. If 1% of JP Morgan's $90 trillion in derivatives came due, it owed $900 billion dollars. It could embezzle every nickel of its deposits, and still be $159 billion short.

Assets include more than just deposits. JP Morgan's total assets were $1.65 trillion. So it'd actually take 2% of its derivatives coming due to bankrupt it. Bank of America had $1.74 trillion in assets and would be bankrupted by a 5% derivative payout. Citibank had $2.2 trillion in assets and would be bankrupted by a 6% payout.

Can this derivative crisis really happen? Could these banks really fail? It already did and they already have. Paying banks' bad derivative bets was and is a huge portion of the bailout. JP Morgan, Bank of America, and Citigroup would be bankrupt if not for the 14-figure bailout.

Let's examine a bank that was allowed to fail, Bear Stearns. Bear Stearns was the 7th largest bank in America. They had $350 billion in assets but held $13.4 trillion dollars in derivatives. They would be bankrupted if forced to pay 3% of derivatives, and were. On some of their derivatives, they bet wrong. On a Monday in March, 2008 they were one of the most respected banks in the world, by Friday the markets turned and they were gone. Poof. Vaporized. This bankruptcy stunned the world, but $13.4 trillion was just the tip of the $1,200 trillion derivative iceberg. And we're on the Titanic. Full speed ahead!

Throwing a mere $750 billion bailout at a problem this big is like chiseling a few cubes off the *Titanic* iceberg to chill a drink, and saying everything's safe. The economy wasn't out of the water by a longshot—and every insider knew it.

"Over-the-counter" (OTC) derivatives, the unregulated kind Speculatos love, are half the outstanding total. There were $72 trillion worth of OTC derivatives in 1998, $683 trillion in 2008. $611 trillion worth of derivatives created in 10 years! Include regulated derivatives like commodity futures traded on exchanges, the increase is roughly $1 quadrillion. $1,000 trillion worth of derivatives created in just 10 years! Now that's greed.

Most people have never heard of derivatives, and few that have truly understand them. Derivatives are de-emphasized by the media. It is easy to see why. The sheer magnitude of the robbery is stupefying. If people were given an honest summary of what happened, they would be not just furious, but murderous.

Derivative contracts were always a fraud because they couldn't be honored. Most everyone peddling them knew this, and understood derivatives were a scam to generate massive commissions. Innermost insiders foresaw the crash, cashed out, converted their fortunes to real assets, and escaped unscathed.

Derivatives were and are unbridled greed. It isn't any harder than that. Sociopaths wanted a fortune, but didn't want to work for it or earn it, so they scammed it.

Derivatives are the largest bubble in world history. They are also the greatest financial crime in history. None of the perpetrators will be brought to justice. They are laughing long jovial laughs, like Santa Claus.

CASTLE OF CARDS

"In my view, derivatives are financial weapons of mass destruction, carrying dangers that, while now latent, are potentially lethal."

—Warren Buffet

The financial crisis was magnified by abusing derivatives, fractional reserve lending, mark-to-market accounting and short selling in a self-reinforcing manner.

Take First Fraud Bank, which bears more than a passing resemblance to Bank of America. First Fraud Bank had $826 billion in deposits in mid 2009. Fractional reserve lending allows it to computer and lend 90% of this $826 billion, or $743 billion. As it continually issues loans, First Fraud Bank would never have all—or even a majority—of its computered money unused, but suppose it has a decent chunk freed up: $100 billion. First Fraud Bank computers $100 billion, which it loans to its investment division. The investment division issues or buys derivatives on 10% margin so pays only 10% of the purchase price. $100 billion created out of thin air is able to buy $1 trillion in derivatives. The $100 billion could also be lent to derivative buyers who put 10% down and borrow 90%. Same end result.

Was that example highly oversimplified? Yes. Was it inaccurate? No.

Derivatives are marked-to-market, overstating worth and understating risk. Each increase in derivative value marked to the ledgers is an asset used to buy more derivatives. Derivatives haven't been paid out yet. If derivatives decline in value and are re-marked-to-market, the profit which was the collateral used for other derivatives suddenly vanishes. More collateral must be obtained or the company is bankrupt.

By marking to market on the upswing, the possible cost of default is kept off the books, potential income is counted. Banks have incurred massive risk, but to anyone but an accounting guru, they look more profitable.

This is how banks create "leverage" in which liabilities far exceed the assets available to honor them. If you exploit the system properly, dotting all I's and looping all holes, astronomical debt can be created out of thin air, generating obscene profits.

Until someone reaches into this skyscraper of cards, plucks one out, and it collapses. Derivative payouts are the economic equivalent of plucking cards. The amount which derivative counterparties owe grows so fast that no one can pay up, leading to an avalanche of derivative defaults. Trillions of dollars of "wealth" vanish as quickly as they were created.

Bubbles will pop naturally. Speculatos usually pop them artificially to make profits off short sales. Knowing a bubble is doomed to pop is different than knowing exactly when it will pop. Speculatos need prices to decline within a limited timeframe to close their short sale positions.

Houses are assets. This grounded the housing bubble. People overvalued their houses, but the houses were worth something. Housing prices plummeted, but when they eventually approach actual values, the freefall will stop, and the system will stabilize.

Derivatives are bets on assets, not assets. They have no intrinsic value. Nothing grounds the derivative bubble. It is a bottomless pit. Banks are like climbers tied to the same rope. One slides into the pit, drags another, and another, and then another. . .

Barthalamou purchased a $100 million credit default swap from First Fraud Bank. His M-BS becomes worthless when millions default on mortgages, as mortgage payments were the income stream of the M-BS. The defaulted M-BS triggers the CDS payout from First Fraud Bank. First Fraud Bank pays it, triggering a payout from a CDS it purchased from Steal Second Bank. Steal Second Bank pays it, triggering a payout from a CDS it purchased from Third Thievery Bank. Third Thievery Bank pays it, triggering a payout from a CDS it purchased from. . . First Fraud Bank, who has now made two massive payouts. And away we go. . .

Half of all houses can't catch fire at once, but half of all CDSs and derivatives can come due. This process of cross defaults repeats over and over and over as bogus investment upon bogus investment vaporizes and CDS "insurance" policies kick in. Everything is leveraged off everything else, so the derivative meltdown reaches critical mass rapidly.

Trillions in payouts are demanded. Some payouts flowing back and forth between banks cancel each other out, but it only takes a 1% or 2% difference to bankrupt most banks. Everyone but the innermost insiders bet the same way, on a market rising forevermore, so the cancellations are limited. If a mere 10% of derivatives must be honored, every bank in America goes under. Poof! The deposits of every American are vaporized. This doesn't take weeks or months, but days. The mighty gears of the financial machine "de-leverage" overextended banks with a vengeance.

If banks are allowed to slide into the abyss, defrauded depositors begin asking difficult questions, the scam is exposed, and reforms are enacted to prevent a repeat of the fraud. Which is why there is a bailout. If banks don't fail, people never institute reforms, and the robbery can be repeated. Any large bank that fails will drag all banks off the cliff in the resulting cross-defaults, so none can be allowed to fail.

Even after receiving "massive" bailouts, banks still don't issue new loans. This confuses people. How can banks receive so much money and still not be lending? Compared to what they owe on derivatives, the bailout is puny. After receiving trillions of dollars in bailouts, they are barely afloat, not rescued. Every nickel they have is being used to cover the money owed on their derivative bets. Extra nickels are set aside for future payments on derivative bets they know will come due. Money or credit is the oil of the economic engine, and with it drained into derivatives, the economy seizes up. The public can't be told the actual cause of the problem, or the real magnitude, or they would erupt.

Trillions more may be required to save the banks. U.S. banks have $180 trillion in outstanding derivatives. They've received about $4.76 trillion in bailouts so far, and guv'ment has issued credit guarantees with a theoretical maximum risk of $13.87 trillion. Assuming all bailout money went to settle derivatives, which it didn't, that leaves roughly $175 trillion. This staggering sum is intricately linked with the continuing economic stagnation, in ways that will be explained in the Master's Degree and PhD sections.

How many derivatives will come due? You can bet your bullocks that banks frantically tried to answer that question, but economy-wide, no one knows. Futures contracts are called futures contracts for a reason, and 90% of derivatives owned by banks are the unregulated over-the-counter variety. Private contracts that haven't been scrutinized by outsiders or regulators.

What should have been done once derivative exposure avalanched and the economy imploded? Courts have consistently held that contracts which are impossible to honor are null & void. Derivative contracts should have been declared fraudulent and impossible to honor, and voided, except perhaps a single "hedge" derivative purchased by the owner of the "insured" security. Insurance for securities should work like normal insurance for cars and homes: only the owner of assets can purchase insurance on them, a single time. This would have eliminated most of the "toxic" assets that burden banks, and made much of the bailout unnecessary. Expecting such a sensible and fair policy is of course naive. Derivatives enrich Speculatos and banks; they own Congress, and they made sure they were bailed out. Limiting the issuance of derivatives would limit the easy money Speculatos can make, and this will never be allowed.

Domino effect. Nuclear reaction. Economic engine. Beneath all the metaphors and confusing economic terminology is still a very simple truth: banks placed massive bets to make easy money, guessed wrong, can't afford to pay what they owe, and expect someone else to foot the bill. Why should they have been saved?

THE GOOD DEPRESSION?

"Liquidate labor, liquidate stocks, liquidate the farmers, liquidate real estate ... It will purge the rottenness out of the system. High costs of living and high living will come down. People will work harder, live a more moral life. Values will be adjusted, and enterprising people will pick up the wrecks from less competent people."
—Andrew Mellon, 49th United States Secretary of the Treasury (1921 – 1932)

"Recessions are therapeutic. They cleanse excess from the economy. Think about excessive risk speculation, leverage, and housing. Recessions are curative: They restore balance..."
—Larry Kudlow, Economist

"It is just as essential for the health of a dynamic economy that dying industries should be allowed to die as that growing industries should be allowed to grow. For the dying industries absorb labor and capital that should be released for the growing industries."
—Henry Hazlitt, Economist

Insiders claim that banks must be saved because too much suffering and chaos would result if they were allowed to fail. Sheeple believe this lie because they do not understand the fraudulent fractional reserve lending and derivatives casino which are the real causes of the current mess.

But still. Depressions are bad. To say otherwise is absurd.

This is true on one level, but on another level Depressions are good. This is counterintuitive, so let's look at a simple example.

Suppose government can no longer create money. Welfare for the poor and rich ends. No one gets paid not to work, no banks get bailouts. The poor stop buying liquor, the rich yachts. Distilleries and yacht makers go bankrupt, their workers lose jobs. But honest citizens no longer paying the inflation tax have more wealth to spend. They purchase more clothes and groceries. Additional jobs in clothes and groceries will be created, though this takes time. If the money spigot is turned back on, liquor and yacht jobs will exist again immediately. Does one want society producing yachts and liquor for parasites, or clothes and food for honest workers?

It is easy to say take the long term approach—until you are the one without a job. Then the tune changes. Screw the big economic words, I ain't got time for jibber jabber, I've got a family to feed and a mortgage to pay, I need work!

The temptation to demand that the money spigot be turned back on during a Depression is powerful. Like a heroin addict in the throes of withdrawal begging to shoot up. This is death for the addict, but initially he is orgasmic again. Unfortunately, addicts have disciplined doctors, economies have politicians.

If a bubble is inflated, huge sums of money are allocated to parasites, and businesses spring up to supply what they demand. Once the money spigot is shut off, it can take years to reallocate resources and supply what workers want. It is not just a question of workers switching jobs or learning new professions. The assets of bankrupt businesses must be sold, and this wealth used to create new businesses which must often be built. A distillery or shipyard cannot easily be converted to a clothes factory or farm.

There is no way to abandon corrupt money and return to a healthy economy without this transition period. Speculatos will tell you otherwise. They are lying. You know why. Most people don't, and are swayed. They may sense a swindle, but without a grasp of the precise mechanisms, this avails them little.

Remember the first lesson in Crusoeville. No one wants the extra apples created after the money supply is increased, but everyone is busy producing them. Is the solution to keep everyone employed making things no one wants just to avoid the pain of a transition to new jobs?

Recessions caused by the failure of businesses are a healthy reallocation of resources. These businesses failed because those running them either did not understand demand, or were not efficient enough to supply demand at low enough prices. If a society is to prosper long term, such incompetents must be weeded out, and resources must be allocated to those who can actually make things people want, and compete in the real world.

Unemployed workers love hearing these sorts of logical arguments. They resonate especially well when made by pasty yuppies who break a sweat bending over to buff their loafers.

So what should have happened? An honest mony system should have been instituted. No fractional reserve lending, no money computered and uncomputered. Without this honest money system, huge banks can never be allowed to fail because this uncomputers mountains of money, which collapses the economy. Speculatos bank on this hostage situation, and use it as justification for bailouts.

After an honesty money system was instituted, no bailouts. Everyone who couldn't pay their mortgage should have lost their house. Every bankrupt bank that issued bogus mortgages or lost at derivatives roulette should have been rupted, which would have been every major bank in America. Speculato "counterparties" owed derivative payments by bankrupt banks would have been shit out of luck, taxpayers and government would not have been pillaged to pay them. Foreclosed houses and bank assets would have been bought up for pennies on the dollar by responsible individuals who had saved money, and can run businesses and live within their means. Enterprising people picking up the wrecks from less competent people.

To sheeple, such a liquidation of malinvestment is cruel and absurd, but it is the only thing that would have restored prosperity quickly. Period. Sheeple believe that there could have been a recovery without this "heartless" and "unjust" free market liquidation of malinvestment. That is why they are sheeple.

Parastic banks that make bogus loans and fritter credit on economically use-less activites like derivatives would have been extinct. The perpetual resource drain and malinvestment they still create, which continues to stagnate the economy, would have been exterminated. To make money, people and businesses would have been forced to return to real, honest economy activity, to produce goods & services which individuals freely demand in the marketplace.

False price signals created by Greenspan's Great Inflation caused America to build a number of houses in 6 years, which it normally would have built over decades. Construction workers made fortunes for 6 years, but now have no work building houses for a decade. The current "solution" is to save banks, doze houses, minimize foreclosures via mortage amnesty measures, and for banks to liquidate accumulated foreclosures gradually. This keeps a glut of cheap, new houses from flooding the market and discouraging new construction which provides jobs. This failed policy is the opposite of what should happen: the rapidest liquidation possible.

Few Americans can spend because they still have massive debt. If people who couldn't make mortgage payments went bankrupt, they would now have disposable income to spend, and the economy would have recovered. Enterprising businesspersons who bought bank resources would be creating new jobs in industries besides housing, producing real goods & services and employing the middle class. Contrast this with vampiric unemployment which pays millions not to work for years.

If banks had been allowed to fail, they would learn that no bailout is coming, and change their ways. Depositors who lost money would learn to choose banks more carefully. Long term everyone would be better off.

Short term, it would have been brutal. No sugarcoating it, doing nothing, pro-viding no bailout, would have allowed massive suffering, but then so has the status quo. Again, sheeple who are used to guv'ment feeding, clothing, and housing them consider it heartless and deranged to let hundreds of millions of people lose their deposits. It is absurd to let the entire banking system fail.

13-figure bailouts are the absurdity. If the banking system can't stay in business without $4,760,000,000,000 in welfare, we need a new system. A system Fed by fraud should be allowed to collapse, so everyone can see it for what it is, and it can be replaced with an honest system. Long term, the big losers would be Speculatos, the big winners we the people.

Sheeple don't see it this way. They condemn future generations to Depression and bailouts rather than taking their medicine and setting things right. Sheeple are ruled by the fear of not being able to feed their families and pay their mort-gages, and Speculatos know it.

AIG, Goldman Sachs, Fannie Mae, Freddie Mac, Citibank and The Big Three should have been allowed to go bankrupt. This was the only real solution. Instead gutless politicians handed the needle back to the addict, preventing recovery, delay-ing the day of reckoning, yet insuring it will be cataclysmic when it finally arrives.

BACHELORS IN BUBBLENOMICS

A Bachelor's Degree is a major accomplishment. Congrats. We covered a lot. A quick summary is difficult. But necessary.

Prior to 1913, America had low taxes, limited government, and few wars. The Federal Reserve and Income Tax were created in 1913, instituting inflation and income taxes which funded a welfare state and military empire. Funding these behemoths made US poorer, so we levied an inflation tax on the world by making the dollar the world reserve currency in 1945. Dollars were backed by gold, other currencies were backed by dollars. Dollars could be redeemed for a fixed weight of gold.

In the 1960s, America created mountains of dollars to fund Vietnam, Medicare and Medicaid. Excessive inflation always causes bank runs, America's came in 1971. Nations redeemed dollars for gold. America didn't have enough gold, so suspended gold redemption, shafting the world. Nations no longer wanted dollars, but America made OPEC sell oil only for dollars. "Petrodollars" allow US to levy a global inflation tax.

American Speculatos computer dollars and lend them to third world Hutvilles. Third world nations use their natural resources as collateral for loans, default on loans, and then American Speculatos seize natural resources. Ever larger loans are issued until American Speculatos own third world nations, third worlders are destitute, and only interest on loans can be paid. Third world nations are minimum-wage workers with 20 maxed credit cards. They hate America.

When America levies a global dollar tax, it creates a global bubble. Foreign factories are retooled to produce luxuries Americans want rather than necessities foreigners need. This is the only way nations can obtain dollars to buy oil. When Americans stop buying foreign goods, foreign factories have no buyers for their goods, and the world economy collapses.

Dollars dwarf the amount of goods America produces. America trades dollars for foreign goods, but foreigners can't trade most dollars for American goods. America defrauds the world.

Foreigners amass trillions of dollars—too many to sell. Selling even a fraction would collapse the dollar. Unsold dollars foreigners hold would then be worthless. The only way foreigners can get something for dollars is to invest them in T-debts that pay more dollars. A monetary Catch-22.

American prosperity depends on a global inflation tax. When the dollar is dethroned, America will no longer be able to levy a global dollar tax, and its prosperity will dwindle.

All fiat monies are unsustainable. Eventually fiat money is inflated so much that it is rejected. America is dependent upon an unsustainable fiat money system. America is unsustainable.

Derivatives are not assets, they are bets on changes in the prices of assets. Derivatives are gambling. They vacuum up most investment in the economy. Why grow apples or make applesauce when you can option and future them for 5 times the profit? Legitimate uses of derivatives are limited. The $1,000 trillion of derivatives created 1998-2008 were a scam. As world GDP is $60 trillion, and everything on Earth is worth $400 trillion, honoring even a fraction of derivatives is impossible. Derivatives were not designed to be honored, but rather to generate commissions for Speculatos.

Banks forced to honor derivatives are rupted, as 3% or 4% of their derivatives exposure exceeds their assets. A huge portion of bailout money covered derivative bets.

Mark-to-market accounting allows the rising market price of unsettled derivative contracts to be marked in ledgers as "profit." This "profit" is used to buy more derivatives. When prices plummet and derivatives are marked-to-market, "profit" vanishes and the bank owes a large fortune which exceeds its capital. To avoid ruptcy, banks commit fraud and don't mark plummeting assets to market. Bank accounting is re-mark-able.

Short sellers "hypothecate" phantom shares of stock and sell them. This collapses the price. The short seller re-buys the stock, "un-hypothecates" it and pockets the price difference. Short selling is counterfeiting. Create all the virtual stock you want, sell it for profit, un-create it. Anything can be shorted (and is), including bonds, mortgages and currency.

Once upon a time, Wall Street helped create agriculture and industry. Now Speculatos concoct bogus transactions which produce paper profits, and convert these profits into assets workers produce. When paper profits are found to be fraudulent, Speculatos have cashed out, and sheeple are holding the bag.

M-BSs were BS. Commercial banks computed mountains of money and issued bogus mortgages which they knew would never be repaid. Insty-bubble. Commercial banks computed another mountain of money and lent it to investment banks that bought the bogus mortgages and resold them as investments called "Mortgage-Backed" Securities. M-BSs.

The first batch of bogus mortgages are off banks' books. The money they were sold for is used to issue more bogus mortgages. Commercial banks computer another mountain of money and lend it to investment banks that buy the bogus mortgages and resell them as BS-ier M-BSs. This process is repeated again and again and again. Each time, there are less qualified borrowers, more minimum wage mansioneers.

Eventually the piles of M-BS start to reek. Speculatos spray Lysol by buying derivative insurance. Individuals selling derivatives obtained commissions, their company obtained policy premium payments, derivative buyers obtained protection from risk. AIG and banks sold derivative insurance to anyone who would buy it.

No one asked if AIG or banks could cough up the trillions of dollars needed to honor all the derivative payouts promised. Innermost insiders knew this was impossible, but didn't care. Too much money was being made to worry about trivialities like sheeple paying mortgages or counterparties paying derivatives.

Investors kept gobbling M-BSs up. M-BSs were insured, why worry? What a joyous fairytale. No one with any risk. Everyone amassing garbage investments worry-free because they bought insurance from the derivative fairy.

Innermost insiders continued selling M-BSs, but also placed derivative bets on M-BS declines. Once the econolypse began, these derivative bets paid out fortunes, but also plummeted prices, triggering additional derivative bets which plummeted prices which triggered additional derivative bets which plummeted prices... Government froze short selling to prevent a total implosion.

Middle class workers can't pay $925,000 mortgages. Mortgage payments were the income of M-BSs, which went rupt. Commercial banks could no longer ship bogus mortgages off their books to M-BSs. As mortgages defaulted, "lie-abilities" were exposed, and derivatives and mortgages were marked-to-market at plummeting prices. The collapse snowballed. Derivatives were triggered and cross-triggered. Counterparty payments that couldn't be honored came due.

Only a person who owns something should be able to insure it or take a derivative bet out on it. Most derivatives should have been declared fraudulent and voided, Speculatos who created them jailed. Instead sheeple agreed to honor the unhonorable. To pay off derivatives for which the world is not enough.

Overextend, pocket loot, engineer a bailout, repeat. Speculatos repeat the same formula century after century.

Most people discussing "solutions" never address the root cause of the housing bubble and Depression v9.2006-201x: a corrupt money system which allows fortunes to be conjured. This is the root cause of all Depressions, and they can only be prevented by reforming our money system and outlawing money conjuring.

How do you end a Depression if you didn't prevent it? Bailouts and stimulus programs worsen Depressions. Depressions can only be cured by rapidly liquidating malinvestment, but this cannot be done because writing off loans and liquidating banks results in mountains of money being uncomputered. Uncomputering mountains of money precipitates Depressions. This insidious paradox is at the heart of our money system, and it was foreseen and engineered by Speculatos so they could hold guv'ments hostage for bailouts. Any proposal for curing Depression v9.2006-201x which does not focus on reforms to our money system is futile. This concept will be explained in much greater detail in the advanced degree sections of *Bubblenomics*.

Sheeple oppose bailouts and wars and welfare, yet feel powerless to stop them. You pay taxes or the IRS takes everything you have. No matter who you vote for, corruption continues and taxes increase. Especially the inflation tax. This is why our Founding Fathers outlawed income and inflation taxes in the Constitution. These taxes were marketed as the economic equivalent of light bulbs and automobiles, advancements that would serve the people. A century later, people serve the income and inflation taxes, and those that levy these taxes are their masters.

Speaking of masters, the Master's Degree is next. It will take you deep into the bowels of the banking beast. Please keep reading no matter how hard it gets. Speculatos need you ignorant to keep shafting you. Don't let them win.

Bubblenomics *II*

To continue your education in bubblenomics, please purchase *Bubblenomics II: A PhD in Common Cents*. It includes:

Master's Degree

Bank frauds are shown on simplified ledgers. The process by which liabilities are transformed into lie-abilities is documented. Modern bankers are shown to be cybersmiths who practice ye old goldsmith scam using computer ledgers. Fed's master ledger is revealed, with entries for each bank. This ledger is the money supply, and banks are shown adding entries to it, increasing the money supply. Bailouts in which Fed creates bank credit are covered, as are the hidden consequences of these bailouts which Fed lies about. Monetization, a Debt Standard of inextinguishable loans, Fed as Inflator of Last Resort, the enslaved market, the Fed Chairman as Inflator General, the actual budget, the GSE guarantee monstrosity, Depression v8.1929-1942 vs. Depression v9.2006-201x. . . These topics and many others are covered.

PhD

Provides transcripts of testimony by Inflator Generals, Treasury Secretaries, and members of Congress which show bubblenomics principles applied in the real world. Includes proof that the bailout was passed to alleviate a $550 billion electronic run on America's banks, an explosive story few Americans have heard, but which all should know. Any one of these interviews is damning by itself, but summed they are a mortifying indictment of our corrupt monetary system and the sociopaths running it. Each of these interviews is a primary source, the unedited testimony of Speculatos who engineered the econolypse.

Post Doctoral Work

Solutions are presented.

Professor BN

Documents the Speculato machinations which caused World War II and shows what Speculatos have planned long term over a multi-century window.

Speculatos most precious commodity isn't yachts, mansions, gold, or even the power to computer infinite amounts of ledger money. It is ignorance. *Bubblenomics II* tells the rest of the truth that Speculatos want hidden.

Information about *Bubblenomics II* is available at www.lawrencerowe.com

INDEX OF PICTURE PAGES

BACHELOR'S IN BUBBLENOMICS